INSIGHTS
ON THE BOOK OF
ISAIAH

INSIGHTS
ON THE BOOK OF
ISAIAH

DR. ALAN B. STRINGFELLOW

WHITAKER
HOUSE

All Scripture quotations are taken from the King James Version of the Holy Bible.

The forms Lord and God (in small caps) in Bible quotations represent the Hebrew name for God, *Yahweh* (Jehovah), while *Lord* and *God* normally represent the name *Adonai*, in accordance with the Bible version used.

Some definitions of Hebrew and Greek words are taken from the electronic versions of *Strong's Exhaustive Concordance of the Bible* (© 1980, 1986, and assigned to World Bible Publishers, Inc. All rights reserved.) or the *New American Standard Exhaustive Concordance of the Bible* (NASC), (© 1981 by The Lockman Foundation. All rights reserved.).

Boldface type in the Scripture quotations indicates the author's emphasis.

INSIGHTS ON THE BOOK OF ISAIAH:
A Verse-by-Verse Study

ISBN: 978-1-64123-302-6
eBook ISBN: 978-1-64123-303-3
Printed in the United States of America
© 2020 by Scott Broeker

Whitaker House
1030 Hunt Valley Circle
New Kensington, PA 15068
www.whitakerhouse.com

2 3 4 5 6 7 8 9 10 11 12 ᴡ 28 27 26 25 24 23 22 21 20

ABOUT PHOTOCOPYING THIS BOOK

CONTENTS

PREFACE

This study is designed to be used for as either a formal classroom curriculum or as a person at-home resource. To receive maximum knowledge and inspiration during the next course of study, I offer this encouragement to both the teacher and the student. They are designed to help you become a disciplined disciple of God's Word.

For the Student

- Read the assigned portion of Scripture at the end of each lesson.
- Take notes on each week's study. Review your notes from the previous week before beginning each study.
- Mark your Bible with key references from one Scripture to another.
- Search the Scripture and mark references in class. Write Scriptures in this book where lines are provided.

Promise the Lord at least two or three hours each week for reading the assigned Scripture and doing your homework. Use the notes section at the end of each lesson to write down any questions that arise while preparing for each lesson. Also, jot down new ideas that are presented during your class time.

The time has come for Christians who mean business for the Lord to devote themselves to the study of His Word in order to master basic biblical principles. Promise yourself and God that you will live up to this standard.

For the Teacher

If you are teaching this study in a formal classroom setting, first, you must prepare yourself spiritually by reading the book of Isaiah in its entirety. These Scriptures will assure you as the teacher that the Holy Spirit will guide you and teach you as you study His Word and impart it to your pupils.

As you teach the course, read the assigned chapters for the next lesson. Take notes and search out Scripture references. You must also be prepared to answer questions, add insight, or promise to research answers to any classroom questions you do not know the answer to. What's more, you must...

- Highlight the subject of each lesson.
- Do not be afraid of being too elementary for your pupils.
- Stay on the major themes, not the minor ones.
- Keep the lessons as simple as possible with all age groups.
- You may add illustrations and ideas, but do not change the major points of the outline.
- Use your own personality and let the Holy Spirit use you as you teach.
- Expect your pupils to do their part by fully participating in the discussion and rigorously completing assignments.

May God bless you, pupil or teacher, as you begin your study in *Insights on the Book of Isaiah*. Let the Holy Spirit teach you both.

Lesson 1
INTRODUCTION

As we enter into this study of the book of Isaiah, we have taken to ourselves a stupendous assignment, but God has called us to teach all of His Word and He will make us sufficient for it.

The Prophetic Portion of the Bible

Beginning with Isaiah and continuing through the Old Testament, there is a section of Scripture that is called the Prophetic Portion of the Bible. Although the predictive element is large in this section, the prophets are more than foretellers. Actually, they were men raised up of God in a decadent day when both the priest and the king were no longer a worthy channel through which the expressions of God might flow. These men not only spoke of the events in the far-off future, but also spoke of local events in the immediate future. They had to speak in this manner in order to qualify for the office of prophet according to God's Mosaic code:

> But the prophet, which shall presume to speak a word in my name, which I have not commanded him to speak, or that shall speak in the name of other gods, even that prophet shall die. And if thou say in thine heart, How shall we know the word which the LORD hath not spoken? When a prophet speaketh in the name of the LORD, if the thing follow not, nor come to pass, that is the thing which the LORD hath not spoken, but the prophet hath spoken it presumptuously: thou shalt not be afraid of him.
>
> (Deuteronomy 18:20–22)

One of the greatest evidences of the fact that these men were speaking the words of God is revealed in the hundreds of prophecies that have been fulfilled literally. Men cannot guess the future. Even the weatherman has difficulty in predicting the weather a day in advance. The examples of hundreds of prophecies that have been literally fulfilled seems to be a genuine appeal to the honest mind and sincere seeker after the truth. Fulfilled prophecy is one of the infallible proofs of the plenary verbal inspiration of Scripture.

The prophets were extremely nationalistic. They rebuked sin in high places as well as low. They warned the nations. They pleaded with proud people to humble themselves and return to God. They had in their message tears along with a great amount of fire, which was not one of doom and gloom alone, for they saw the day of the Lord and the glory to follow. All of them looked through the darkness to the dawn of a new day.

The Man Isaiah

We know very little about the man Isaiah. The world knows little about its great men. Even Shakespeare we know very little about and we know practically nothing about Homer. So it is with the prophets. We know little about Amos, Hosea, or Isaiah. Maybe the Lord hid away the man in order that the voice might be heard. It is the message and not the man God wants us to notice. Consider for a while the man Isaiah.

- Isaiah was a man of the city. He was an urbanite. He lived all of his life in a city. He labored in the city. His long ministry of over fifty years was in a city—from 750 B.C. to 700 B.C. Isaiah's references are always from the standpoint of a city man.

- He was the court preacher. He is the first of a long line of city preachers—Jeremiah, Paul, etc.

- His city was Jerusalem. He was an aristocrat. He was cultural. Tradition says that his father, who was Amoz, was a brother to Amaziah, the king, who was a father to Uzziah, the king. In that event, he was a first cousin of the king. (This could explain the first part of chapter 6 when we get to it.)

uncle/cousin -kings

- Isaiah always seemed at home in the king's court. He moved among the leaders. He grew up in a day of influence and prosperity.
- King Uzziah of Judah and Jeroboam of Israel (northern kingdom) brought the people to the highest heights of prosperity. They rivaled the power and the glory of the united kingdom under David and Solomon. Attendant to prosperity were the vices that accompanied it.

When I read the book of Isaiah, I think of America. The youth of our land have known nothing but wealth and plenty. Isaiah lived in a like day of financial abundance and saw his people plunge into sin. But Isaiah walked around in a garment of hair cloth like Elijah, calling the people back to repentance. He walked through Jerusalem in that garb calling people back to God.

Isaiah's Message

- Isaiah was a great poetic genius as he declared his message of the Lord God.
- He was a great speaker and he was a perfectionist with words.
- His figures of speech are from the Lord.
- Isaiah is the messianic prophet of the Old Testament. He pictures the birth, death, and the golden age of the millennium in this book 750 years before it came to pass.
- Isaiah talks about the Lord as though Christ was there with him. He talks about the virgin birth, the virgin-born Savior, and the crucifixion as though he were standing there.

Isaiah's Family

- Isaiah had a wife (see Isaiah 8:3) and he was the father of two sons.
- His first son was named Shear-jashub (see Isaiah 7:3), which means "a remnant shall return."
- His second son was named Majer-shalal-hash-baz, which means "speed the spoil" meaning a speedy doom for Judah's enemies.

The Name Isaiah

- Isaiah means "the salvation of Jehovah."
- Wherever you find the name ending in -iah, you can attach the name Jehovah to it. For example, Jeremiah means "whom Jehovah hath appointed"; Uzziah means "the might of Jehovah"; Zedekiah means "the justice of Jehovah"; Zechariah means "whom Jehovah remembers"; Uriah means "the light of Jehovah."
- So, the name Isaiah means, "the salvation of the Lord God."

The book as it stands bears every evidence of being preserved in its divinely arranged order. It is only unbelieving ignorance that could lead any to think to rearrange and dissect it in the manner of modern critics. George Adam Smith, author of *Isaiah in the Expositor's Bible*, is the most commonly known specimen among that crowd. It is a virtual denial of inspiration to destroy the true prophetic character of the Messianic portions of the magnificent prophecy.

Many professing Christians pay little or no attention to the prophetic word, but in neglecting that which forms so large a part of the holy Scriptures, they wrong their own souls and dishonor Him who gave His Word for our edification and comfort. The real value of prophecy is that it occupies us with a Person, not merely with events. That Person is our Lord Jesus Christ, who came once to suffer and is coming again to reign. Of both these advents Isaiah treats, and that in a way plainer and fuller than do any of the other Old Testament prophets.

Similarities Between Isaiah and the Bible

Those who are interested in the curious things concerning Scripture have long noticed that in Isaiah, in a sense, you have the miniature Bible:

+ The Bible consists of sixty-six books: Isaiah has sixty-six chapters.
+ The Bible is divided into two testaments, Old and New; Isaiah is divided into two parts, the first having to do largely with Israel's past condition and the promise of the Messiah's coming and the second dealing particularly with their future deliverance.
+ The Old Testament has thirty-nine books: the first half of Isaiah has thirty-nine chapters.
+ The New Testament has twenty-seven books: the second part of Isaiah has twenty-seven chapters.

These similarities, of course, are mere coincidence because it was not the Spirit of God but human editors who divided the book in this way; nevertheless, it is interesting and quite suggestive when you realize that Isaiah deals in a very definite way with that which is the outstanding theme of all the Scriptures—God's salvation, as revealed in His blessed Son.

Like other prophets, Isaiah wrote at the command of the Lord and then searched his own Scriptures, the Scriptures then available, as to what manner of time the Spirit of Christ that was in him did prophesy when he testified beforehand concerning the sufferings of Christ and the glories that should follow. The portion that deals with the sufferings of Christ, which took place at His first advent, have become amazingly clear in the light of the New Testament Gospels.

With that background about the man and a little about the book in general, let's take now to the background from which Isaiah wrote the prophecy.

God and Government

There is not a piece of literature that excels Isaiah in oratorical excellence. He spoke from a background of history that you must understand briefly. For you to get a background from which Isaiah wrote the book, we must understand these four men and remember a little about them. We will take the men and try to understand them by looking at the political and nation life.

1. Uzziah

    + Uzziah reigned for fifty-two years.
    + He was an able and gifted administrator and military strategist.
    + He was king of Judah, the southern kingdom, at the same time that Jeroboam II was king over the northern kingdom of Israel, commonly called Ephraim, of which Samaria was the capital. Jerusalem was the capital of Judah.
    + These two men, Uzziah and Jeroboam, brought the nation back to the glorious height of prosperity that it knew under the united kingdom.
    + Uzziah prospered in everything to which he placed his hand. He did so as long as Zechariah, the prophet, lived. (Now there are twenty-eight different Zechariahs in the Bible and when we think of Zechariah, we think of the prophet who wrote the eleventh of the twelve minor prophecies in the Old Testament, the next to the last book. This is not he. That Zechariah returned to Zerubbabel back from the Babylonian captivity. This Zechariah is an unknown prophet—about the only thing we know is that he had a tremendous influence for good upon King Uzziah and as long as Zechariah lived, Uzziah served the Lord faithfully and well.)
    + When Zechariah died during the older days of Uzziah, he turned away from the Lord. Uzziah entered the temple, the holy sanctuary of God, and sought to abrogate unto himself the services that belong to the appointed priests (all of this is found in 2 Chronicles 26).

- The high priest, Azariah, and eighty of his priests entreated Uzziah not to do it, but the hard-hearted king was determined to set aside the ministry of the priest and when he did so, he was stricken with leprosy and he lived separate and apart, dying a leper for the remainder of his reign.
- It was during the prosperous reign of Uzziah that the young man Isaiah grew up. It was in the last year of Uzziah—the year of his death—that Isaiah saw the glorious vision recorded in the sixth chapter.
- Uzziah, leprous, set apart, and hidden away, had a son—his name was Jotham.

2. Jotham
- Jotham was co-regent with Uzziah until the death of his father.
- Jotham was a good man and a good king.
- He continued the prosperity that had started under his father.
- Jotham was a devout man of the Lord because he extended the courts of the temple.
- Doubtless Amos and Hosea, prophets of the northern kingdom, and Micah and Isaiah of the southern kingdom, had a great affect upon Jotham.

3. Ahaz
- Jotham was followed by Ahaz, and without an understanding of Ahaz and the time of Ahaz, we could never understand Isaiah and the words he brought from the Lord.
- The little kingdom of Judah in the south was surrounded by these:
  a. On the east were Moab and Edom.
  b. On the south, the ancient kingdoms of the Egyptian Pharaohs.
  c. On the west were the states of Philistia.
  d. To the north, the unfriendly state of Israel known as Ephraim.
  e. To the northeast was Syria with her capital of Damascus.
  f. To the ultimate north covering the horizon from side to side was the growing, colossal empire of Assyria, with its famous capital on the Tigress River named Nineveh. There in oriental splendor reigned what he called himself, the king of kings, in whose eyes the little kingdom of Judah and Ephraim were but as grasshoppers. This mammoth empire numbered its hosts by the myriads. Its chariots and horses covered lands like the locusts. Four times in the lifetime of Isaiah did this mighty force of Assyria overthrow Judah.
- How is it that Assyria was introduced to Judah? And how is it that Assyria came into the political and national life of Judah? It came about by this King Ahaz.
- Pekah, the king of Israel, the northern kingdom, and Rezin, king of Syria, formed a conspiracy to dethrone Ahaz, overrun Judah, and set up a puppet government there. That confrontation is called the Syro-Ephraimite War (recorded in 2 Chronicles 28).
- Ahaz, instead of turning to God, purposed to find help from some other source. Isaiah came to Ahaz and said, "Don't be afraid of Pekah of Israel or Rezin of Syria—they are but smoking fire brands—or the ends of burned out logs." (See Isaiah 7:4.)
- Isaiah told Ahaz to trust in God and that He would destroy Pekah and Rezin, but Ahaz had already purposed in his heart some other form of help. Isaiah stood before him and said, *"Ask thee a sign of the Lord thy God; ask it either in the depth, or in the height above"* (Isaiah 7:11), so Ahaz said, *"I will not ask, neither will I tempt the Lord"* (7:12).
- It was then that Isaiah delivered the Messianic Prophecy of Isaiah 7:14, looking beyond King Ahaz, he saw the Messiah—and told Ahaz that before that child was old enough to know very much, Pekah and Rezin would be destroyed forever.

- Ahaz had already purposed to find help from some other source. He turned to Tiglathpileser, King of Assyria, who was ruthless and merciless. He was one of the great conquerors of all times. It did him good to extend his power all over the southern kingdom. He was the one who devised deportation.
- Ahaz was more impressed by Tiglathpileser than by the power of God. So, with gladness and eagerness did Tiglathpileser come and the Assyrians not only destroyed the northern kingdom and Syria, but he also destroyed the city of Judah. Had it not been for the intervention of God, Assyria would have destroyed Jerusalem, the holy city, along with the temple.
- It was Ahaz who invited Tiglathpileser to come. Ahaz did not listen to the prophet, Isaiah.
- Under Ahaz, Judah was walked over. Ahaz journeyed to Damascus and met Tiglathpileser there and brought back idolatry that he saw there and he closed the temple. (See 2 Chronicles 28; 2 Kings 16.)
- Ahaz was followed by Hezekiah.

4. Hezekiah
- Hezekiah began his reign at twenty-five years of age and reigned twenty-nine years.
- He was like David—after God's own heart.
- The first thing he did was to call the people to revival, repentance, and reformation.
- Hezekiah opened the doors of the temple and invited the remnant of the northern kingdom to come and to celebrate with them the first Passover observed in a generation. (See 2 Chronicles 30.)
- When the Assyrians came—as they always did to a new government—they came under Sennacherib. (See 2 Chronicles 32; Isaiah 36, 37.) They came and destroyed the cities of Judah and surrounded Jerusalem. Hezekiah took the letters from Sennacherib demanding abject surrender. He took these demands before God and spread it out before the Lord in the temple (see Isaiah 37:14) and Isaiah said to the king in essence, "The Lord said, do not be afraid of the words that you have heard from the king of Assyria. Behold I will send a blast (put a spirit into him) and he will hear a rumor and return to his own land and I will cause him to fall by the sword in his own land." (See Isaiah 37:21–38.)
- Trusting the mighty arm of the Lord—this was the good king Hezekiah.
- Then something happened that brought disaster to the nation and to us. God sent Isaiah to Hezekiah and said, "*Thus saith the LORD, Set thine house in order: for thou shalt die, and not live*" (Isaiah 38:1). Hezekiah wept and Isaiah responded with the Word of the Lord, saying, "*I have heard thy prayer, I have seen thy tears: behold, I will add unto thy days fifteen years*" (Isaiah 38:5).
- Two things happened during those fifteen years:
  a. Merodach-Baladan—the upcoming king of Babylon who was getting ready to destroy Nineveh and Assyria—heard of Hezekiah's recovery and sent an embassy there supposedly to congratulate him on his recovery. But actually, it was to form a conspiracy against Nineveh. Hezekiah was flattered so he opened the treasures, the temple, and the cities to Merodach-Baladan and God sent Isaiah to Hezekiah and said to him, "*Behold, the days come, that all that is in thine house, and that which thy fathers have laid up in store until this day, shall be carried to Babylon: nothing shall be left*" (Isaiah 39:6). Then he said, "*And of thy sons that shall issue from thee…shall be eunuchs*" (Isaiah 39:7) and Daniel was a eunuch in Babylon. (See Daniel 1:3–7.)
  b. Second, Manasseh was born, the son of Hezekiah. Manasseh was twelve years old when he came to the throne and he reigned for fifty-five years in Jerusalem. (See 2 Chronicles 33 and 2 Kings 21.) Of all the kings there was none so mean and sinful as Manasseh. It was because of the sin of Manasseh that God destroyed Judah and sent her into the Babylonian captivity. It was God's judgment upon Judah because of Manasseh—a recurring theme in the story of

Scripture. The hatred of God for Manasseh can be seen in Jeremiah 15:1–4 as well. When was this man born? He was born in that fifteen-year period that God gave to Hezekiah. Because of his wickedness, God destroyed Judah and Jerusalem.

Now if you will take your Bible in hand, we will start through the book of Isaiah and teach it by sections and by verses as we go through the book. With this background knowledge of the book's layout, Isaiah himself, and the political circumstances, we are ready to dive into the Scripture found in the book of Isaiah.

How Much Do You Remember?

1. Although little is known about the man Isaiah, recall what we can gather about this prophet.
2. How is layout of the book of Isaiah similar to the layout of the Bible?
3. Recall the political lineage described in this historical background.

Your Assignment for Next Week:

1. Review your notes from this lesson.
2. Read Isaiah chapters 1–3
3. Underline your Bible.

Lesson 1 Notes

Lesson 2
CHAPTERS 1, 2, AND 3

CHAPTER 1
1. VERSE 1
   - The book is introduced by the first verse.
   - Here, Isaiah says that what he sees is a vision.
   - He identifies himself as being the son of Amoz and what he saw was concerning Judah and Jerusalem in the days of the four kings mentioned.
   - Other nations are also the subjects of his prophecies but only the relationship to the Jews indicated in chapters 13–23.
   - The ten tribes of Israel, the northern kingdom, are introduced only in the same relation—chapters 7–9.
   - Jerusalem is particularly specified because it is the site of the temple, the center of theocracy, and will be the future throne of the Messiah.
   - The Old Testament prophecies interpret spiritually the history given to us in other books just as the New Testament epistles interpret the Gospels and the book of Acts.
   - There is much spiritual correspondence between Isaiah and Romans—Isaiah being "the salvation of Jehovah" and Romans being "the gospel of God."

2. VERSE 2
   - Here begins the vision of Isaiah. The first word in the vision is significant: *"Hear."*
   - People who do not hear never learn, so the prophet utters the words of the vision when he says, *"Hear, O heavens, and give ear, O earth: for the LORD hath spoken, I have nourished and brought up children, and they have rebelled against me."*
   - Here a grand setting is before us. It is in the form of a court, the Lord God is the complainant and His case is against the defendants, Judah and Jerusalem.
   - The two words you should remember are these: "children rebelled." Those that He loved and brought up now had turned their back upon the Creator.

3. VERSES 3–8
   - *"The ox knoweth his owner, and the ass his master's crib: but Israel doth not know, my people doth not consider"* (verse 3).
   - Now these two animals are not especially known for their intelligence and yet the Lord says that they have more sense than those children that He had loved.
   - They owed their love and allegiance to the Lord God from their childhood in Egypt to the very moment that we speak of here—just as we in this dispensation owe our allegiance to the crucified one.
   - Our master's crib is the Word of God, a part of which we have before us now.
   - In verse 4, the words *"Ah sinful nation"* means nation-people-seed-children. The Holy One of Israel is the one that they have sinned against and in so doing, they are now hearing the judgment of the Lord upon them.
   - They are in a backslidden condition and the Lord says that they are *"laden with iniquity"* (verse 4). That expression sends us down the course of time and we hear the Man of Galilee saying, *"Come*

unto me, all ye that labour and are heavy laden, and I will give you rest" (Matthew 11:28). Now we know what the word "laden" means.

- You will notice, in verse 5, that sin always makes one sick in the head and makes the heart weak, which results in total moral depravity from the foot to the head (verse 6). He sees nothing but sores, bruises, and wounds caused by sin.

- Judah has become desolate (verse 7). Strangers devour it in the presence of its own people and this is all a part of the degradation of Judah. They are helpless and abandoned, just like a hut in a vineyard or a shanty in a cucumber field (verse 8).

4. VERSE 9

- Here we see the doctrine of the remnant: "*Except the L*ORD *of hosts had left unto us a very small remnant, we should have been as Sodom, and we should have been like unto Gomorrah.*"

5. THE DOCTINE OF THE REMNANT

- Let's look at that doctrine of the remnant in Isaiah: Isaiah 10:20–22, Isaiah 11:11–16, Isaiah 37:1–4, Isaiah 37:31–32, and Isaiah 46:3.

- In Romans 9:25–29 you find similar wording because Paul is quoting Isaiah 1:9 and also Isaiah 10:20–22.

- In Revelation 12:17 a little remnant of Jews is described.

- Thus far in Isaiah we have seen the sin and the judgment of God; but for a remnant, God would have destroyed Judah as He did Sodom and Gomorrah. Hope and salvation lie in the remnant always. The judgment could not fall on Sodom until Lot was taken out of there. The small remnant—the elect—God always sees and He always cares for.

- In Matthew 24:22 because of the "elect" the days of judgment will be shortened.

- In Revelation 7:3, we see these words: "*Hurt not…till we have sealed the servants of our God in their foreheads.*" God never chooses a majority. He looks upon His own—a small remnant.

- In Judges 7:2–7, Gideon had an army of 32,000 and God told Gideon to reduce it. So the fearful and fainthearted turned away and their total 22,000 turned back and left only 10,000. The Lord said to Gideon that the army was still too large, so God reduced them to three hundred and the Lord said, "*By the three hundred men that lapped will I save you, and deliver the Midianites into thine hand*" (verse 7).

- Of the twelve tribes, ten were lost. Only two were left and only a small remnant returned to Jerusalem with Zerubbabel (about 42,000).

- Jesus worked with *twelve* and only left 120 in the Upper Room.

- In the days of Noah, only Noah and his family, a total of eight, were saved.

- There will be a small remnant when the church is raptured, and I would dare say it would be very small compared to what we think it might be. The remnant will be so small that we can say "except for a very small remnant." That is the doctrine of the remnant in minute form.

6. VERSES 10–15

- Now the Lord applies the words of Sodom and Gomorrah to Judah and Jerusalem. Can Judah rightfully be called Sodom? In Revelation 11:8 it says so.

- It is they—Judah and Jerusalem—who are as Sodom and Gomorrah. The same people who faithfully observed all of the ordinances that the Lord God had appointed—the same people who offer all sacrifices—and the Lord asks after they have offered all those sacrifices and kept all of those ordinances, "for what purpose?" (See verse 11.)

- Then the Lord makes some interesting observations in verses 12–15. He speaks very bluntly and He talks in words that even we can understand.

- Action and doing is not enough. I think we can learn something here. If we observe ordinance as an outward act, seeking God's approval, it is in vain. But if we do it for Him, in the right spirit, it blesses Him and it blesses us.

- We should never rest in any ordinance because in so doing, we emphasize the act of the ordinance itself and not the precious blood of Christ as our only confidence.

- We must *see through* the ordinance—the Lord Jesus. It causes us to "remember" what He did for us on the cross.

7. VERSES 16–17

- *"Wash you, make you clean; put away the evil of your doings from before mine eyes; cease to do evil; learn to do well."* That sounds like John the Baptist saying, *"Repent ye.... Bring forth therefore fruits meet for repentance"* (Matthew 3:2, 8).

- But first fruits, new fruits, means a new life and a new tree.

- How can we be clean, washed, and cease to do evil?

- Only through the grace of our Lord Jesus Christ are we washed and made clean.

- The new life in Him is the righteous requirements of the law fulfilled. (See Romans 8:4.)

8. VERSE 18

- One of the most stirring and moving verses in all Scripture is here in verse 18. Look up this verse and copy it down:

_____

_____

_____

_____

_____

- This is the great invitation of God. It is the word of grace. It seems that God condescends and He reasons with the man.

- The revelation of this book is reasonable and right. The religion of our Lord is reasonable and rational.

- The whole first chapter of Isaiah is a court case. His arraignment to Judah and Jerusalem is found in the first part of the chapter and He called them to trial. This is His plea toward those people He loves. His hurt turns into love. This is a blessed proclamation of full amnesty. It is the judicial cleansing of every repentant soul.

9. VERSES 19–20

- Blessing follows obedience and vice versa and He seals this judgment with the last phrase of verse 20: *"For the mouth of the Lord hath spoken it."*

10. VERSES 21–31

- Here we find indictments, warnings, and promises.

- The Lord looks back on the city in tenderness as He remembered Jerusalem, but now it must be likened to a harlot.

+ Once in a place of righteousness, now murderers are there. In place of silver (speaking of atonement) was the dross of complacency and self-sufficiency. Wine of joy diluted with foul water.

+ The princes—the leaders—were rebellious and they were bribe lovers. Because of this, the Lord would judge and pour out vengeance on those who were enemies of the Lord.

+ Notice the strong language of verse 24, where we find: "*Therefore saith the* Lord, *the* Lord *of hosts, the mighty One of Israel.*" He emphasizes who He is.

+ The discipline of the Lord is real. Here we see that He has the effect of removing the unjust and unholy, purging the nation from its dross and sin, from all that was base and unpleasing to God, after which He would restore their judges as at the first.

+ Then, redeemed with judgment, Zion will be called once more the city of righteousness (see verse 26), the faithful city.

+ This will be their final blessing as other Scriptures show us, after the long years of their dispersion and the bitterness of the last great tribulation have come to an end. Their sufferings must go on until the unrepentant transgressors and willful sinners are utterly destroyed. Fierce judgment is always indicated when people turn away from the Lord God.

+ The warnings of this section have been fulfilled in Israel's history and will be completely fulfilled in the tribulation.

+ The promises look toward the millennium. The "oaks" of verses 29 and 30 are connected with idolatress worship.

+ And finally, let me paraphrase the last verse: "The strong man among you will disappear like burning straw and your evil deeds are the spark that sets the straw on fire and no one will be able to put it out." So, the word "tow" means straw.

CHAPTER 2

In this chapter, we find a millennial scene. Jerusalem is the world's center of government and instruction concerning God. When Christ comes to reign, Jerusalem will be the world capital and the center of worship. The peace described, for instance, in verse 4 can only come when Christ returns in glory.

Chapter 2 begins the second vision—the second of the three that we will find in chapters 1–6. The vision in this chapter will last throughout chapters 2, 3, 4, and 5. Looking over the background that was taught during the first lesson and looking over the sinfulness of Judah and Jerusalem, Isaiah sees the last days of the Lord in verses 1–5 and these verses should be a parenthesis.

1. VERSES 1–5
   + Let me emphasize here that what Isaiah sees in this vision is exactly what he saw.

   + Notice the words in verse 1: "*The word that Isaiah the son of Amoz saw concerning Judah and Jerusalem.*"

   + "*And it shall come to pass in the last days*" (verse 2). Isaiah sees through all of the troubles, destruction, and sin and the Lord gives to him a vision of what it will become.

   + The vision begins with an outlook far beyond the present condition of sin and suffering in the earth to a day in which Judah and Jerusalem are not only restored, but shine with a far more exceeding and eternal weight of glory than they ever have.

   + In verse 2, we have the supremacy of that beloved people, Israel, when fully restored to the favor of Jehovah.

   + Jerusalem will then be the center, spiritually and politically, as she is physically now the center of all the earth. She will have no rival in the capitals that now surpass her. The Lord will take Israel in that day and restore them to their land and Jerusalem will be His throne city.

- Notice in verse 2: "*...the mountain of the Lord's house shall be established in the top of the mountains, and shall be exalted above the hills.*" The mountain is the city itself. This is a common prophetic symbol. Mountains signify governments and throne cities, and Jerusalem will be "*the city of the great King*" (Psalm 48:2; Matthew 5:35), and "*all nations shall flow unto it*" (Isaiah 2:2).

- This will be fulfilled literally in the coming millennial reign after the present work of grace has come to an end. Right now, according to Acts 15:14, He is visiting the Gentiles to take out of us a people for His name. When this special work is completed, He will "*build again the tabernacle of David*" (Acts 15:16), and through restored Israel, bless all the nations. Then will be the time when "*many people shall go and say, Come ye, and let us go up to the mountain of the Lord, to the house of the God of Jacob; and he will teach us of his ways, and we will walk in his paths*" (Isaiah 2:3).

- You see, in that day of His power, the law will go forth from Zion and His Word from Jerusalem. He will rule all the nations in equity and put down every opposing thing. Just think, Israel and Jerusalem, trodden down and small, will head all of the nations, nevermore to lose that place of supremacy, for she will be established with the Messiah.

- The times of the Gentiles at that time will be over. The Lord will settle all the disputes and nations will convert their weapons of war into instruments of peace and there will be no more war nor will they learn anything about war anymore.

- Then this parenthetical statement ends with a plea, "*O house of Jacob [Israel], come ye, and let us walk in the light of the Lord*" (verse 5).

It is very evident that the verses that we have been considering (verses 1–5) are parenthetical, for there is no apparent connection between verse 6 and what has gone before. It is refreshing spiritually to see beyond the dark, present judgment of God's people and to know that Isaiah was not only prophesying about the present for Judah and Jerusalem, but he was also seeing beyond that into the glorious future, which he calls "*in the last days*" (verse 2).

2. VERSES 6–9

- Now we come out of that glorious vision of the future back into reality and the then present conditions to which Isaiah addressed himself.

- He begins that word of chastisement from the Lord by saying, "*Therefore thou hast forsaken thy people the house of Jacob, because they be replenished from the east, and are soothsayers like the Philistines, and they please themselves in the children of strangers*" (verse 6).

- Here we see east and west both contributing to draw Judah and Jerusalem away from the Lord God. The Scripture says, "*from the east*" and then you will notice the soothsayers are from the Philistines. The Philistines were to the west of Judah and Jerusalem.

- Wealth came from the east and the soothsaying and the idolatry from the west, and we notice that God's people are attracted to both.

- On the eastern border of Judah dwelt the Moabites and the Edomites, who over and over again made inroads into the land of Judah and brought its people into humiliating bondage. From the opposite side, there were also evils from the Philistines. Wealth came from one side; idolatry, black magic, ritualism, and superstition came from the other.

- In verse 7, you note the condition of Moab and Edom with lots of money and lots of gold.

- In verse 8, you will notice the condition of the Philistines with all the idols, the word of their own hands, their soothsaying, and their idolatry.

3. VERSES 10–22

- Here the prophet speaks of the day of the Lord when God will arise in His might and His indignation to deal with wickedness and corruption wherever it is found.

- Men may seek to enter into the rocks and hide themselves in the ground (verse 10) but their hope of escaping the anger of the Lord will be in vain for *"The lofty looks of man shall be humbled, and the haughtiness of men shall be bowed down, and the Lord alone shall be exalted in that day"* (verse 11).

- The day of the Lord is in direct contrast to the day of man—this present age when God is permitting men to take their own way and to try out their own plans independently of His authority.

- In verse 12, we read, *"For the day of the Lord of hosts shall be upon every one that is proud and lofty, and upon every one that is lifted up; and he shall be brought low."* What is the day of the Lord? It is that period of time that we have studied in the book of Revelation—namely God dealing with man during the tribulation (we will not be here).

- This judgment of men upon the earth is expressed very vividly in verses 12–14. Notice in verse 13, cedars and oaks—the noblest of all trees—are only figures of men high up on the social scale.

- Note also, in verse 14, the mountains and the hills, which means all organized governments and states.

- Note, in verse 15, the tower and wall, which means military preparedness.

- Verse 16 mentions ships and pleasant pictures—meaning all forms of commerce and art.

- In that day, all of man's achievements and his pride will be brought down and only the Lord God will be exalted.

- In verses 18 and 19, the prophet turns to the root evil of that time—idolatry. The Lord has been forsaken; idols have replaced Him. All that men have put in the place of God will be abolished, and in their terror, men will hide in the holes, rocks, and caves of the earth hoping to find shelter from the wrath of the almighty God (verse 19 and 21).

- We see here the fulfillment of the statement of the Lord when He said in Luke 23:30: *"Then shall they begin to say to the mountains, Fall on us; and to the hills, Cover us."*

- Surely both New and Old Testaments alike lift up their voices to proclaim our Lord Jesus to be Jehovah, the Lord of Hosts, the King of Glory. Man is nothing and so the Lord, through Isaiah says, *"Cease ye from man, whose breath is in his nostrils: for wherein is he to be accounted of?"* (verse 22). Man alone has life only as he breathes, but the Christian has something more than just breath because Christ is Himself *"a quickening Spirit"* (1 Corinthians 15:45) and is *"able also to save them to the uttermost that come unto God by him, seeing that he ever liveth to make intercession for them"* (Hebrews 7:25).

- In other words, we should never have confidence in the flesh at all, but always rejoice in the Lord for He is worthy.

CHAPTER 3

In chapter 3, we have a continuation of the vision that Isaiah saw at the beginning of chapter 2. This vision will continue on through chapter 5. The judgment we see here in chapter 3 is merely a continuation of chapter 2, so it continues on as if there was no chapter division. The judgment is leveled in particular against Judah and Jerusalem. It is intense and severe. This prophecy is a picture of Isaiah's day and it was fulfilled in the past. However, this does not exhaust its meaning. These conditions will prevail again in the end time and will call down the wrath of God.

1. VERSES 1–7

- In verse 1, you will notice the title of the Lord: *"For, behold, the Lord, the Lord of hosts, doth take away from Jerusalem and from Judah the stay and the staff, the whole stay of bread, and the whole stay of water."* The word *"stay"* means supply, or that which remains. Wouldn't it be awful if the Lord said that to us? Because you see Christ is our Bread of Life (see John 6:35), and He is also the Water of Life (see

John 4:14). There was a famine in verse 1 and this was a form of judgment from God toward Judah and Jerusalem.

- There was also a famine of mighty men, soldiers, judicial leaders, prophets, and the prudent (verses 2–3) and there were no respectable men among the leaders of the army nor among honorable men, and the counselors and the eloquent speakers were not to be found. In other words, there was a lack or a famine of leadership. Qualified men for high positions were lacking. This likewise is a judgment from God.

- In verse 4, we see a terrible situation and the Scripture says, *"And I will give children to be their princes, and babes shall rule over them."* In other words, men with the mental level of children will rule over the people. Their incompetency is likewise judgment from God.

- The situation continues; God is dethroned and anarchy always follows. In verses 5–7, we find that in desperation, men were ready to follow anyone who might be able to point out a way of escape from the present misery and one who might promise to bring order out of the chaotic condition then prevailing. Those whom they turned to for guidance were in utter bewilderment themselves.

- You will notice in these verses that they were mad at each other, neighbors and relatives. They had no honor for the older generation and anyone that had the proper clothing would be called a ruler and be allowed to have charge of the government. But no one wanted to lead, they all wanted to follow, fuss, and sin. The ones who were asked to be the leaders did not want to be the healers because they themselves were in a poor plight and very bad condition.

- All of these verses 1–7 are the judgments of God upon Judah and Jerusalem.

2. VERSES 8–11

- The root cause of all of the trouble is indicated in verse 8: *"For Jerusalem is ruined, and Judah is fallen: because their tongue and their doings are against the LORD, to provoke the eyes of his glory."* Thus, they had brought down judgment upon their own heads and so we hear the solemn woes pronounced against them.

- There are two of these solemn woes in this chapter found in verses 9 and 11, and another six "woes" can be found in chapter 5.

- The first woe is found in verse 9: *"Woe unto their soul! for they have rewarded evil unto themselves."*

- Then in verse 11: *"Woe unto the wicked! it shall be ill with him: for the reward of his hands shall be given him."* This is simply another way of saying, *"Whatsoever a man soweth, that shall he also reap"* (Galatians 6:7).

- In between these two woes is a promise in verse 10 for deliverance of His people—the righteous remnant that God will care for and will protect in a day of storms and stress. Copy down this promise from verse 10 below:

_____

_____

_____

_____

_____

_____

3. VERSES 12–15

- In verse 12, we hear the voice of the Lord God saying, *"As for my people…. Oh my people…."* Jehovah sees His people being oppressed by women and by rulers with boys' minds and as He cries out to His people, it reminds us of that same tender tone that we find in Matthew 23:37, which says, *"O Jerusalem, Jerusalem, thou that killest the prophets, and stonest them which are sent unto thee, how often would I have gathered thy children together, even as a hen gathereth her chickens under her wings, and ye would not!"*

- It is indicated in verses 13–14 that Jehovah must stand up, intervene, and judge.

- Then the Lord asks this question: *"What mean ye that ye beat my people to pieces, and grind the faces of the poor?"* (verse 15). This question is the reason for His judgment because it refers to His people.

4. VERSES 16–24

- In verses 16–24, we find the subject to be women and the appearance of women.

- You will note that there are twenty-one items of feminine attire mentioned in these verses. At least eighteen of these were worn by the Babylonian goddess called Ishtar, whom the Hebrew women were idolatrously trying to copy.

- The vain women are rebuked. In their pride and empty headedness, their one great concern was personal adornment. They sought to add to their beauty by every device known.

- In verse 16, where the daughters of Zion are haughtily walking with stretched forth necks and lustful eyes, you can see that it is not just a matter of dressing properly and keeping in style, but rather the difficulty here lies in the inner life.

- God took note of all the ornaments and apparel that they relied upon to make themselves attractive. Remember also that in the New Testament, careful instruction is given to women that their adorning should not be focused on the outward appearance, but rather that meekness and grace, which is the adornment of the heart, should be apparent. (See 1 Timothy 2:9–15; 1 Peter 3:3.)

- Verses 25 and 26 should actually be a part of chapter 4, so they will be included in the next chapter's study.

How Much Do You Remember?

1. Describe Isaiah's vision concerning Judah and Jerusalem in the days of the four kings mentioned in the opening verses.
2. Describe the doctrine of the remnant.
3. Why is it that Judah and Jerusalem can be likened to Sodom and Gomorrah?
4. Consider verse 18, the verse you copied down. What implications does this have for your life and your faith walk?
5. How can chapter 1 as a whole be related to a court case?
6. Describe the vision for Judah and Jerusalem found in Isaiah 2:1–5. What is the outlook for these cities beyond their present condition?
7. Describe the idolatry happening in chapters 2 and 3. What are the people putting before God? Where are these influences coming from?
8. As described in chapter 2 verses 10–22, what will be man's reaction to the judgment of God?
9. Recall the judgments of God found in verses 1–7 in chapter 3.
10. Amidst the two "woes" found in chapter 3, what is the promise given for God's people?

Your Assignment for Next Week:
1. Review your notes from this lesson.
2. Read Isaiah chapters 4 through 6.
3. Underline your Bible.

Lesson 2 Notes

_____

_____

_____

_____

_____

_____

_____

_____

_____

_____

_____

_____

_____

_____

_____

_____

_____

_____

_____

_____

_____

_____

_____

_____

_____

_____

_____

_____

Lesson 3
CHAPTERS 4, 5, AND 6

CHAPTER 4

1. VERSES 3:25–26; 4:1

    ❖ As we left the study of chapter 3, I stated that verses 25 and 26 of that chapter should rightfully belong in chapter 4. When you read verses 25 and 26 of chapter 3 along with verse 1 of chapter 4, you get the meaning of the whole passage:

    > *Thy men shall fall by the sword, and thy mighty in the war. And her gates shall lament and mourn; and she being desolate shall sit upon the ground. And in that day seven women shall take hold of one man, saying, We will eat our own bread and wear our own apparel: only let us be called by thy name, to take away our reproach.*

    ❖ These verses depict the conditions during the tribulation and the remainder of chapter 4 sets forth the preparation for entering the kingdom.

    ❖ This section could be called prophecy in two ways—the conditions would prevail not only in the days following the threatened Babylonian captivity but also in the dark days of the tribulation; they are followed by verses 2–6 as all millennial prophecy.

    ❖ Because of the men being killed in battle, there would be and there will be a shortage of men. There is but one man left to seven women and the women begged to be taken into a man's household at no expense only to be called by the man's name. The Scripture says, *"to take away our reproach."* What is reproach? Look up this word and define it below:

    Reproach: _____

    _____

    ❖ To die childless was to the Hebrew the acme of misery, but over and above this misery, being unwedded or childless was especially felt by the Jewish women who were looking for "the seed of the woman." Jesus Christ is called the *"branch"* in verse 2. A Hebrew woman's desolation could go no further.

2. VERSES 2–6

    ❖ This section of verses describes a vision of the future kingdom.

    ❖ In verse 2, we find the words *"branch of the Lᴏʀᴅ."* It is called a sprout in other portions of the Scripture. He is also called in this verse *"the fruit of the earth"* and in this, we see Him in His spotless humanity sprouting forth in the middle of all of the death and desolation of Adam's race.

    ❖ In all of the ruin, war, and desolation there is one single star of promise, hope, and blessing. For there will be a remnant of Israel described here in verse 2 as *"them that are escaped of Israel."* These will be left after the burning judgments of Jehovah have passed and every one included in this remnant will be written in the Book of Life.

    ❖ In verses 3 and 4, everyone that is left in Jerusalem and everyone whose name is written among the living will be a holy people and dedicated to Him.

    ❖ All these verses from 2 through 6 indicate that this then is the beginning of what is termed the millennium, when Israel's Messiah, our Lord Jesus Christ, will reign over the earth. It is the dispensation of the fullness of time, when indeed all things will be under His control that are in heaven or on earth. (See Ephesians 1:10.)

- ✦ In verse 5, we see that the Lord will create upon every dwelling place in Mount Zion and upon all of the assemblies a cloud of smoke by day and a shining, flaming fire by night.

- ✦ In verse 6, there will be a tabernacle for a shadow in the daytime from the heat and for a place of refuge and cover from storm and rain. This speaks of the great Shekinah glory of God, which is a parallel thought given to us in Exodus 13:21–22. This is the presence of God when the Messiah will be with His people and be their stay and their guide, their refuge and their protection.

Throughout this chapter, we have seen first tribulation and then beyond the tribulation into the millennial reign of Christ.

CHAPTER 5

You will recall that this vision of Isaiah began at the first part of chapter 2 and now we are in the last chapter of this same second vision. This chapter is called Jehovah's vineyard. The vineyard comes from one of the two figures taken from the botanical world to represent the whole nation of Israel. (The other is the fig tree.) Our Lord gave a parable of the vineyard before His death that obviously referred to the whole house of Israel. (See Matthew 21:33–46.) Isaiah announced the imminent captivity of the northern kingdom into Assyria and the southern kingdom into Babylon. The Lord Jesus Christ showed that God gave them a second chance in the return from the seventy years of Babylonian captivity, but the rejection of the Son of God would usher in a more extensive and serious dispensation.

Here Isaiah compares Israel with the lovely vineyard planted by the Lord, which instead of producing luscious fruit, yielded only wild and worthless grapes.

1. VERSES 1–7

- ✦ In verse 1, the Lord says, *"Now will I sing to my wellbeloved a song of my beloved touching his vineyard. My wellbeloved hath a vineyard."* The Lord says that He will sing to His well-beloved. Who could that be? Only the Lord Jesus. "My beloved touches His vineyard." What could that be? It means that Jesus touches the house of Israel. Then again, "My well beloved has a vineyard." That says the same thing. The meaning can be found from knowing who is speaking, and also by reading verse 7, which gives us further clues: *"For the vineyard of the LORD of hosts is the house of Israel, and the men of Judah his pleasant plant."* Isaiah looks beyond and he sees the Lord Jesus centuries before His coming.

- ✦ In verse 2, we see that the vineyard is fenced and all the stones were gathered out of it and the land was planted with the choicest vine—Israel. He built a tower in the midst of it and also made a wine press only to find that there was no fruit suitable to His holy desires. That is, instead of bearing fruit for God, Israel brought forth that which only grieved His heart and dishonored His holy name.

- ✦ And so, addressing Himself directly to the inhabitants of Jerusalem and the men of Judah, He asked, *"Judge, I pray you, betwixt me and my vineyard. What could have been done more to my vineyard, that I have not done in it?"* (verses 3–4).

- ✦ After all the care He had lavished upon Israel, His loving provision and His gracious forgiveness that was extended to them over and over again and now—how could it be possible that there would be no suitable fruit for Him?

- ✦ All of this was a manifestation of a heart that had departed from the living God and so, after giving them one opportunity after another to repent and to judge themselves in His sight, He finally decided to give them up saying in verses 5–6:

    I will tell you what I will do to my vineyard: I will take away the hedge thereof, and it shall be eaten up; and break down the wall thereof, and it shall be trodden down: and I will lay it waste:

it shall not be pruned, nor digged; but there shall come up briers and thorns: I will also command the clouds that they rain no rain upon it.

+ Here we see in plain language that God had indeed planted Israel and shielded her from everything and yet her rewards were only wild grapes. Israel and Judah would be strongly and sternly disciplined by God.

2. VERSES 8–23

+ In these verses, we have the six dreadful woes upon Israel. These six woes foretell the execution of judgment. The predictions in this chapter of Israel and Judah has occurred exactly with man as a race because the Lord God sang a song of love and joy over His creation back in Genesis 1. But all of those who have followed Adam, the first Adam, have taken on the nature of sin and iniquity; but praise God, there is a second Adam—and the song over Him never ceases.

   a. The first woe

   + In verses 8 to 10, the first woe is directed against the lust of the eye—the coveting of houses and lands. The people are never satisfied. Having acquired one house or field, they had to have another.

   + The Lord speaks clearly at this point when He gives the indication that the penalty will correspond to the offense. For instance, in verse 10: *"ten acres of vineyard shall yield one bath,"* or about eight gallons. If we are to covet, we are to do it scripturally, and the Scripture does say to *"covet earnestly the best gifts,"* that is, those that will make least of ourselves and will edify our brethren. (See 1 Corinthians 12:31.)

   b. The second woe

   + In verses 11 to 17, we find the second woe is directed against the lusts of the flesh, against those who from the beginning of the day until the cool of the evening pursue strong drink until wine pursues them.

   + This is combined with the more refined form of sensuous pleasure, music— which from the Day of Jubal has been one of the chief delights of the children of Cain.

   + These—wine and music—are their whole lives. Body and soul are provided for, but what about the spirit that can never be satisfied without God? They regard not the work of the Lord and they care nothing about the operation of His hands (verse 12)

   + In verse 13, they seem to have no knowledge of God and their men of honor are famished and they are dried up with thirst. In other words, you can't drink enough of that stuff because you are always thirsty.

   + Note again the correspondence between the sin and the penalty in verse 14: *"Therefore hell hath enlarged herself, and opened her mouth without measure: and their glory, and their multitude, and their pomp, and he that rejoiceth, shall descend into it."*

   + In all the severity of the judgment, the Lord of hosts will be exalted and He will be sanctified in righteousness.

   c. The third woe

   + We read about the third woe in verses 18 and 19. This is upon those who openly defy the God of Israel and this is clearly directed against those who, boasting of liberty, are really but yoked beasts of burden and the wagon that they are pulling is their own sin.

   + They challenge the Lord God to carry out what He has long threatened to do when they say, in verse 19: *"Let him make speed, and hasten his work, that we may see it."* In other words, they are the ones who did not think prophecy could ever be fulfilled nor could they comprehend it.

d. The fourth woe
+ The fourth woe is found in verse 20, and this is upon those who fail to distinguish between good and evil, righteousness and unrighteousness.
+ They put darkness for light and light for darkness. They put bitter for sweet and sweet for bitter. In other words, they make no distinction between that which honors God and that which dishonors Him. They are neither cold nor hot but utterly indifferent to divine truth.

e. The fifth woe
+ The fifth woe is found in verse 21. This woe is upon those who are wise in their own eyes and prudent in their own sight. Each considers himself competent to rule God out of his own life. This is the pride of life.
+ This woe is the sin of pride, which God hates above all else. (See Proverbs 16–17.)

f. The sixth woe
+ The sixth woe is found in verses 22 and 23. It is to those who are so inflamed with wine that they lose all sense of righteousness and judgment.
+ This is not a repetition of the second woe, for these heavy drinkers are on the judgment seat, and show their incompetency for the place they have assumed by reversing all justice—acquitting the guilty and condemning the innocent.

3. VERSES 24–30
+ Now, in verses 24–30, the penalty is announced. God's indignation would be aroused against those who repudiated His law and despised His Word.
+ At God's summons, swift and powerful troops would descend upon Judah (verses 26–29).
+ Her people would be smitten (verse 25). The nations from afar would be an instrument of vengeance in the hands of an outraged God (verse 26).
+ The immediate application of these stirring words is to the marching, triumphant hoards, first of Assyria, which would lead Israel captive—that is, the ten northern tribes—in 722 B.C., and then of Babylon, which would later overwhelm Judah.
+ No effort on Judah's part would enable them to turn back the power of the enemy when the appointed hour had come for the destruction that had been so long predicted. Like a roaring lion would the eastern nations rush upon their prey and carry it away triumphantly, and in that hour of distress, they would cry to the Lord in vain, for darkness and sorrow were destined to be their portion.
+ Notice the words in verse 30: "*in that day*," linking this with the previous chapters and justifying connecting them together. It is good to remember that although nations may be influenced by all kinds of motives, little do they recognize that God is still moving upon the scenes. His mighty hand can be seen even in our present day as we see these truths and other truths of the Word of God being brought to pass and being fulfilled in our day.

CHAPTER 6

We have now come to the third vision of Isaiah. The first vision was found in chapter 1, the second vision began in chapter 2 and continued through chapter 5, and now in chapter 6, we take up the third vision. Just as the third book of the Bible, Leviticus, takes us into the sanctuary with the glories of Christ passed before us in all of its types, so in our book here in Isaiah, we are now coming to the third vision. Here in this chapter, we see the Lord Jesus in His glory fully manifested, which is the very meaning of "three."

This portion of prophecy is greatly hallowed to us by the words recorded in John 12:36–41. Jesus said,

While ye have light, believe in the light, that ye may be the children of light. These things spake Jesus, and departed, and did hide himself from them. But though he had done so many miracles before them, yet they believed not on him: that the saying of Esaias [Isaiah] the prophet might be fulfilled, which he spake, Lord, who hath believed our report? and to whom hath the arm of the Lord been revealed? [See Isaiah 53:1.] *Therefore they could not believe, because that Esaias said again, He hath blinded their eyes, and hardened their heart; that they should not see with their eyes, nor understand with their heart, and be converted, and I should heal them.* [See Isaiah 6:10.] *These things said Esaias, when he saw his glory, and spake of him.* [See Isaiah 6:1.]

There are many reasons given why this call came in chapter 6 to the prophet Isaiah. I think there are two reasons for this vision appearing here in chapter 6 and not at the beginning of the book. The first five chapters were sad, tragic, and full of judgment, whereas the sixth chapter is placed here for Isaiah to bear a message of hope to the people. It is also the introduction to the great section of Scripture we call the book of Immanuel in chapters 7 through 11. This could never be considered a "second blessing" of Isaiah. What is said here in chapter 6 is only a divine seal of authority upon the preceding chapters as well as a guarantee of the validity of all that follows.

The vision might also be considered as a renewed, transforming, enlightening experience graciously given to one already summoned into divine service. Such experiences were granted, for example, to the apostles Peter and Paul. (See Acts 10:9–16; 18:9–10.) So regardless of the theory as to the reason why this vision is placed here in chapter 6, it is for our learning and for God to bless us as we study it.

1. VERSES 1–5

   + In verse 1, we see the time of the vision. It took place *"in the year that King Uzziah died,"* which was about 740 B.C. This ruler, inflicted with leprosy as a result of disobedience, never recovered from that disease and died a leper.

   + Isaiah opens with a sad note by mentioning the death of this king, but ends on a victorious note when he adds, *"I saw also the Lord sitting upon a throne, high and lifted up, and his train filled the temple"* (verse 1).

   + Isaiah went into the temple and discovered that over and above and beyond the dead king, there was one true king of the nation Israel who was not dead. Isaiah saw the Lord with all of His majestic splendor sitting upon the throne that was high and lifted up. This was the same temple in which Uzziah had tried to take and do away with the service of the priests. Isaiah was familiar with that temple because he had been there many times. This may therefore teach us that it takes the eyes of the soul to see God and the ears of the heart to hear Him.

   + In verses 2–3, we read that above the throne there stood seraphim. This is the only time that word is used and it is used in the plural. This is an unusual order of angels. Each one had six wings; with two they cover their face, with two they cover their feet, and with two they did fly. These seraphim cry out, *"Holy, holy, holy"* (verse 3). This refers to the three in the Godhead: God the Father, God the Son, and God the Holy Spirit. In that light of God, Isaiah knows the seraphim at once, insofar as to give them that name. The word *saraph* means "to burn"—but not to burn as we would burn incense. This word means to consume as in the judgment of God. It is always in connection with a sin offering, which is consumed without the camp. This gives us some of the significance of the seraphim. They express symbolically the active, searching, burning holiness of God. Remember that it is the glory of Jesus that Isaiah looks upon and the three-fold ascription of praise by the angels when they say *"Holy, holy, holy"* guarantees that *"in him dwelleth all the fulness of the Godhead bodily"* (Colossians 2:9).

- In verse 4, as the song of worship sounded forth, the very posts, doors, and foundation begin to sway in a responsive awe to His glory. Now we come to the personal part of the vision, where we see the Lord preparing a vessel unto honor for His use.

- We now come to the most detailed call of God to a man that is recorded in the Word of God. In those days of Uzziah's fleeting moments, Isaiah saw beyond that king, and he saw the great Lord—Jehovah—Jesus—and His presence filled the temple. We turn now to the man, Isaiah, and we see the Lord preparing a vessel unto His honor and His use.

- Verse 5 is the first step of the call, and notice the words of Isaiah: *"Then said I, Woe is me! for I am undone; because I am a man of unclean lips, and I dwell in the midst of a people of unclean lips: for mine eyes have seen the King, the Lord of hosts."* The first step then is that he is brought into that holy light in which he sees everything clearly, exactly as it is and at once he cried out that he is undone and a man of unclean lips. The light of the Lord Jesus causes us to stop and reveals in us first of all that we are sinful and unclean, yet the light that shines around us is the light of the Lord and in His presence all of us are as filthy rags. Isaiah instantly recognizes that it is his own lips that are unclean, not merely those of his neighbors. He is of the same makeup as all of the rest of us. In the light of that glory of the Lord, there is no difference between us, for all of us have sinned and come short of the glory of God. (See Romans 3:23.) The only difference between the lost and the saved is the fact that we have confessed that Christ makes the difference.

2. VERSES 6–7

- In verses 6 and 7, we find that one of the seraphim came to Isaiah and he had a live coal in his hand that he had taken off of the altar and he laid that live coal upon the mouth of Isaiah and said, *"Lo, this hath touched thy lips; and thine iniquity is taken away, and thy sin purged"* (verse 7).

- In the presence of God, Isaiah saw himself as being unclean. Always the closer we are to Him, the more we realize the sin that is in our life.

- Let's look at that coal off of the altar.

  a. The word *"touched"* here was not a casual, inoperative thing, but the word conveys the same significant meaning as we find in Luke 8:45 when the Lord felt the light fingertip and asked, *"Who touched me?"* In that touch, there is always an effect—a communication of virtue.

  b. The glowing coal then is our Lord Jesus Christ, but not on the high throne that was lifted up, but the Lord Jesus lifted up on the cross. Here we see in one scene what historically took place in two actions on and after the final entry into Jerusalem in Luke 19. Then He came to sit upon His throne, but the people were not ready for Him as their king. He came unto His own and His own received Him not, so He steps, as it were, from off the throne and laying Himself upon the altar, becomes the Paschal Lamb, or the glowing coal.

  c. There are two altars where this coal could've come from—the *golden altar* standing in the holy place, called the altar of incense, or the *brazen altar* standing at the very entrance of the court and called the altar of the burnt offering. Since the glowing coal clearly speaks of the means by which sin was put away and forgiven, that coal could not have come from the altar of incense. That altar was provided for worship for those whose sins had already been forgiven. It was the brazen and not the golden altar.

  d. The fire by which the coal glowed must then have been the fire, not of complacency and delight of which incense always speaks, but it was the fire and the coal of judgment. The burning in that coal was the same as you find in the name of the angelic host called seraphim. It was burning like "seraph."

- It must be different for us today; it was quite natural with the character of dispensation in which everything was external that Isaiah's lips should be touched, for the lips are the external manifestation of what we really are. (See Matthew 12:37.) But it is the inner man that must now be affected or touched by that coal of fire, for it is our Lord Jesus suffering, burning, and being consumed for our heart to be cleansed. Once the heart is changed in our present dispensation, then we have freedom and joy to talk and walk with the Lord and to make joyful confession and to be used for service.

+ It is not at all necessary to look upon the prophet Isaiah here as taking the place of an unforgiven sinner—far from it. He was surely a saint (believer) long before this. It is not Isaiah's regeneration that is figured here, but his being made ready for the Master's use in accord with all the Scripture that follows.

+ Never confuse these two truths: there is a cleansing that is accomplished at once by divine grace—then there is the progressive, daily learning and responsibility pressed upon us by the glowing coal of Christ touching us in prayer, in Bible study, in worship, etc.

3. VERSE 8

+ In verse 8, Isaiah *"heard the voice of the Lord, saying, Whom shall I send, and who will go for us? Then said I, Here am I; send me."* When you are close to the Lord, you always listen to the Lord and you hear what He says. Isaiah was close to the Lord there in the temple and he heard the words.

+ Notice that the question is not addressed to great ranks of angelic beings. No seraphim nor cherubim offers. The Lord God had one man in mind and He was getting him ready for His own use.

+ Notice the wording in verse 8, when the Lord God says, *"Whom shall I send, and whom will go for us?"* The word *"us"* here is plural and God the Father, God the Son, and God the Holy Spirit are all revealed in that one word called *"us."*

+ Just what did Isaiah look upon there in the temple? He actually saw the manifestation of the Son of God.

+ Then Isaiah volunteers. Once he had been cleansed and touched by the Lord Jesus, he was ready to receive the call and the call always comes in a different way. God always calls and appears to us if we will but listen. A man feels a call from God. The call is the need and the need is the call. This is always true in Scripture.

+ Isaiah volunteered and he kept on going for another fifty years of preaching and prophesying.

4. VERSES 9–10

+ In this passage, the Lord tells Isaiah,

    Go, and tell this people, Hear ye indeed, but understand not; and see ye indeed, but perceive not. Make the heart of this people fat, and make their ears heavy, and shut their eyes; lest they see with their eyes, and hear with their ears, and understand with their heart, and convert, and be healed.

+ When the seraphim came and cleansed Isaiah, and Isaiah volunteered for the service of God, the Lord said to him, "Go."

+ Isaiah was to tell the people the message of the Lord, but the Lord said in these two verses that they wouldn't hear, see, or understand. It seems like a strange and sad thing that the prophet Isaiah is sent to a blind, deaf, and hard-hearted people, yet we may safely say at once that God never hardens hearts that would otherwise be soft. He does not blind the eyes of those who would see.

+ This can be likened to carrying a bright light into a dark barn at night. At once, all of the unclean creatures of the darkness like the rats and mice to whom the darkness is congenial—these things flee from the light and scatter to darkness again. But the birds and creatures of light will fly toward the light just like a bug at night. The lantern comes into the darkness for judgment and exposes the true state of all and what they really are. But the light did not alter any of the creatures, it only revealed them. It did not turn what was otherwise clean into unclean—so the gospel is the same way.

The same sunlight that hardens the clay also melts the wax—so grace rejected is what hardens. It is not wrath, but the riches of His goodness and long suffering that would lead us to repentance. If that goodness is rejected and despised, then the heart is hardened and is increased with hatred toward God.

5. WOE, LO, GO
   - I want to point out three words before continuing on in this passage. First, in verse 5, we find the word *"woe."* In verse 7, we find the word *"lo."* In verse 9, we find the word *"go."*
   - This is the way God usually works in all of our lives; "Woe, lo, go."

6. VERSES 11–13
   - Isaiah knows the conditions of the heart of Judah, and in verse 10, we saw that the Lord God told him that Judah will not understand, see, perceive, or hear, so Isaiah cried with a loud voice, "How long?"
   - The desolation of Judah was near as we see in verse 11. The Lord directed Isaiah to tell the people, *"Until the cities be wasted without inhabitant, and the houses without man, and the land be utterly desolate."* Isaiah was to do everything he could to reach the people as long as they were present and able to hear him and before a catastrophe struck such as the captivity of Judah.
   - You will note that even while God describes Judah's doom, He also inserts a note of mercy. No matter how terrifying Judah's future might be, the Lord promises never to forget His faithful remnant. Here the remnant is called *"a tenth"* and a *"holy seed"* (verse 13).
   - God would deal with the faithful remnant with lovingkindness. He would someday restore them to the land. This happened in the days of Ezra and Nehemiah. This remains true today—He will remember His ancient covenant with Israel and is bringing her anew to a place of blessing.
   - In our day, this same thing applies. Judgment will surely fall upon those who reject the Lord Jesus. We know not when our Lord will return for His saints. He is always faithful, however, to the remnant in our day, which is the church.
   - It is important to reemphasize the significance of the words "a tenth" and "return." Never will Israel perish totally any more than a living seed perishes when buried in the earth. The life germ within the seed causes it to survive even though its outward frame or shell is often dissolved.
   - The figure of speech used in verse 13 indicates that even though an oak tree has been cut down, it still has life in its roots and a fresh sprout springs up and in that sprout the tree continues to live—it all depends upon the life principle being in that rooted stump.
   - So, other nations may pass away altogether and they have because they lacked the divine life's germ, but as for Israel, *"the holy seed"* has been promised and it has been perpetuated as a nation and this is the life's germ of the rooted stump, which God promised in His earlier covenants with Israel.

How Much Do You Remember?
1. In the ruin and desolation, what is the single promise, hope, and blessing that remains for Israel?
2. What does the term "millennium" mean?
3. Recall the six woes described in chapter 5.
4. Describe Isaiah's vision in the temple from chapter 6.

Your Assignment for Next Week:
1. Review your notes from this lesson.
2. Read Isaiah chapters 7 through 9.
3. Underline your Bible.

Lesson 3 Notes

Lesson 4
CHAPTERS 7, 8, AND 9

CHAPTER 7

Now we begin what is called "the book of Immanuel" and this begins in chapter 7 and continues through chapter 12 verse 16. This entire section is called the book of Immanuel and for a background study, let me just set the stage for you as we consider verse 1:

> *And it came to pass in the days of Ahaz the son of Jotham, the son of Uzziah, king of Judah, that Rezin the king of Syria, and Pekah the son of Remaliah, king of Israel, went up toward Jerusalem to war against it, but could not prevail against it.*

There was no greater administrator than Uzziah and his son, Jotham. But the sorriest of all was Ahaz, the son of Jotham and the grandson of Uzziah. He was idolatrous. He was sinful. At one of the most critical junctures in the history of Judah, there was Ahaz like a big toad upon the throne in Jerusalem.

Ahaz—in the face of a threat from Rezin, king of Syria, and Pekah of the northern kingdom of Israel—secretly turned over his kingdom to Tiglathpileser, king of Assyria (see 2 Chronicles 28:16–25) instead of turning to God for help and for strength and wisdom. It was upon this occasion that God sent Isaiah to confront Ahaz and to plead that he not find refuge and help from the Assyrians, but that he find help and refuge in almighty God.

Before we enter the verse by verse study of chapter 7, it would be wise for us to consider the law of double reference as seen in these chapters—particularly in four areas. First, the Hebrews' persecution at the hands of foreign rulers is described—that is, Isaiah's day and also of the great tribulation still in the future. The second double reference, the judgment of the nations, both of Assyria and of the marshalled hosts at Armageddon, is described. Third, God's dealing with the Jewish remnant, both after the Babylonian captivity and after the great tribulation. Fourth, the advent of the Messiah, both His virgin birth and His future return to the earth in glory. This is gloriously portrayed. The book of Immanuel is called that because it deals at length with the Messiah who indeed is "God with us."

1. VERSES 1–3
   - Chapter 7 opens with two enemies who have always acted independently against Judah—now being united they are advancing toward Jerusalem. Word of this advancement was brought, not exactly to Ahaz personally, but in verse 2, to the *"house of David"* that he represents.
   - As the news was given, the heart of Ahaz was moved and the heart of his people *"as the trees of the wood are moved with the wind"* (verse 2). In other words, they were terror-stricken and they trembled.
   - In verse 3, the Lord speaks directly to Isaiah and He says, *"Go forth now to meet Ahaz, thou, and Shearjashub thy son, at the end of the conduit of the upper pool in the highway of the fuller's field."* You'll note the detail that the Lord gives to Isaiah as to where he was to meet Ahaz.
   - Almost nonchalantly the son is mentioned. Since the lad neither said nor did anything, the whole significance of his presence had to be in his name. The name Shearjashub means "a remnant shall return," and it is clearly a link with the last words of the previous chapter that says, *"In it shall be a tenth, and it shall return"* (Isaiah 6:13). So the son of the prophet is a sign of the fulfillment of Jehovah's word to the prophet.
   - Note the words in verse 3 as to where Isaiah was to meet Ahaz. He was to meet him at the end of the conduit of the upper pool in the highway of the fuller's field. Now what does all that mean? Isaiah

is to go to the very end of the water supply where it pours its life-giving waters into Jerusalem. That water supply comes from the same meaning as "the most high" and it is the upper pool. This is all meaningful because Christ alone is the conduit or the channel whereby the blessing of God can come to all of us. The place was "to the end of the conduit." Christ, who is the antitype of this conduit, not in His incarnation as being born of the virgin, or in His life, but only when He was raised from the dead, symbolically breathed that life into His disciples. To this day, it is only as having died and being raised that He is the end of the conduit. All of this points to Christ as the Water of Life. (See John 4:6–14.) The fuller's field was where garments were washed and it became a place of cleansing.

- In verse 3 also, you will find that phrase "*in the highway of the fuller's field.*" The highway is a path clearly defined by being raised up above the surrounding land in order that the people may walk. It is noted that the highway is raised up and it characteristically led upward for it is called "*the causeway of the going up*" (1 Chronicles 26:16). Thus, if the conduit is the way by which the waters of blessing came down, the highway is the clean and holy path leading up to the source of all blessing.

- Proverbs 16:17 gives us still a more clear and moral truth when it says, "*the highway of the upright is to depart from evil.*" Then another time we find in Isaiah 35:8, "*And an highway shall be there, and a way, and it shall be called The way of holiness.*" The lesson here is the blessing of life comes down in sovereign grace and it is the "conduit." The life received leads upward by the path of the raised highway. Our Lord is both highway and conduit as well as cleanser or "fuller."

2. VERSES 4–9

- Here we see a part of the remaining statement of Isaiah to Ahaz. That statement was begun in verse 3 and then Isaiah says to Ahaz:

> *Take heed, and be quiet; fear not, neither be fainthearted for the two tails of these smoking firebrands, for the fierce anger of Rezin with Syria, and of the son of Remaliah. Because Syria, Ephraim, and the son of Remaliah, have taken evil counsel against thee, saying, Let us go up against Judah, and vex it, and let us make a breach therein for us, and set a king in the midst of it, even the son of Tabeal: thus saith the Lord GOD, It shall not stand, neither shall it come to pass. For the head of Syria is Damascus, and the head of Damascus is Rezin; and within threescore and five years shall Ephraim be broken, that it be not a people. And the head of Ephraim is Samaria, and the head of Samaria is Remaliah's son. If ye will not believe, surely ye shall not be established.*
>
> (verses 4–9)

- Ahaz sees two victorious armies coming toward him. The Lord God says, in essence, "No, they are only two tails of torches that are at the point of being extinguished altogether. They are only smoking and not aflame." If Ahaz was to believe the Lord, then he was to look ahead sixty-five years and one of his enemies would cease to be a people altogether and the throne would be taken over by one who would be called the son of Tabeal (verse 6). That word, when pronounced correctly as Tabeal, means "the good for nothing god," but if it is pronounced Tabeel, it then means "the good god." Will Jehovah allow the house of David to be set aside for the "son of a good for nothing"? The answer is no!

- The next verses would open the eyes of anyone because the Lord says, "*neither shall it come to pass*" (verse 7). Then He goes on to explain that Syria is headed up in its capital of Damascus and that they may be seen in the head of Damascus, Rezin, and when one looks upon Rezin, they really see Syria. Rezin is in league, or partnership, with Ephraim and within sixty-five years, Ephraim will be smashed to pieces. This has a twofold meaning; Ephraim was scattered then (and they are the ten tribes of the north) and Ephraim or Israel was scattered throughout all of the years until 1948. The head of Ephraim is Samaria and the head of Samaria is Remaliah's son Pekah. When you see a man unworthy of a name such as "Remaliah's son," you see all of Ephraim.

3.   VERSES 10–12

   +   The second time Isaiah confronts Ahaz with the words of the Lord is in verses 10 and 11.

   +   Isaiah said to Ahaz in essence, "Just trust in God and He will destroy Pekah and Rezin." But Ahaz had already purposed in his heart some other form of help—the help of Tiglathpileser—and Isaiah stood before him again and said, *"Ask thee a sign of the LORD"* (verse 11).

   +   Ahaz responds in verse 12 by saying, *"I will not ask, neither will I tempt the LORD."* The true reason for declining the offer was the fact that Ahaz has resolved not to do God's will, but to negotiate with Assyria and to continue in the idolatry described in 2 Kings 16.

4.   VERSE 13

   +   In verse 13, the Lord says, *"Hear ye now, O house of David; is it a small thing for you to weary men, but will ye weary my God also?"* This prophecy is addressed to the whole house of David and we find therein a continuing prophecy addressed to the Davidic family.

   +   The word *"weary"* means "to try the patience of" and the word *"men"* speaks of the prophets.

   +   Isaiah as of yet had given no outward proof that he was from God, but now God is offering a sign, which Ahaz publicly rejects. The sin is therefore not now merely against men, but openly against God and we see Isaiah's manner and his total approach change from mildness to bold reproof. Since Ahaz would not ask for a sign from heaven, the Lord said, "I will give you a sign and you will always remember it."

5.   VERSES 14–16

   +   It was then that Isaiah delivered the Messianic prophecy of Isaiah 7:14. Looking beyond King Ahaz, he saw the Messiah—and that sign was to the whole house of Israel. Copy down the Messianic prophecy found in verse 14.

   _____

   _____

   _____

   _____

   _____

   +   The word for "virgin" has always been a point of controversy. The Revised Standard Version has attempted to take the word and do away with its full significance by translating it "young woman." They put in the footnote the word "virgin." This should be reversed. There may be occasions when this word may be translated "young woman," but not here. Obviously, it would be no sign from God if a young woman had a son. That was commonplace. Even if a young woman had a son out of wedlock that would not be so unusual. Obviously, Isaiah intended that the meaning of the word in the original should be "virgin."

   +   Looking back upon that statement during this dispensation, we see that Isaiah used exactly the words that the Lord God placed upon his heart and that 750 years after his prediction, the prophecy came to pass. (See Matthew 1:23.) From this passage, there is no room for question about Isaiah's prophecy of a Messiah.

- For faith, the sign is Jesus and Jesus alone. But when we consider the context that there was a sign offered to and in spite of the sin of Ahaz, then we consider the apparent close connection between verse 14 and verse 16. The prophecy reads on the surface that before the very son of the virgin will know how to refuse evil and choose the good, that is, apparently before Immanuel had arrived at the age of discretion—both Syria and Ephraim would be devastated and it is of this devastation that the supernatural birth of the child should be a sign.

- There is always a meaning in prophecy of the almost present and of the far-off final fulfillment. In this case, there must have been a nearby historical fulfillment for Ahaz himself. This is true here in this case because in the next chapter, you will find the immediate fulfillment in the birth of a son of Isaiah and the mother—the prophetess—whom we will study in chapter 8, but he was not called Immanuel. This is the nearby fulfillment, but it by no means satisfies the requirements of verses 14 and 15. That boy in chapter 8 was not called Immanuel, nor has any other child ever been called such a name, but the boy in chapter 8 was called Maher-shalal-hash-baz, which means "speed to spoil" or "haste for the reward." Under the divine direction of the almighty God, the child's name that was to be born of a virgin was to be Immanuel, which means "God with us." There has never been another child called by this name. While it is true that many children have been called Jesus—it was not and is not to this day an uncommon name, in fact Joshua is but a form of it—but this child means "God with us" or "Savior" and it is the manifestation of God Himself.

- There should not be any emphasis placed upon the mother here except that she was a virgin. She became the mother of the humanity of our Lord Jesus Christ.

- The sign of this fulfillment would not be totally fulfilled during the days of Ahaz because the prophet immediately added, "Butter and honey shall he eat, that he may know to refuse the evil, and choose the good. For before the child shall know to refuse the evil, and choose the good, the land that thou abhorrest shall be forsaken of both her kings" (verses 15–16). The expression "butter and honey shall he eat" is very striking for it indicates the true humanity of the child to be born of the virgin. While he was to be supernaturally conceived, He would have a real physical body that would be nourished by proper food as in the case of others. Butter was the best of animal food and honey the best of vegetable food. With such as these, the holy child was to be nourished that He might grow from infancy to manhood in a normal way.

- When we turn to the New Testament records, we do not read of some remarkably different child whose early activities were different from those of other small boys. He increased in wisdom, statue, and in favor with God and man. Feeding upon the food provided, He grew from childhood to youth and from youth to manhood. Our Lord's humanity was exactly like that of others, apart from sin—totally apart from sin.

- Don't forget the immediate meaning of this prophecy outlined in chapter 8 by the son of Isaiah and the prophetic meaning that was to come hundreds of years later by the Lord Jesus Christ being born of a virgin.

6. VERSES 17–25

- In verses 17–25, we see a prediction of an impending invasion of Judah. This is explained in more detail in 2 Chronicles 28:1–20.

- Notice in verse 17, the promise that the Lord would bring upon the people of Judah had not come upon them from the day that Ephraim (the northern kingdom) departed from Judah and this would come by way of the king of Assyria.

- Judah was to be the bone of contention between two great powers—Assyria and Egypt. Egypt is described as a menacing fly and Assyria is described as a stinging bee and both of these would descend upon Judah at the summons of the Lord God. As they came, they would come in vast hordes spreading across the whole land even into the valleys and the caves (verse 19).

- In verse 20, we see that Assyria is described as a razor who was hired to shave everything they had—their land, their crops, and their people. The great cities of Judah would fall and only thorns and briars would be left where once there had been flourishing industries, plantations, and vineyards.
- In verse 21—when is it all over—a man will be fortunate to have a cow and two sheep left and there will be enough land uncultivated that even these three creatures will give him the milk and butter that he needs. Anyone who wanted to survive lived on milk, butter, and honey (verse 22).
- Judah will be wretched in that day for in the place of vineyards, having a thousand vines, each worth a silverling—or about twenty-five cents—the land will be covered with briars and thorns taking the place of grapes. These briars and thorns afford a jungle for the wild beasts as you will see in verse 24.

CHAPTER 8

As we begin chapter 8, you will recall that we have studied first about Isaiah's first child, Shearjashub in chapter 7, verse 3. Then we ascended to the Son—Immanuel—and now we descend again to the second lad—the second son of Isaiah called Mahershalalhashbaz. Later, we will proceed in chapter 9 up again to the Child called Wonderful and all the other names given to Christ.

1. VERSES 1–3

- In the beginning of chapter 8, Isaiah is addressed directly and he is to take a large tablet such as could be hung up prominently for all to see and he is to write upon it with a man's pen. Concerning his second son—he is to write his name before he is born and so he writes the words *"Maher-shalal-hash-baz"* (verse 1).
- In verse 2, by divine direction, he selects two witnesses—the necessary number for a competent testimony—whose names are given to us here in the Scripture and therefore we are quite sure that those names are significant. The witnessing names are Uriah, the priest, which means "Jehovah is my light" and the second one is Zechariah, which means "Jehovah remembers." Zechariah was the son of Jeberichiah, which means "Jehovah will bless." Thus, the one witness says by his name "Jehovah is my light" and the other indicates that the Lord God is to bless and that God will never forget His people.
- Why did Isaiah take the two witnesses and write down the name of his second son before the son was even conceived? When Assyria devastated Syria and Ephraim, the two witnesses would then testify that the prophet's tablet or paper had been exposed for about twenty months, bearing that one strange word—the name of his son—a name that no one would give to a child unless he was divinely ordered to do so. That name was to foretell what they saw taking place before their eyes and all of this was to take place rapidly.
- If you recall, I mentioned in chapter 7 that there was double meaning to many of the things that we read in this book of Immanuel from chapter 7 through chapter 12. Here, we find part of a double meaning explained. In chapter 7, there was a sign given that a virgin should conceive and she should bear a son and his name be called Immanuel. That was the long range meaning and it was to come to pass some 750 years after Isaiah wrote those words. Here in chapter 8, we see the immediate meaning that completes the double meaning in the birth of the second son of Isaiah. Immanuel, you will remember, means "God with us," whereas Mahershalalhashbaz means "haste ye to the spoil" or "your enemies will soon be destroyed." In our own language it simply means "God is against those who are against us who are for God."

2. VERSES 4–8

  + In verse 4, you see another double meaning in the fact that before this child, the child of Isaiah, will have knowledge to cry the words "my father and my mother," all of the riches of Damascus or Syria and the ruins of Israel, the northern kingdom, will be taken away by the king of Assyria.

  + In verses 5 through 7, you find the words of the Lord speaking to Isaiah: *"Forasmuch as this people refuseth the waters of Shiloah that go softly, and rejoice in Rezin and Remaliah's son; now therefore, behold, the Lord bringeth up upon them the waters of the river, strong and many, even the king of Assyria, and all his glory: and he shall come up over all his channels, and go over all his banks."*

  + That word *"Shiloah"* means "sent." This is another name for Christ so let's explore that for just a moment. Shiloah flowed between Mt. Zion and Mt. Moriah. Zion tells always the story of grace as in contrast with Sinai, which tells the story of law. Moriah tells the same story for it is here that God provided Himself a lamb. (See Genesis 22:2, 8.) It was on Mt. Moriah that the temple was built where those sacrifices that were offered pointed toward the Lamb of God. Now Shiloah is at the base of both these mountains. Could anything speak more clearly of Christ who is the true Shiloah, the sent one, being at the base of all God's goodness, mercy, and grace?

  + While talking about verse 6, I want to say a word about the names of Rezin and Remaliah. These names too are very significant.

      a. Remaliah is a word made up of "rem," meaning "lofty or lifted up," along with the preposition "I" and the easily recognized "jah" or Jehovah—the whole word reading "lifted up to Jehovah." Now it means just the opposite of what you may think. It means that he, Remaliah, would lift himself up to be like Jehovah. Remaliah then is a name that is intended to lead our thoughts to Lucifer or to Satan.

      b. Rezin, the king of Syria, means "self-will." The name of his kingdom can be misunderstood when we leave the Hebrew word "Aram" unchanged into the Greek called "Syria." Aram is precisely the same root as the first syllable of Remaliah and means again "lifted up." So, when we put all this together, we find that the self-willed one, Rezin, is the king of Aram, those lifted-up people, the children of pride.

  + We find here in this Scripture that Syria and Samaria had refused to recognize the value of having an association with Judah and so they spurned the waters of Shiloah and had joined forces with Rezin and Pekah and the Lord was bringing against them the armies of the king of Assyria, which would flow over their lands like a great river and would even reach into Judah also thus overspreading Immanuel's land. (See verse 8.) That is the land promised by covenant to Abraham and his seed. *"Thy land, O Immanuel"* refers to the land of Palestine, the land of Jehovah, which He had claimed as His own when He declared, *"The land shall not be sold for ever: for the land is mine"* (Leviticus 25:23).

3. VERSES 9–17

  + In this section of Scripture, Isaiah exhorts, *"Sanctify the LORD of hosts himself; and let him be your fear, and let him be your dread"* (verse 13).

  + In verse 14, they were to fear God above and look to Him. He will be their salvation or their stone of stumbling. This was literally fulfilled in Christ in 1 Corinthians 1:23, where Paul says, *"But we preach Christ crucified, unto the Jews a stumblingblock, and unto the Greeks foolishness."* The words *"sanctify the LORD of hosts himself"* in verse 13 is a strange injunction and you will find a similar statement found in 1 Peter 3:15 and it means simply that God needs to be made holy in the hearts of His children.

  + After announcing the approaching apostasy in the Ephesian church, Paul said in Acts 20:32, *"I commend you to God, and to the word of his grace."* So here, in verses 16 and 17, Isaiah is speaking in

God's behalf and exclaims, *"bind up the testimony, seal the law among my disciples."* To those who are willing to be taught of God, the word becomes increasingly precious as the days grow darker.

4. VERSES 18–22

    + In verse 18, we find a very important verse. Isaiah and his family were called to be a testimony to all Israel: *"Behold, I and the children whom the LORD hath given me are for signs and for wonders in Israel from the LORD of hosts."* That means that all of the family of Isaiah were for signs and so what does that mean? *Isaiah* means "Jehovah will save." *Shear-jashub* means "a remnant shall return" and *Maher-shalal-hash-baz* means "your enemies must soon be destroyed." So, all of the family of Isaiah were for signs and for wonders in Israel.

    + In verse 19, there is a warning against spiritualism. God forbids His people to dabble in this Satanic system. When people turn from God, they generally go after the occult and the abnormal. Notice in verse 19 it says, *"familiar spirits, and unto wizards that peep, and that mutter: should not a people seek unto their God? for the living to the dead?"* That means in essence, "So you're trying to find out about the future by consulting spirits and witches that mutter, can you talk to the dead? Why don't you ask God?"

    + Then, in verse 20: *"if they speak not according to this word, it is because there is no light in them."* Now you will find some reference to these things we've talked about in verses 19 and 20 in Deuteronomy 18:9–12 and Leviticus 20:27.

    + Verses 21–22: God's sure Word abides and if any speak contrary to it, it is because they are in darkness themselves. That is, when the day dawns for the eternal blessing of the redeemed, there will be outer darkness for those who spurned the light of truth only to be misled by falsehood. They will be exposed by the Word of God. Those who are in darkness and who dabble in this Satanism will only find trouble, anguish, and dark despair and they will be thrust into outer darkness.

CHAPTER 9

The opening verses of chapter 9 form a continuance of what just took place in chapter 8. We know this because the first word of chapter 9 is *"Nevertheless."* Chapter 9 is one of the all-important chapters in the entire Word of God. Most of you are familiar with this chapter because it contains a portion of Scripture that is read quite often.

Don't forget the historic and geographical background in which chapters 8 and 9 are given to us. It is important for you to remember what has been taught in chapters 7 and 8 in order to understand this chapter.

1. VERSES 1–3

    + This chapter begins with a verse that is ordinarily hard to translate, but when we take it in the entire context of the Word of God, it does not become difficult for us to understand. It is as though Isaiah could look down through the ages and see the Lord Jesus full of grace and truth, making known the wonders of God and His redeeming love to those who heard and accepted the Light of Life.

    + When we read verse 1 and then compare it to Matthew 4:15–16, the meaning seems to be very clear. Galilee was the despised area and a place where Gentiles had congregated. The Lord Jesus passed by Jerusalem, the religious center of the day, and made His headquarters in the despised periphery of the kingdom. Zebulun and Naphtali were located in the north, with Naphtali along the west bank of the Sea of Galilee and Zebulun adjoining Naphtali on the west. Nazareth was in Zebulun and Capernaum, which was the headquarters of Jesus, was in Naphtali.

    + Regardless of the translation and interpretation of verse 1, it is obvious that the people in Galilee, who were in the darkness of paganism, did see a great light, even Jesus, the Light of the world. (See John 8:12.) This was fulfilled at the first coming of Christ, referred to in verse 2.

- In verse 3, Isaiah looks on to a day when once more the nation will be recognized by God as in a covenant relationship with Himself. Note that it is His people, Israel, that is in question in verse 3 and not the Gentiles. It seems evident that here the word "not" should be omitted. Really, the prophet was saying, "thou has multiplied the nation, and increased the joy." This passage actually looks forward to the future blessing of Israel when they will be restored to the Lord and to their land and will have learned to know the Messiah. There is a parenthesis of time between verse 2 and verse 3. Verse 2 is the first coming of Christ, verse 3 is the second coming.

2. VERSES 4–5

- Verses 4 and 5 contemplate the conditions that were to prevail in the world through the long centuries of the dispersion of Israel. These verses had a local application to the destruction by the Assyrian army. The prophet describes the sad conditions destined to be the portion of the nations until Christ comes again.

- Verse 5 agrees with the words of our Lord as recorded in Matthew 24:6–7 where He says, "*And ye shall hear of wars and rumours of wars: see that ye be not troubled: for all these things must come to pass, but the end is not yet. For nation shall rise against nation, and kingdom against kingdom: and there shall be famines, and pestilences, and earthquakes, in divers places.*" So these verses look beyond the immediate of Isaiah's day to the great tribulation.

3. VERSES 6–7

- Verses 6 and 7 give us one of the most complete prophecies concerning our Lord Jesus that is to be found anywhere in the Old Testament.

- We have seen in the last two verses that the thought goes beyond the present conditions of Isaiah's day and looks forward to the period of the great tribulation.

- With that background, we find verses 6 and 7, which say:

    For unto us a child is born, unto us a son is given: and the government shall be upon his shoulder: and his name shall be called Wonderful, Counsellor, The mighty God, The everlasting Father, The Prince of Peace. Of the increase of his government and peace there shall be no end, upon the throne of David, and upon his kingdom, to order it, and to establish it with judgment and with justice from henceforth even for ever. The zeal of the LORD of hosts will perform this.

- This is as complete a prophecy of Jesus Christ as chapter 53 of Isaiah. The reference here is to the second coming primarily—as chapter 53 is to the first coming. These verses continue the thought of verses 3–5 and they look forward to the second coming of Christ. The question arises of how "a child is born" at His second coming. First of all, let us clearly state that He was not born "unto us"—that is, the nation Israel, at His first coming. John tells us, "*He came unto his own, and his own received him not*" (John 1:11). He was born at Bethlehem the first time, but this is not the reference here. Christ will be born to the nation Israel at His second coming. Perhaps it may be better to state it this way—they will be born as a nation at once. This is made perfectly clear in the last chapter of Isaiah, chapter 66 verses 7–8, where we read:

    Before she travailed, she brought forth; before her pain came, she was delivered of a man child. Who hath heard such a thing? who hath seen such things? Shall the earth be made to bring forth in one day? or shall a nation be born at once? for as soon as Zion travailed, she brought forth her children.

- Israel is to be delivered of a man child in the future, not by His birth, but by *their* birth. This will be the *new birth* of the nation Israel when He comes. Verses 6 and 7 refer to the second coming of

Christ, but there is no serious objection to interpret it for God's children today, for it teaches His virgin birth.

- The thought to remember here is, Israel is the nation in verses 3 through 7, and it is their future if we compare Scripture with Scripture. When the nation Israel is thus new born, it will be as if Messiah were just then born to them as a nation, although the literal birth occurred two thousand years before. The birth they will celebrate, is the birth *to them* at that time.

- So the words "unto us" refer, beyond all question, to the only nation ever elected as a nation—the only people among whom the prophet could put himself in saying "unto us." When all Israel does awaken to the mighty truth that the Lord is his—when for the first time, he really knows that he is a sinner and is the object of the redeeming love of the Lord, then it is, and not until then, that the Lord is born to him.

- Now let us look at the names of glory found in verses 6–7, that the Spirit of God adorns the man child with. They are like bells on the high priest's garment for they ring His praise.

  a. "WONDERFUL." This is not an adjective. This is His name. He is wonderful not only in what He says or does, but in the great mysteries of His own person for *"no man knoweth the Son, but the Father"* (Matthew 11:27). He is wonderful in every way.

  b. "COUNSELOR." He never sought counsel of man nor did He ask for their advice. Paul says in Romans 11:34: *"For who hath known the mind of the Lord? or who hath been his counsellor?"* Never in the life of Christ was there one hesitation, never a reversal, never a regret for anything He had to say.

  c. "THE MIGHTY GOD." He is the one to whom all power is given. He is the omnipotent God. Even that little baby on Mary's bosom was helpless there, but He held the universe together.

  d. "THE EVERLASTING FATHER." It simply means that He is the Creator of all things, even time, the ages, and the far-off purpose of all things. *"All things were made by him; and without him was not any thing made that was made"* (John 1:3). In Hebrews 1:2, we read: *"Hath in these last days spoken unto us by his Son, whom he hath appointed heir of all things, by whom also he made the worlds."*

  e. "PRINCE OF PEACE." There can be no peace on this earth until He is reigning. His government is not static. There is increasing growth. He will occupy the throne of David. Justice is dominate in His rule. There is no peace nor will there ever be a world without war until Christ comes again.

4. VERSES 8–12

- After this burst of joy caused by the announcement of Jesus as the true Messiah, we return to the land of the prophecy broken off. We come then to verses 8 through chapter 10 verse 4, in which the Assyrian is used as the rod of Jehovah.

- The prophet now turns back to local conditions. Those of the north kingdom were vaunting themselves. In spite of the calamities that were surrounding them, they would arise above them and become once more a strong and secure people, but the Lord declared that He would raise up adversaries from among these Assyrians who had been their allies and from among the Philistines, the ancient enemies of His people who would devour Israel with an open mouth. His anger was toward them only on account of their sins but His hand stretched out in judgment. You find this recorded in verses 8–12.

5. VERSES 13–17

+ On Israel's part, there had been no exercise because of the chastening hand of God upon them; rather there was their own resentful pride. They dared to boast themselves even against God and against His servants who came to instruct them in His truth.

+ The leaders were terribly guilty in that they misled those who were subject to them causing them to err and so led them to destruction because of their unrepentant condition.

+ Their continual waywardness called for further judgment, and we see this described in verses 18–21.

6. VERSES 18–21

+ *"For wickedness burneth as the fire: it shall devour the briers and thorns"* (verse 18). Men may think lightly of the sin and pay little or no attention to the solemn warnings God gives concerning its vital effects, but if they persist in rebellion against God, they will find that wickedness does indeed burn as a fire and if they refuse to turn to God, they will soon find out that they will have to endure the judgment that they have brought upon themselves.

+ God's holy nature will not permit Him to condone iniquity. So *"Through the wrath of the Lord of hosts is the land darkened, and the people shall be as the fuel of the fire"* (verse 19). Famine and pestilence added to their own wretchedness and misery. Yet, instead of turning to Him, confessing their sin, and seeking forgiveness, they blamed one another for the troubles that had come upon them.

+ Manasseh turned upon Ephraim and Ephraim upon Manasseh and both together turned upon Judah. All of this was the sad result of forsaking the way of the Lord. The chapter closes with the solemn refrain repeated for the *third time*, *"For all this his anger is not turned away, but his hand is stretched out still"* (verses 12, 17, and 21).

How Much Do You Remember?

1. What were the four double references found in chapter 7?
2. What is the significance of the name of Isaiah's son, Shearjashub, given in chapter 7?
3. Recall the Messianic prophecy, given in 7:14.
4. In verse 18 of chapter 8, what was meant for the family of Isaiah?
5. In chapter 9 verse 3, what can be looked forward to?
6. Recall the names of glory describing Jesus Christ and their significance found in Isaiah 9:6–7.
7. What is the refrain that closes chapter 9 (and was used three times throughout the chapter)?
8. Recall the historical background and political history found in these three chapters.

Your Assignment for Next Week:

1. Review your notes from this lesson.
2. Read Isaiah chapters 10 through 13.
3. Underline your Bible.

Lesson 4 Notes

_____

_____

_____

_____

_____

Lesson 5
CHAPTERS 10, 11, AND 12

CHAPTER 10

It is a well-known principle of Scripture interpretation to recognize the double application or fulfillment of many prophecies. Conditions through which Israel and the other nations have passed already often depicts and portrays something that is yet to be faced in the future. We see this set forth in the present chapter, which deals primarily with Assyria and Judah—but also looks forward to the time when the great tribulation and the time of Jacob's trouble will take place in Immanuel's land. Only as we keep these two applications of the prophetic word before us can we understand what is set forth here in chapter 10.

1. VERSES 1–2

   + Here we see another woe pronounced upon those who in their pride and selfishness decree unrighteous decrees in order to legalize their oppression of the poor and enrich themselves at the expense of the fatherless.

   + Monopolies are not a recent thing. In Judah, as in our own civilized lands today, there were those who counted it good business to take advantage of others in adverse circumstances and profit by the ruin of their less fortunate countrymen. All of this is hateful to a God of judgment.

2. VERSES 3–4

   + In verse 3, we find a warning concerning a day of reckoning. The unjust judges must stand before the great Judge. This verse looks beyond to the final day of reckoning.

   + Then, in verse 4, we find those same words that we have found in three other verses of Scripture. *"For all this his anger is not turned away, but his hand is stretched out still."* God seems to find a way always to judge and He even permits things to happen for chastening the people who have sinned.

   + God shows us in the next section of Scripture just how He can use the Assyrians, for instance, to accomplish what He wants.

3. VERSES 5–12

   + Notice that it is when the Lord has performed His whole work on Mt. Zion and Jerusalem that the Assyrian is to be punished. This needs to be kept in mind as we study this passage.

   + When King Ahaz was threatened with utter ruin by the kings of Israel and Syria, he went to the king of Assyria for help—only to find later that this covetous ruler aspired to have complete control over all of the lands, including Judah.

   + Later on, Sennacherib descended on the land like a mighty torrent, his army driving all before it until it was destroyed by a pestilence in one night as it besieged Jerusalem in the days of Hezekiah. This terrible enemy became the type of godless foe which, in the last days, will attempt to bring Palestine under its control only to be destroyed by omnipotent power on the mountains of Israel.

   + As the rod of Jehovah's anger, from Assyria was used, as other nations had been used before and since, to chasten the people of God because of their turning away from Him; but in the day of their repentance, He would destroy the enemy that had brought disaster upon Judah. As far as Assyria was concerned, there was no realization of the fact that it was a rod in the hands of God and Assyria was to learn a bitter experience that after they had been used to punish *"an hypocritical nation"* (verse 6) that they, Assyria, were doomed to utter destruction.

- Jehovah's whole work upon Mt. Zion and upon Jerusalem will mean the return of His people to Himself. Then, in the days that He takes them again as a nation, He will deal with the Assyrian and with all who have afflicted Israel.

4. VERSES 13–19

- Since Assyria did not understand that God was using them, they vaunted themselves as though they had accomplished everything and had won all of the victories because of their own wisdom and prudence.

- Assyria had robbed and oppressed the nations, including Israel and Judah, ruthlessly and heartlessly. To them, all of the people were as eggs in the nests of birds, opened to be spoiled, and their armies were as helpless as the mother birds when their nests were robbed.

- Not knowing that God was using them as an ax in His hand, the Assyrians boasted as though the power and might were all their own. Therefore, in the reckoning day that was coming, God would deal as sternly with Assyria as He had dealt with others and as they had sown hatred and cruelty, so they would also reap indignation and judgment.

- In the day of Jehovah's triumph, He will vindicate the remnant in Israel who have put their trust in Him and they will be as a flame to devour the nations that have sought their destruction. The Word of God will be fulfilled concerning His promise that while He would punish His people in measure for their sins, He would never break His covenant with them—a covenant made first with Abraham and confirmed to David.

- Although a full end will be made of many of the nations that have afflicted Israel, He will never make a full end of Israel as we will see in the next section of Scripture.

5. VERSES 20–23

- Notice in verse 20: *"And it shall come to pass in that day, that the remnant of Israel."* When the judgments of God are being poured out upon the earth in the dark days of the great tribulation, a remnant of the Jews will turn to the Lord in deep repentance and in living faith. These will prove the greatness of His mercy and the faithfulness of His promises. No longer relying for help on the powers that persecuted and failed them in the hour of their need—they will find their resource and protection in God Himself.

- The prophetic word is clear and free of all obscurity. Only unbelief can deny its definite application to a literal remnant of the sons of Jacob when they turn to the Lord in the time of their greatest trouble. Then He will come and be their help and He will save the nation because of the remnant.

- We need to remember that they are not all Israel that are of Israel. The great majority *"as the sand of the sea"* (verse 22) will go into utter apostasy and be destroyed in their sins, but a remnant will return and be acknowledged by God as His people. And so, we learn in chapter 11 of Romans: *"All Israel shall be saved"* (verse 26). For this remnant will be the true Israel in that day of Jehovah's power.

6. VERSES 24–27

- In clear and definite terms, the prophet predicts the overthrow of the enemy who was hammering at the very gate of Jerusalem. God will prevent fear on the part of His people from the Assyrians.

- Literally all was fulfilled in due time so far as the prophecy had to do with the Assyrians of the past. When in the last days, another mighty army comes again against Israel from the same region in the north, His doom will be just as certain as was that of the Assyrians in the past.

- The progress of the Assyrian army marching down through the land is depicted graphically in the verses that close this chapter.

7. VERSES 28–34

+ Prophecy is history written beforehand and here Isaiah foretold the path that the Assyrians would take as they marched through Palestine, wrecking city upon city, but the closing verses tell of his defeat at last when the Lord of hosts intervened with His mighty power for the deliverance of those who cried to Him in the hour of their distress.

+ There is a remarkable prophecy here and it will be for the future as well as the past. It works out the route of the future invader from the north, but don't forget that this same route was taken by the Assyrians hundreds of years ago:

  + Aiath is about fifteen miles north of Jerusalem.

  + Migron is south of Aiath and is the pass where Jonathan got a victory over the Philistines. (See 1 Samuel 14.)

  + Gaba and Ramah are about six miles north of Jerusalem.

  + Anathoth was about three miles north of Jerusalem.

  + Laish is the extreme north of Palestine in the tribe of Dan (this is as far as the screams should go).

  + Madmenah, which means dung hill, is just north of Jerusalem.

  + Gebim, just north of Jerusalem, the exact site is not known.

  + Nob is north and in sight of Jerusalem.

+ This passage charts the march of the enemy from the north, which brings a state of paralysis and defeat to Jerusalem.

CHAPTER 11

In chapter 11, we find as the main theme the "person and the power of the king" and the character and the quality of the kingdom. Chapters 11 and 12 are the continuation and culmination of the prophecy that started back in chapter 7. Chapter 10 concluded with the coming of the king to deliver the remnant in Jerusalem from the king from the north. In this chapter, the person of the king is introduced and the nature of his kingdom is given.

This is one of the great prophecies concerning the millennial kingdom of Christ. Pay particular attention here to the details of the kingdom. A literal interpretation of this chapter must be considered as the details will be null and void if this is not the case.

1. VERSES 1–5

+ Verse 1 is very meaningful and important. A live sprout comes forth from the line of David. David is not mentioned, but mention is made of his father, Jesse. The royal family had drifted back to the level of Jesse's day. We find here a reference back to the *"branch"* of Isaiah 4:2. This is one of the titles given to Christ. Again, we will see Christ set before us as the branch in Isaiah chapter 53.

+ In verse 2, we have the One who is presented in Revelation 1:4 as having the seven spirits of God, that is, the Holy Spirit in the sevenfold fullness of His power. Coming by virgin birth through David's line, Christ is the branch out of the root of Jesse, the father of David. Upon Him rests: (1) the spirit of Jehovah; (2) the spirit of wisdom; (3) the spirit of understanding; (4) the spirit of counsel; (5) the spirit of might; (6) the spirit of knowledge; and (7) the spirit of the fear of the Lord. All of this is found in verse 2.

+ In verses 3–5, the fear of Jehovah is the spirit of reverence. We are told in John that the Father gives not the spirit by measure to His beloved Son. (See John 3:34.) From the moment of His birth, the Lord Jesus was under the controlling power of the Holy Spirit. He chose not to act in His own omnipotence, but as the servant of the Godhead. After His baptism in the Jordan, the Spirit was seen descending upon Him as a dove. This was the anointing of which Peter spoke, in preparation for his gracious ministry. Never for one moment was He out of harmony with the Spirit. It was this that made it possible for Him to grow in wisdom, stature, and in favor with God and man. This mystery is great. The Father revealed His will to Jesus from day to day so Christ said, *"I am in the Father, and the Father in me"* (John 14:10). Scripture guards carefully the truth of the perfect manhood of our Lord. We see Him here as the servant of Jehovah speaking and acting according to the Father's will. His judgment and His understanding are perfect.

+ The character of the reign of Christ is depicted in these verses and in that day, the government of this world will be just and right because He, Christ, is reigning. The long, selfish misrule of earthly rulers will have come to an end and Israel and the nations will enjoy the blessings of the Messiah's gracious and faithful reign—then all the wickedness will be dealt with in unsparing judgment and the meek of the earth will be protected and enter into undisturbed blessedness.

+ We have now looked at chapter 11, verses 1–5, very briefly. Now let us go back and try to put these events in the proper perspective and try to explain for our own understanding exactly what we feel that the Holy Spirit is saying.

+ If you go back to chapter 10, verse 33, and forget the chapter division into chapter 11, it all reads like one great story. This is a glorious prophecy. All of it arose in the day in which Isaiah lived and Assyria held the then-civilized world in an iron grip. Assyria was a merciless empire. It was Assyria that, in invading Palestine, destroyed the northern kingdom (Israel) with the capital city of Samaria. Four times in the life of Isaiah did Assyria ravage and try to overrun Judah. Had it not been for the prayer of good King Hezekiah, they would have destroyed Judah. This prophecy begins and ends in a violent yet distinct contrast.

+ First, we find the prophecy concerning Assyria in verses 33 and 34 of chapter 10. The Lord will cut it down like a cedar of Lebanon. Second, then he speaks of the resurrection of Israel when he says, *"there shall come forth a rod out of the stem of Jesse, and a Branch shall grow out of his roots"* (Isaiah 11:1). When you contrast these two trees, you find that we are talking about a cedar and an oak. When a cedar is cut down, there are no shoots—no life stems—just a stump that stays in the ground and rots. So completely did the Assyrian Empire vanish from the earth that centuries later, Alexander the Great marched over Nineveh, the capital city of Assyria, and was not even aware that he was walking on the land where that city once stood. God completely kept His word in reference to the cedar—no shoot, no growth from the Assyrian Empire. Then the prophet speaks of Israel as an oak tree. When an oak is cut, there are still roots—shoots of life—and a small stem will come out from the top of the stump. That will become a Branch and He will be the Lord God of righteousness.

2. VERSES 6–9

+ In verse 6, we see the beginning exhortation of the quality of the kingdom. Now it is that kingdom that we want to speak of for just a moment.

+ First, that kingdom is coming in time and history and it is coming slowly, gradually, but it is indeed coming. The hand of the Lord is always in history and His purpose is always carried out. The kingdom is coming slowly, surely, but that kingdom cannot be seen. As Luke records in chapter 17 verses 20–21: *"The kingdom of God cometh not with observation: neither shall they say, Lo here! or, lo there! for, behold, the kingdom of God is within you."* This actually means that we can't see it, but we know that it is happening and in the Greek, the words "within you" mean "in the midst." The kingdom in its outward form, as the Davidic Covenant says and as it was described by the prophets, had been rejected by the Jews so that during this present age, it would not come with observation or literally an outward show, but it would come in the hearts of men. Meantime, the kingdom is actually "in the midst of." Ultimately, the kingdom of heaven will come with outward show.

- Second, the kingdom will come openly, suddenly, swiftly, and gloriously as a literal kingdom openly in the earth. Romans 11:25 tells us: *"For I would not, brethren, that ye should be ignorant of this mystery, lest ye should be wise in your own conceits; that blindness in part is happened to Israel, until the fulness of the Gentiles be come in"*—then the blindness and the mystery surrounding God's people will be removed.

- Those of us who are Christians and who live in this dispensation are heirs and are now present holders of a passport into the literal kingdom of our Lord. That kingdom is described here in chapter 11 in detail.

- The one who reigns as king is Christ, our Lord. He will set up His kingdom and that will be His government. Isaiah 9:6 says, *"The government shall be upon His shoulder."* What government? This government that we are talking about here in chapter 11 and described so vividly as being a place that is literal and is peaceful.

- Now we take the quality of the kingdom found in verses 6 through 9. This is a lovely picture. It is all creation of God to be delivered from the bondage of corruption into which it was plunged by sin. Romans 8:21 says, *"Because the creature itself also shall be delivered from the bondage of corruption into the glorious liberty of the children of God."* Isaiah says, in verse 9, *"for the earth shall be full of the knowledge of the Lord, as the waters cover the sea."* So it is literal. The earth and the creatures therein will be as they are described here in verses 6 through 9.

3. VERSE 10

- In verse 10, are the words *"in that day there shall be a root of Jesse."* Those words are familiar to you by now because they talk about a future day. Christ is the root of Jesse as well as the branch of Jesse and He will be manifested in such majesty as to be a banner or an ensign. He will rally about Him all of the people and He specifically says, *"to it shall the Gentiles seek."* The whole earth then shares in the joy of Him who is both the root and the offspring of David.

- Notice those last words of verse 10: *"and his rest shall be glorious."* Christ will find His resting place in that kingdom—and Christ is our rest.

4. VERSES 11–13

- In verses 11–13, we find those words again *"in that day."* The Lord will set His hand *"the second time to recover the remnant of His people."* Notice the words *"the second time."* Notice He is gathering them from every country to which they have scattered. This suggests two questions: One, when did He gather them the first time? And two, is the second gathering final or will there be a third?

- There can be but one answer to the first question. It was Jehovah's hand alone that recovered His people from Egypt the first time. With His hand, He brought them out of this first deliverance, when His hand will again be active—only the second time it will not be only over Egypt, but over the entire earth. Then it follows that the second recovery of Israel will be as much the direct work of God as the first was from Egypt. He alone can truly restore His people a second time.

- It is indeed true that all of prophecy tells us that the same nation must be in the same land as was in that place at the rejection and crucifixion of the Lord. Its people, Israel, must return to the land in order that prophetic Scriptures may then begin to be fulfilled. Until they are there, no direct fulfillment can take place. God is now permitting, in a providential way, a return to the land of Israel, but they are returning in the same unbelief in which they left and they are not going back to a never-ending blessedness, but to a time unparalleled in history that is called the great tribulation.

- Verses 11 and 12 then speak of the final gathering of all of the tribes of Israel, the two of the southern tribes called Judah and the ten of the northern tribes called Israel, and that regathering is not to be followed by a third. It is the sweeping hand of the Lord over all the earth that gathers every one of His earthly people, Israel, back into the land.

- Many have thought in days past that the promise of Israel's restoration were fulfilled long ago when a remnant returned in the days of Zerubbabel, Ezra, and Nehemiah. But here we are informed definitely with the words *"the Lord shall set his hand again the second time to recover the remnant of his people"* (verse 11)—and we learned that they will return not simply from Babylon as they did before, but from all the lands where they had been dispersed throughout the long centuries of their sorrow and suffering.

- Israel and Judah, no longer divided, will be drawn to the Lord Himself who is the Ensign to be set up in that day and they will flow together to the land of their fathers, no longer as rival nations but as one people. Such change will take place so that Ephraim will not envy Judah and Judah will not vex Ephraim. The Lord's gracious hand will be extended to both Ephraim and Judah and they will be His people.

5. VERSES 14–16

- In verses 14–16, we find more details as to the manner of their return to Palestine, assisted by the nations that were once their enemies. Certain geographical changes are indicated here that no doubt will be affected when the feet of our Lord will stand again upon the Mount of Olives and there will be a great earthquake with far-reaching results as foretold in Zechariah chapter 14.

CHAPTER 12

In this chapter, we find the worship of the Lord in His kingdom. This brief chapter of only six verses reads like a Psalm. Here is set before us the praise of a people under the direct and personal reign of Christ. This is pure praise from redeemed hearts to God because of His salvation and creation. With the curse removed from the earth, there will be a great occasion to praise God for His display of goodness.

1. VERSE 1

- Notice the words *"In that day thou shalt say, O LORD, I will praise thee: though thou wast angry with me."*

- The tribulation is past and the storms of life are all over. Now they have entered into the literal kingdom of our Lord and Savior.

- This is an occasion for praise. All of us who are Christians should meditate long on this short chapter and think of the joys of heaven after the pilgrim journey on this earth is over. What a day of joy that will be!

2. VERSES 2–3

- Notice in verse 2 the words *"God is my salvation."* They will not say that God *provided* salvation, but that He *is* salvation. Salvation is a person, not a program.

- In verse 3, we note the abundance, joy, and satisfaction that there will be in salvation. Wells that never run dry because the Word is the water that washes us clean from the wells of salvation that were so long spurned by the self-righteous Jew who sought to save himself by his own efforts. Then the returned remnant will draw the Water of Life as they call upon His name and bear witness before all the world to the salvation that He has given.

3. VERSE 4

- Verse 4 begins a new thought. The first three verses, which is the first part of this chapter, speak of Israel's abounding joy and then beginning in the fourth verse through the sixth, this joy runs over to all the nations of the earth.

- This song remains to be sung in the future for "that day" has not yet come nor can it possibly be sung while the Jews are still wandering in strange lands. To this very day, Jehovah is unmistakably angry with the nation Israel; not on account of its idolatry for which it was originally banished to Babylon for seventy years, but He is angry far more for the crucifixion by "lawless hands" of His beloved Son and for not accepting Him as Messiah. Therefore, they have been banished for 2,000 years and are still wandering.

- ✦ But even that anger of the Lord has a limit as is indicated in chapter 10, verse 25. I do not see that the song here in chapter 12 permits any extended exposition because it is a simple thing to understand. The returned, the renewed nation, first quenches its own thirst at the fountain of salvation and then the waters overflow for all the peoples of the earth to share in those springs of happiness.

4. CONCLUDING THE BOOK OF IMMANUEL
- ✦ Now we come to the end of the book of Immanuel. It began at chapter 7 with the birth of Immanuel and traces His path till He is seen reigning as king in chapter 9. Then, after the rise of the Assyrians digging their own graves and threatening Jerusalem, the remnant of Israel finds new life in the Sprout. With His introduction as the Branch, Israel rejoices and the kingdom with a king is seen in the final chapters of this section.

How Much Do You Remember?

1. In chapter 10, how does God use the Assyrians to accomplish His will?
2. What is the main theme of chapter 11?
3. Describe the character of the reign of Christ mentioned in the beginning of chapter 11.
4. Contrast the prophecy concerning Assyria as a "cedar" in chapter 10 with the resurrection of Israel as an "oak" in chapter 11.
5. Explain why chapter 11 verse 11 speaks of God recovering the remnant of His people for a "second time."
6. Why is chapter 12 a response of praise?

Your Assignment for Next Week:

1. Review your notes from this lesson.
2. Read Isaiah chapters 13 and 14.
3. Underline your Bible.

Lesson 5 Notes

_____

_____

_____

_____

_____

_____

_____

_____

_____

_____

_____

Lesson 6
CHAPTERS 13 AND 14

CHAPTER 13

1. A PREVIEW OF THE NEXT SECTION OF ISAIAH

   + Isaiah chapters 13 through 23 contain burdens or judgments on nine surrounding nations. All of these nations had some contact with Israel and most of them were near her borders. Israel suffered at the hands of some of them and will suffer again in the future. While this section, for the most part, is yet future, nevertheless, the chief characteristic is that much has been fulfilled and stands today as an evidence of fulfilled prophecy. All of this adds interest and importance to these eleven chapters. The Assyrian is no longer the oppressor—those of other nations take his place.

   + A burden is a judgment. It was not pleasant to the prophet to deliver the message, for it made him the unpopular preacher of "bad news" and his message became a burden to the nation for which it was intended.

   + Babylon, as the subject of the first burden, is suggestive of many things to the reverent student of the Word of God. First of all, the literal city of Babylon is the primary consideration. This is indeed remarkable, as Babylon, in Isaiah's day, was an insignificant place. It was not until a century later that Babylon became a world power. God pronounced judgment on Babylon before it became a nation. It is also well to note that this new section does not end with the burden on nine surrounding nations, but extends on through six woes to be found in chapters 28 through 33 and concludes with the calm and the blessing after the storm in chapters 34 through 35.

   + The burdens of this section, chapters 13 through 23, are related particularly to Babylon in chapters 13 and 14; to Moab in chapters 15 and 16; Damascus, the capital of Syria, in chapter 17; some unnamed power (Cush or Ethiopia in Africa) in chapter 18; Egypt in chapter 19; Egypt and Ethiopia in chapter 20; Edom and Arabia in chapter 21; Jerusalem in chapter 22; and Tyre in chapter 23.

   + In chapters 13 and 14, Isaiah looks on into the future, predicting what he saw: the destruction that would come upon Babylon as a result of the Medo-Persion invasion. It may seem strange to you that Babylon should occupy the place it does in these prophetic visions in as much as it was an insignificant power in the days of Isaiah, completely overshadowed by Assyria, but the spirit of prophecy enabled Isaiah to look on to the time when these two would be combined in one great dominion of which the city of Babylon would be the capital.

2. VERSES 1–6

   + Verses 1 and 2: The literal city of Babylon in history is in view in this chapter and also in chapter 14. Babylon as a symbol of rebellion against God is also to be remembered. The tower of Babel is where it all began and the end is before us here and in Psalm 2.

   + In verse 3, the word *"sanctified"* means "set apart" for a specific use by some agency. God will use the Babylonians as He did the Assyrians, as instruments for punishing His people.

   + Verse 4 offers a satisfactory explanation of those sanctified ones. Babylon will come against the southern kingdom of Judah as Assyria did against the ten northern tribes of Israel. We see this reemphasized again in verse 5, where the Babylonians will likewise be the rod of God's indignation.

   + Verse 6 looks beyond anything that is now or has been in history and is projected into the day of the Lord, for the great tribulation is the reference here.

3. VERSES 7–10

+ When God's judgment falls upon Babylon, it will be as painful as the extreme suffering of a woman in labor. The fierce anger of the Lord will lay the land desolate—that is, Babylon. Once again, we are speaking of things that are yet to be—the great tribulation.

+ All of the constellations of the heavens will not give light, the sun will be darkened, and the moon will not shine. When the wrath of God is active, the heavens add terror to that wrath when the Lord God causes all to be in total darkness.

4. VERSES 11–16

+ Notice that the Lord will punish the world for their evil in verse 11. Though that wrath will be centered in Palestine, the whole globe comes under the visitation of the judgment of God.

+ Shaking the heavens are a part of the judgments of God. So large a portion of the human race will be destroyed in the conflicts and natural catastrophes of those days that a man will be more precious than gold. Fear and terror will take hold upon all of the inhabitants of the earth.

5. VERSES 17–22

+ Here the prophet reverts to the literal destruction of Babylon, which was in the immediate future, and he identifies those who will destroy Babylon—"the Medes."

+ This punishment was not consummated until some centuries later, when that proud city was leveled to dust with its palaces destroyed, its hanging gardens ruined, and its destruction made so complete that in all the centuries since, it has never been able to rise again.

+ It is true that from time to time, small villages have been built near the site of the ancient city, but the ruins of Babylon recently uncovered by archaeologists show how completely the prophet's words have been fulfilled. Even to this day, the Arabian refuses to pitch his tent there, thinking that demons prowl by night among the ruins of the city.

+ God has decreed in verse 20 that Babylon will never rise again. The Babylon of the apocalypse is a symbolic picture of the great religious, political, and commercial organization of the last days that will become fully developed after the true church has been caught up to be with the Lord. This commercial organization called Babylon—like that of the ancient city—will soon be consummated and it too will fall, never to lift itself up again against God and His people.

+ In verse 21, you will notice the word *"satyrs,"* which means "demons." Babylon was the headquarters for idolatry in the ancient world. They, along with the wild beasts, apparently reside there.

+ The doom described here in chapters 13 and 14 that fell upon Babylon was an illustration of the terrible fate that awaits the godless Gentile powers. It should be noted that many of the expressions used in these verses are practically identical with those of other prophecies concerning the Day of the Lord and with the events that follow the breaking of the sixth seal in the book of Revelation.

CHAPTER 14

In chapter 14, we see a continuation of the burden of Babylon that we began in chapter 13. Great issues are at stake in this chapter because we see that God links Israel's future restoration with the doom of Babylon. Though centuries were to elapse between the two events, through the decree of Cyprus, a remnant was permitted to return to Jerusalem, thus fulfilling a part of the divine predictions concerning the recovery of Judah, so their final restoration is linked with the complete overthrow of everything that is godless, commercial, and that which is described in Revelation and in Daniel.

1. VERSES 1–2

+ In verse 1, we have a clear statement of fact about how God will deal with Israel. Some people say that God is through with His chosen people, yet in this verse it says, *"For the Lord…will yet choose*

Israel." Also, a great company of Gentiles will yet be saved outside of the church after the church is removed; and they are designated here as "*strangers.*"

- In verse 2, the words "*the people*" actually mean Gentiles. The Gentiles will return the remnant to Palestine rather than hinder them as they are doing today: "*And they shall take them captives, whose captives they were.*" This phrase throws some light on the controversial statement in Ephesians 4:8 that says, "*He led captivity captive.*" This statement is quoted from Psalm 68:18. The same thing occurs in Judges 5:12. You will find it all through Scripture that the one they thought had been made captive—Christ—actually became the victor.

2. VERSES 3–8

- The kingdom of Babylon seems to be used here as a synonym for all the Gentile powers that have taken part in the persecution of God's ancient people. When the last great enemy will be destroyed, they will be able to rejoice in the manifestation of Jehovah's power. Just as Israel sang on the shores of the Red Sea as they viewed the destruction of Pharaoh and his host, so in that coming day will they be able to raise the song of Moses and the Lamb as they see all their enemies brought down. Then the whole earth will be at rest and will be at peace; there will be singing and the trees will rejoice. In other words, we will be in the kingdom and we will know the joy of the kingdom.

3. VERSES 9–15: LUCIFER

- We come now to something that enables us to understand how sin began in the heavens and also to comprehend something of the unseen powers that, throughout the centuries, have dominated the minds of evil, disposed men—seeking to thwart the purpose of God. The fall of Lucifer portrays the fall of Satan. The passage links very closely to Ezekiel 28, which should be carefully considered in the effort to understand this fully.

- The words of verses 9 through 15 cannot apply to any mere mortal man. Lucifer, meaning the light bearer, is a created angel of the very highest order, identical with the covering cherub of Ezekiel 28. He was, apparently, the greatest of all the angel host, and was perfect before God until he fell through pride. It was his ambition to take the throne of God for himself and become supreme ruler of the universe.

- Note the five "I wills" in this section of Scripture. It was the assertion of the will of God in opposition to the will of the creature that brought about his downfall and so an archangel became the devil! Cast down from the palace of power and favor that he had enjoyed, he became the untiring enemy of God and man. Throughout the millennia since, he exerted every conceivable device to ruin mankind and to rob God of the glory due to Him.

- It is of him our Lord speaks in John 8:44. The Lord there shows that Satan is an apostate having fallen from a position once enjoyed and we know from the other Scriptures how he goes about as a roaring lion seeking whom he may devour. We know from Luke 10:18 that the Lord saw Satan fall from heaven. From other passages we learn that Lucifer was not alone in his rebellion (see 2 Peter 2:4) and our Lord speaks of "*the devil and his angels*" (Matthew 25:41), which is confirmed in Revelation 12:7, where we read of this war in heaven between Michael and his angels and the dragon and his angels. These evil angels are the world rulers of this darkness. (See Ephesians 6:12.) They seek to dominate the hearts and minds of the rulers of the nations, stirring them up to act in opposition to the will of God.

- Those five "I wills" of Lucifer is sin in its embryonic stage. This is the evolution of evil. There is no evolution of man, but there is evolution of sin. It began by a creature setting its will against the will of God. As a free moral agent, the creature must be allowed to do this. This is man's original sin, "*All we like sheep have gone astray; we have turned every one to his own way*" (Isaiah 53:6). Those words "*his own way*" means that all of us "*have gone astray.*" Lucifer thought in his heart to lift himself to the rank of God.

+ In verse 12, the name Lucifer, son of the morning, is this king of Babylon, king over confusion, and the name is given to him that literally rendered means "bright shining one, son of the dawn." Thus, the whole meaning is the very close parallel to "bright morning star."

+ As surely as students of Scripture have seen him who is now called Satan behind the king of Tyre in Ezekiel 28, there is equal reason for discerning the same personage behind the king of Babylon. Tyre was a representative of commerce—as Babylon was of the religion of the world. Tyre represents the material side of this one's activity, ever desiring to possess the earth, while Babylon represents the spiritual that would aim at heaven. As in those early days when rebellious men would build both a city and a tower, Tyre would correspond with the city that was to cover the earth and Babylon with the tower that was to reach heaven. Both the king of Tyre and of Babylon evidenced the same sin of pride and this is the same heritage of all of us as fallen from the Lord. This character that would ascend "*above the stars of God*" (verse 13) can but suggest that these two are one and that one is Satan.

+ I want to quickly ponder the question about the source of evil, sin, suffering, and sorrow. Where did all this moral and physical disorder and confusion come from if the one Creator of all is good? Can God then be the author of confusion that is not good? Can good produce evil? It would equally be intelligent to ask such a question as, "Can the sun give out darkness?" If we take then simply as a working hypothesis, that as God is the source of all that is good—so the devil is the source of all that is evil—we have narrowed the question down to, "Where did the devil come from?" Thank the Lord, Scripture is clear about this. God created one long before man that was a spirit creation, perfect in all his ways, and as God does create all things, that one—that spirit creation—had absolute liberty to go in any direction, not compelled, but with power of free choice to walk in any direction, moral as well as physical. Having been created by the Creator's hand, what name could be given him? It must at least express what he then was, not what he afterward make of himself. No "devil" was he then. No "Satan" could, or did God make, but a brilliantly shining one, the very star of the morning amidst the hosts of the heaven did God made him. It would be absurd then to trace sin and all the consequences of sin to the source of all good—that being God the Father—because Satan was not created Satan, but the bright star of the morning.

+ One may say that it is hard to understand the presence of evil in the creation of a God that is only good, and that gives rise to another question—where could that evil suggestion come to him, Lucifer, when there was no evil present then in all the universe? It certainly could not have come from anywhere external to him for there was none there. True, but the Bible suggests a clear answer in these words from Ezekiel 28:17: "*Thine heart was lifted up because of thy beauty, thou hast corrupted thy wisdom by reason of thy brightness.*" It was self-born—it came from self-occupation with his own creative beauty, ignoring his dependence upon his Creator. You and I may learn much from this. Complacent self-occupation, even with what God might work in us, is filled with grave danger. Only when our minds and thoughts are kept on the Lord Jesus Himself—His beauty, His perfection, His love—can we find safety, joy, blessing, and true holiness.

+ The name "son of the morning" or "bright morning star" having been given to the one who has turned light into darkness may give rise to a certain sense of resentment since we know it as justly belonging to another one who claims it and in whom alone all light is focused: the Lord Jesus. He is for us who are Christians "the bright and morning star." There is no sound reasoning for questioning that Lucifer, the son of the morning, was the original and worthy name expressing the creative beauty and dignity of him who was afterwards named as expressing his own self-acquired character that is the devil, Satan, that old serpent, and the dragon. Therefore, there is no rivalry between the names for he to whom that name was first applied, lost it forever, and gained these other names that tell us that he is now the ruler of this world, the ruler of darkness, and has taken on the name of devil, Satan, serpent, and dragon.

+ When you trace the ambitious path of this Lucifer, it reads like a storybook of pride. Notice *"I will exalt my throne above the stars of God: I will sit also upon the mount of the congregation, in the sides of the north: I will ascend above the heights of the clouds; I will be like the most High"* (verses 13–14). He will ascend above the Lord God Himself; he will sit upon the mount and notice how strikingly suggestive that phrase is of that other mount called Har-Mageddon for that also means, when translated, "Mount of the Assembly" or "gathering," but the last part of the word "Mageddon" has in it the idea of a military gathering of troops in undisguised warfare and speaks to the final gathering of all the children of pride in open conflict with him that sits on the horse described in Revelation 19:19.

+ When Lucifer made this statement, all angelic assemblies were in willing submission to the throne of God. It is with this assembly in mind that Lucifer aims to place his throne in the extremity of the north—the highest possible elevation. The word "north" in the Hebrew properly means "hidden" or "obscure." As Israel's foe ever came from the literal north, so do the attacks upon our faith come from these dark obscure places.

+ The "north" is not dark for us who now see and know the true, bright, morning star, for He, the Lamb, is there and will enlighten it as is expressed in Psalm 48:1–3, which says, *"Great is the* Lord, *and greatly to be praised in the city of our God, in the mountain of his holiness. Beautiful for situation, the joy of the whole earth, is mount Zion, on the sides of the north, the city of the great King. God is known in her palaces for a refuge."*

4. VERSES 16–23

+ In this portion of Scripture, we should not be surprised to find in these few verses that the King of Babylon was confounded with Lucifer. The actual meaning, of course, is that he was controlled or dominated by him.

+ In verses 16–23, we find a highly poetical section of Scripture but a description in no uncertain terms of the utter destruction of the last great enemy of Israel in the Day of the Lord. You will find this also in Ezekiel 31:16–18. None who dared to rise up in pride and arrogance to defy the living God has ever been able to escape the inevitable result.

5. VERSES 24–27

+ In the Assyrian of the last days, we see it as it were the incarnation of all the persecuting powers who have distressed Israel since their dispersion among the Gentiles. When the nations are gathered together for the Armageddon conflict, the Lord Himself will destroy the Assyrian with every other enemy of Christ and His truth. Israel will be completely delivered and God glorified in the kingdom to be set up in righteousness.

6. VERSES 28–32

+ Now in the last five verses of the chapter, we have a separate prophecy given in the last year of King Ahaz, which relates to the Philistines and its people.

+ This is considered the second burden, the burden of Palestine.

How Much Do You Remember?

1. Which nation is the burden related to in chapters 13 and 14?
2. What is Babylon a symbol of?
3. In chapter 13 verse 21, what does the word *"satyrs"* mean, and what was Babylon a headquarters for in the ancient world?
4. In chapter 14, what does God link the final restoration of Jerusalem with?
5. Recall the five "I will" statements of Lucifer in chapter 14.

Your Assignment for Next Week:

1. Review your notes from this lesson.
2. Read Isaiah chapters 15–18.
3. Underline your Bible.

Lesson 6 Notes

_____

_____

_____

_____

_____

_____

_____

_____

_____

_____

_____

_____

_____

_____

_____

_____

_____

_____

_____

_____

_____

_____

_____

_____

_____

Lesson 7
CHAPTERS 15, 16, 17, AND 18

CHAPTER 15

This brief chapter records the burdens of Moab and it continues on throughout the chapter and into chapter 16. Literally, this is the third burden since you will find the burden of Palestine recorded at the end of chapter 14.

It is difficult to see at first that this prophecy concerning a small nation in a faraway place, in a distant day, could have any bearing upon us today. How could the temporary distress of these obscure people convey a message to us? We will find here, as well as in every Scripture, that there is a message for us as *"All scripture is given by inspiration of God, and is profitable"* (2 Timothy 3:16).

Moab was the nation that came from Lot through the incestuous relationship of his eldest daughter. The illegitimate son of this sordid affair was the father of the Moabites. (See Genesis 19:33–38.) These people became the inveterate and persistent enemies of the nation Israel. Balak, their king, hired Baalam, the prophet, to curse Israel for Balak feared them when they passed through the land of Moab. David sought refuge there for his parents from the hand of Saul. Moab is representative of those who make a profession of God, but actually they have no vital relationship with Him. They finally become enemies of God's children and will seek to do them harm. You might say that modern "Moabites" are described in 2 Timothy 3:1–5 and in Jude, verses 14–16.

Judgment came upon ancient Moab. The destruction of Moab was sudden and devastating. It led to a long night of weeping and no joy in the morning. It begged for the sympathy of the prophet because it was a frightful burden. This destruction was wrought first by Assyria and later by Babylon.

There are only nine verses to this chapter and we will notice that the first four verses describe the sudden destruction of Moab and that the last five give to us a sad spectacle that elicits the sympathy of the prophet of Zoar.

1. VERSE 1
   + This burden of Moab came suddenly *"in the night."* This expression is repeated twice to emphasize the suddenness of the storm that struck the nation. The storm came at night and their night of weeping never ended.
   + At first, they were numbed by the suddenness of it all and there was silence. The silence was broken by an eternal howling and wailing.
   + The word *"Kir"* is now "Kerak" on a mountain peak about ten miles from the southeast corner of the Dead Sea.

2. VERSE 2
   + It is well to note the number of proper names given in this chapter that refer to the geographical places. Dibon is where the Moabite's stone was found. Bajith means "house."
   + Here, it evidently refers to the Temple of Chemosh. In this time of trouble, the people flocked to the temple. During days of distress, people seek for relief in religion and they crowd the temples and churches. This is merely the fleshly instinct of the old nature and is the conduct of those who are professors.
   + The Moabites turned to a heathen temple and pagan god. Modern man goes to a liberal church. Neither comes to the living God in genuine obedience. Religion is merely an escape mechanism from the tragedies and raw realities of life.

3. VERSE 3
   - The impressive fact of this realism is the deep sorrow of the people as they survey the awful aspect of the total destruction of the nation. *"Weeping abundantly"* means to be "drowned in tears."
   - There is no hymn singing here. Ancient Moabites and modern Moabites only sing the blues. If there were any of God's children here in much affliction, there would likewise be the joy of the Holy Spirit.

4. VERSES 4–5
   - In verse 4, it is not necessary for us to locate the geographical positions of these cities. It simply means that all the great centers of Moabite culture were involved in this havoc that was wrought by the enemy.
   - In verse 5, we see that although Moab was the enemy of Israel, the prophet's heart goes out in sympathy to Moab because of the terror that has come upon them. This reveals the heart of God. In spite of the people's sin, God still loves and will extend mercy.
   - "Zoar" is the place where Lot took refuge at the destruction of Sodom and Gomorrah. (See Genesis 19:18–32.) The Moabites will take refuge in Zoar as Lot did of old.

5. VERSES 6–9
   - In verses 6 through 9, we find a detailed description given of the further ravaging of the land of Moab. It is like unto a flood that covers the land.

CHAPTER 16

The prophecy concerning the judgment of Moab continues in this chapter. Perhaps it may seem out of all proportion to the reader in ratio with the importance and size of the nation. Moab was a more formidable nation in that day than we are willing to concede. Its prominence to the nation Israel at that time cannot be overestimated. This chapter opens with a last call to Moab to avail herself of the mercy God has provided for her. They are enjoined to pay tribute to Israel according to their arrangement. (See 2 Kings 3:4–24.) This was an acknowledgment of God and a tribute to Jehovah. In the great tribulation a nation's faith in God will be determined by their attitude and action toward Israel.

Because of pride, Moab failed to obey God. The final judgment is predicted in a short time in this chapter.

1. VERSE 1
   - The lamb was the animal of sacrifice that best depicts Christ. Sela referred to here is "Petra," the capital of Edom. From the southern border to the northern border, the lamb is to be sent as a tribute to Israel. This would be an acknowledgment of the authority and position of Israel. It was a tax that would require humbleness on the part of Moab to comply with its terms.

2. VERSES 2–5
   - This section is projected into the great tribulation and the kingdom—as the fifth verse shows by its direct reference to the tabernacle of David.
   - During that time of trouble, the nation Israel will be in grave difficulty. (See Jeremiah 37.) They will seek for refuge from their enemies. As some nations seek sanctions against them, they will seek for sanctuary among the surrounding nations.
   - Satan, cast out of heaven at this time, will vent all his anger against them. (See Revelations 12:13–16.)
   - Those who befriend these people by so much as giving a cup of cold water will be rewarded of God.

3. VERSES 6–8
   - Pride will be the cause of Moab's rejection of God's offer of mercy, as seen in verse 6.

- In verses 7 and 8, we read about how judgment will inevitably fall upon Moab. Only Moab will howl for Moab now.

4. VERSES 9–11

- The prophet's heart is again touched and he weeps as he anticipates the coming judgment upon Moab. God never delights in judgment. It is His strange work. He would rather extend mercy.

5. VERSES 13–14

- The coming judgment is dated. Notice the words *"within three years."* Here again, Isaiah proves he is a true prophet of God. The Assyrians shortly thereafter invaded the land of Moab. We find again that Isaiah qualified in all points in reference to Deuteronomy 18:22: *"When a prophet speaketh in the name of the LORD, if the thing follow not, nor come to pass, that is the thing which the LORD hath not spoken, but the prophet hath spoken it presumptuously: thou shalt not be afraid of him."*

CHAPTER 17

Now we come to consider the burden of Damascus. Closely linked with Damascus, we have the nation of Israel called here "Ephraim" after the break they had with Judah. Because of the fact that they had formed an alliance with Syria, of which Damascus was the capital, they must share in the judgment that was about to fall on that proud city. Damascus is sometimes said to be the oldest city in the world. This may or may not be so, but it has certainly existed through many thousands of years and has passed through many wars and distressing experiences—yet it stands today as a great commercial center in that part of the world. Israel is linked with this judgment or burden that is pronounced upon Damascus. Partners in crime mean partners in punishment.

1. VERSE 1

- Here we see the burden of Damascus: *"Behold, Damascus is taken away from being a city, and it shall be a ruinous heap."*

- This verse presents a real problem, it appears, in the fact that it states that Damascus will be *"taken away from being a city"* and yet historians state that Damascus is the oldest city in existence today. There are two possible explanations for this:

    a. Historians are not accurate in making such a bold and general statement. The many ruins that are found around Damascus have been caused by the many wars that have taken place there.

    b. In view of the fact that Damascus is called the oldest city and has withstood the ravages of war, it will cease from being a city in the coming destruction of the great tribulation.

- However, it is interesting to note that Damascus is still a city, and there always has been a city and Syria is still a nation. At the time when Isaiah prophesied this, Sennacherib's hosts were rapidly moving toward Israel and Syria and it is of this onslaught that the first verse speaks.

2. VERSES 2–3

- In verse 2, we read of Aroer, which is a suburban area near Damascus.

- In verse 3, the northern kingdom of Israel must bear her share of the burden pronounced upon Damascus because of their alliance. Both Israel and Damascus were besieged by the Tiglathpileser, as recorded in 2 Kings 15:29 and finally deported by the Assyrian, Shalmaneser, as recorded in 2 Kings 17:6.

- This was the near-immediate future and was a partial fulfillment of Isaiah's prophecy.

3. VERSES 4–5

- Isaiah's prophecy looks beyond the near future or the day of the Assyrian—the prophecy looks toward *"that day"* when the nation Israel will again be besieged by the enemy from the north, east, and west. Again, they will turn to an alliance and not to God. Israel will make a covenant with a world ruler as recorded in Daniel 9:27.

+ All of this has a prophetic tone of that which will take place again in the last days when God will deal once more both with Israel and with the nations. In that time, a remnant of Jacob will be preserved who will seek the face of God.

4. VERSES 6–8

+ The remnant described in this passage is distinguished in many of the books of the prophets and comes before us clearly again in the New Testament. A remnant will turn to God. A remnant will be saved and this remnant is the true Israel *"for they are not all Israel, which are of Israel"* (Romans 9:6).

+ Again, Paul says, *"And so all Israel shall be saved"* (Romans 11:26). The entire nation is not intended here—it is only a remnant as Isaiah states it. It is the remnant in whom God recognizes the true seed of Jacob. Abhorring idolatry, they will find their resources in the God of their fathers and as they look to Him for protection, He will undertake for them.

5. VERSE 10

+ This verse has a spiritual application, but it is likewise interesting to note how this land in our day has been planted with pleasant plants and trees.

+ The forest of the cedars of Lebanon will have almost all been removed. There were many trees in that land and the Mount of Olives was covered with them. The enemy removed many of them. While the Turks controlled Palestine, they extracted a tax on trees. The people cut down practically all the trees in the land and it was almost denuded of greenery. After World War I, England began a movement to plant trees in Palestine that were later destroyed by Arabs. The subsequent governments of Israel continued this policy and literally millions of trees have been set out. Today in Israel, you will find olive trees and orchards of fruit—greenery everywhere.

6. VERSE 11

+ *"In that day"*—what day? The day that Scripture depicts as a terrible trial such as Jacob has never known in the past. Surely the harvest will be a day of grief and desperate sorrow. How this should move our hearts to cry for God for the salvation of Israel and to pray for the peace of Jerusalem.

7. VERSES 12–14

+ While these words also have had a primary fulfillment in the destruction of Israel's foes in the past, notably Assyria of Isaiah's day and the Chaldeans later on, they also coincide with what our Lord Himself prophesied concerning the great tribulation, preceded by the time when *"nation shall rise against nation, and kingdom against kingdom"* (Matthew 24:7); when the sea and the wave will roar, and there will be earthquakes in diverse places, and their hearts will fail them for fear.

+ As the closing hour of the tribulation strikes, the nations will be gathered together against Jerusalem. The hosts of the Gentiles will come from the east, north, and west to engage in bloody conflict seeking to obtain possession of Emmanuel's land, but the appearance of the Lord Jesus Christ in glory will bring the last great war to an end.

CHAPTER 18

Chapter 18 is the burden of the land beyond the rivers of Ethiopia. The exact nations that Isaiah had in mind in this chapter have not been definitely ascertained. This is obvious from the many interpretations that scholars give to it. It could hardly be Egypt since the description of this location does not fit Egypt. The Bible says, *"beyond the rivers of Ethiopia"* (verse 1) and that is not an apt location of Egypt. There is a separate burden in chapter 19 concerning Egypt and it would be unusual to have this particular burden described and not mention Egypt. We believe that Ethiopia best suits the text of Scripture.

Another problem arises at this point, however, and that is—which Ethiopia is intended? There are two Ethiopias in Scripture. The word for Ethiopia is Cush. There is one on the Euphrates in Asia described in Genesis 2:13 and there is another in Africa. (See Isaiah 20:3–5.) We conclude, therefore, that the Ethiopia in Africa is the one intended here in the Scripture.

Missionaries to that particular land tell us that it is known and noted as the land of birds and is called the land of wings (you'll find this in verse 1). This passage of Scripture is not all judgment—or a burden—because as we will see, many favorable things are said in Scripture concerning Ethiopia. (See for example, Psalm 87:4 and Amos 9:7. In Amos, God proves His love to His people by saying He loves them as He loves the Ethiopians.) It is interesting to note that one of the first converts—Gentiles to be saved in the church—is recorded in Acts 8 and that was the Ethiopian eunuch.

1. VERSE 1
   - Even though the chapter begins with the word *"woe"* it is an unfortunate interpretation here. The word should be "ah." It is definitely not a woe or a burden that is referred to in verse 1.
   - The words *"shadowing with wings"* might be better rendered by "rustling with wings." Special attention is called to the noise that is made.

2. VERSE 2
   - It is assumed from the statement that the ambassadors are sent by sea, that this would be a great sea power. *"Vessels of bulrushes"* has likewise been a stumbling block in interpretation. Some have indicated that those words mean a steamboat. *"A nation scattered and peeled"* is Israel. This is potentially evident and most of the sound students of the Word of God concur in this.
   - *"Whose land the rivers have spoiled"* presents a difficulty. There is only one river in Palestine and it has never flooded the land. But when you look at the African Ethiopia where the Nile rises, then you have a totally different picture.

3. VERSES 3–6
   - An ensign lifted up in the land will be the signal for the returning to Palestine of those who through the centuries have wandered among the Gentiles. We may see this being fulfilled already. They are now in the land and recognized by other nations as an independent republic. One could well hope that their sufferings were over, did we not know that even greater distress awaits them in the future when the horrors of the great tribulation will burst upon them in all of their fury. Then a remnant will be distinguished from the masses and with this remnant Jehovah will be identified.

4. VERSE 7
   - This verse coincides with the actual return of the Lord when He will arise to deal in judgment with the enemies of Israel and will recognize the remnant as His people. The great trumpet will be blown, and the outcasts of Israel summoned to return from every land of the earth to their ancient territory. Surely, we see in all that is going on at the present time in reference to Israel how readily all these things will have their complete fulfillment as soon as the church of God has been taken out of the scene and caught up to be with the Lord.
   - God's heart is ever toward Israel and while He has permitted them to pass through such terrible sufferings throughout the long centuries of their dispersion because they knew not the time of their visitation, the day will surely come when, their transgressions forgiven and their hearts renewed, they will be restored to Him and planted again in their own land.
   - This land has been spoiled many times by invading armies that are often pictured as overflowing, destructive rivers. Through 2,000 years since the rejection of Christ and the destruction of Jerusalem and the temple that followed about forty years later, this land has undergone war after war. In all of these stresses, Israel has been an almost continual battleground—Assyria, Babylonia, Persia,

Greece, Egypt, Rome, and later the Turks all have fought over this land and whoever has won, the Jew has always been the loser until when, in God's due time, a nation was established.

  + God has been working providentially toward the fulfillment of His purposes for Israel. Their reliance has been, however, upon their own wisdom and might, assisted at times by the Gentiles, rather than depending upon God Himself. So there have been many disappointments and there will be more in the future, until that day when Israel will be born in a day.

How Much Do You Remember?

1. Describe the burden of Moab found in chapters 15 and 16.
2. In chapter 16, what will be the cause of Moab's rejection of God's offer of mercy?
3. What nation is Damascus' partner in crime and punishment for this burden of Damascus?
4. After studying the clues found in Scripture, which region can be deduced to facing the burden of Ethiopia found in chapter 18?

Your Assignment for Next Week:

1. Review your notes from this lesson.
2. Read Isaiah chapters 19, 20, and 21.
3. Underline your Bible.

Lesson 7 Notes

_____

_____

_____

_____

_____

_____

_____

_____

_____

_____

_____

_____

_____

_____

_____

_____

_____

_____

_____

Lesson 8
CHAPTERS 19, 20, AND 21

CHAPTER 19

This chapter is the burden of Egypt. No nation figures so prominently on the pages of Scripture besides Israel than does Egypt. She has a longer history than any nation mentioned in Scripture, including Israel. Egypt was one of the most ancient of the great nations of the past. It is in existence today and plays a prominent part in world events. It has a glorious future predicted on the pages of Scripture. This chapter contains all elements that enter into the history of the nation—its past, present, and future.

Egypt comes into prominence early in Scripture when Abraham ran away to Egypt and got into difficulty. Later, Joseph was sold into Egypt and during a famine, Jacob and his twelve sons went down into Egypt with their families. There, Israel became a nation in the slavery of the brick yards of Egypt. Ahaz and Hezekiah both made an alliance with Egypt and found her an unreliable ally. When Jesus was born, He was taken down into Egypt. The gospel made many converts in Egypt during the first three centuries of the Christian era. Mark established the first Christian community in Egypt in Alexandria. In Alexandria, the Hebrew Scriptures were first translated in 285 B.C. Simon, the zealot, was the first preacher in Alexandria. Another name for ancient Egypt is Mizraim. (See Genesis 10:6–13.)

1. VERSES 1–4

    +   The idolatry of Egypt is the chief target of God's condemnation of this nation. Perhaps no people were ever given over to idolatry more than the Egyptians, with the possible exception of the Babylonians. The very fountainhead of idolatry, Egypt, because of her long history, is a perfect example of Romans 1:21–23 (read these verses).

    +   The people were originally monotheistic, but they gradually lapsed into the basest sort of idolatry where every creature was worshipped: the bull, the frog, the scarab (a beetle), the fish, and all sorts of birds.

    +   The contests of Moses and Pharaoh to let Israel go resolved itself about a battle of the gods. Jehovah struck at all forms of idolatry in Egypt—from the sun and the River Nile, to frogs and lice. Now He comes down again in a cloud like a chariot to destroy the idols of Egypt.

    +   It is interesting to know that idolatry has long since disappeared from what it was in that land. This has been fulfilled literally.

    +   Verse 2: A Pharaoh arose about the time of Isaiah who could no longer control this great kingdom and the army no longer obeyed him. This caused the setting up of weak city governments that were self-governing for a period of time.

    +   Verse 3: This proud nation that had advanced in civilization so much farther than other nations was brought down to a low level. The people turned to their idols to no avail and finally in desperation resorted to spiritism.

    +   Verse 4: The *"cruel lord"* referred to here is generally identified as one of three or four of the ancient rulers. The identification is not important but the effect of the Lord is important.

2. VERSES 5–10

    +   Verse 5: The sea refers to the River Nile that was the main artery of the nation and the rivers are the canals that were built especially at the mouth of the river.

- Verse 6: The brooks are the outlets to the sea and most of them are filled up today. All vegetation of a valuable nature was to disappear from the brooks of the river. Because they are dried up, only the delta region is now known as the fertile soil of Egypt.

- Verse 7: The *"paper reeds"* are the papyri that was used in that day as paper. It was one of the main industries of Egypt and afforded a great volume of Egypt's wealth. It disappeared and no longer grows along the banks where it was indigenous and where Moses was hidden along the River Nile.

- Verse 9: The linen of Egypt was world renowned. Linen taken from mummies is superior to any linen that is made by the mills of Ireland even today. The fine twined linen was used in the construction of the tabernacle in the wilderness by Moses. That industry disappeared and this prophecy was literally fulfilled.

- Verse 10: The entire fishing industry was to disappear. This has been fulfilled literally. Egypt's wealth practically consisted in her river. Because of its volume, it is here called a sea.

3. VERSES 11–15

- Verse 11: Zoan is the Tunis of secular history. Mental weakness as well as material depletion was to be a judgment and this was fulfilled.

- Verse 12: All the leadership would disappear from Egypt.

- Verse 13: Noph is Memphis as we know it today.

- Verse 14: This is a vivid picture of the reduction of Egypt to a base kingdom.

- Verse 15: Industry and commerce would die and poverty and wretchedness would overtake the nation. This continues to be the plight of Egypt and we see that God's Word has been literally fulfilled in this regard.

The first section of what we have covered in chapter 19 could be divided up as follows:

  a. Failure of false religions (verse 1–4).
  b. Failure of material resources (verses 5–10).
  c. Failure of spiritual power (verses 11–15).

4. VERSES 16–25

- *"In that day"* (verse 16) places this section in the future. These words occur six times. This verse surely characterized Egypt in the more recent conflict with Israel. The armies of Egypt crumbled and fled.

- In verses 17–18, this could likewise have a present-day application. This entire section looks toward the Day of the Lord for a complete fulfillment.

- Verses 19–20: *"An altar to the LORD"* has been interpreted by some of the cults as the pyramid. The pyramid is neither an altar nor a pillar but a monstrous mausoleum for the burying of a king and his queen. The cross will yet be the place to which Egypt will look instead of to a heap of stone.

- Verses 21–22: Egypt has a glorious future. The nation will enter and enjoy the kingdom with Israel. How different from the present hour.

- Verse 23: This freeway will not be for soldiers and armies but for those going to Jerusalem to serve Christ, the king.

- Verse 24: Note the exalted position of Egypt in the kingdom.

- Verse 25: Note this statement and it is one of the most amazing statements in Scripture—*"blessed be Egypt."* A blessing is yet to come to this despised and debased nation. Now we will proceed with a more detailed study of verses 16–25.

5. A MORE DETAILED STUDY OF VERSES 16–25

- In verses 18–25 of chapter 19, we have a broad and yet thorough look at both the Jew and the Arab.

+ Had this prophecy been read a few decades ago, a critic could have said, "You are crazy, for there is no state of Israel nor has there been a state of Israel for centuries and centuries." But God said that the people would return to the land and that there would be a nation called Israel. In more recent history, we have seen that prophecy come to pass as the prophecy concerns the state of Israel.

+ The prophecy also concerns the enemies of Israel and of each other. One of those is Egypt and the other is Assyria. Today, we don't call Assyria by that name because the great empire has been broken up and therefore today, we would say Iraq, Jordan, Syria, and Saudi Arabia—or what the media refers to as the "Arab world." These are the enemies of Israel. To the north was Assyria and to the south, Egypt. Between these two great empires in those ancient days was the little tiny nation called Israel and it became the common battlefield. She was destroyed, ravaged, and invaded by first one and then the other. From the south, there were the pharaohs and the Ptolemies. From the north, there were leaders such as Tiglathpileser and the Antiochus Epiphanes. The ancient story boils down to the ravaging of the land of Israel.

+ The modern story of Israel has been the same thing. There has been no moment in the state of Israel that they did not face the prospect of war or war itself and this is the way it will be until Christ comes. Israel is surrounded by fifty million Arabs who say and think that Israel should not exist— while Israel is a tiny country of less than seven million Jews.

+ It is hard to realize the pertinency of this prophecy and that such a thing should ever come to pass as is described here in this passage. The prophet Isaiah lifts up his eyes to the golden tomorrow, to the millennial kingdom of our Savior, and thus does he write, in verse 18, that the land of Egypt will speak the language of Canaan and they will swear to the Lord of Hosts, that is, pledge allegiance to the great God—and in that day there will be an altar of the Lord in Egypt.

+ Egypt will cry unto the Lord because of the oppressors and God will send them a mighty one even the Lord Christ and Egypt will know the Lord in that day. And the Lord will smite Egypt for whom He loves He also chastens. God will smite Egypt for her transgressions but He will also heal Egypt. In that day there will be a highway out of Egypt to Assyria and they will go back and forth and the Egyptians will serve God with the Assyrians. In that day, Israel will be a blessing in the midst of the earth along with the other two.

+ Can you imagine such a thing as that—when there will be peace and comradeship between these peoples? What is this that God is promising to the Arab world?

+ God never forgets His covenants with anyone. This prophecy concerns a prophecy God made with Abraham for His son, Ishmael. All the Arab world looks to Ishmael as their patriarch just as the Jews look upon themselves as the descendants of Isaac and Jacob.

+ What is this covenant that God made with the Arab world? We read it plainly in the book of Genesis. In Genesis 16, Sarah is barren and she brings to Abraham her handmaiden, Hagar, and she makes him consent to have a child by Hagar. When Hagar conceived, Sarah became jealous and she and Abraham sent her away and she wandered in the Negev Desert. Expecting a child, an angel appeared and spoke to her that God would make of her child, Ishmael, a great nation. The angel told her to go back to her mistress and she obeyed. In Genesis 17, the lad Ishmael is thirteen years of age and God makes a covenant with Abraham and He promised Abraham a son by Sarah. But God also heard Abraham's cry for his son Ishmael, and God said that He would make of Ishmael a great nation and people and that He would multiply exceedingly and that He will be the father of twelve princes and of a great nation.

+ In the Genesis 21, Isaac is born, meaning "laughter." Ishmael laughed at the child and so once again Hagar is cast out and she went to the desert and there God repeated the covenant that He had made before. (See Genesis 21:17–21.)

- In Genesis 25, Isaac and Ishmael are together burying their father, Abraham. In that chapter, Ishmael is the father of twelve sons, just as Jacob had twelve sons. Ishmael is also the father of one daughter who married Esau (see Genesis 36:3) and thus was laid the foundation for the Arab world as we know it today. God is remembering His promise to Ishmael. We are beginning to see some signs of that as we approach the days of the return of the Lord. As you look at Saudi Arabia, it is a desolate, barren land, and yet it is second only to us in individual wealth. Who put that oil there? Billions of barrels of it are there in that land. God put it there and this, I think, is a part of God's blessing and a part of God's covenant.

- Would it always be that those cousins will forever hate each other and fight against each other? Would it always be that the Western World will be in the middle trying to find peace? The prophet lifts up his voice and he prophesies of the glorious millennial kingdom of our Savior. Israel will be in that and a part of that. You will find this in Zechariah 12–14. The prophet says that there is coming a time when the Lord Jehovah, the Messiah, will appear to the nation Israel. They will be back in their own land when Christ appears to them. Then will come to pass Romans 11:26: *"And so all Israel shall be saved."*

- There are others also that will be saved. Look at the prophecy here in chapter 19 verses 20–21:

  And it shall be for a sign and for a witness unto the Lord of hosts in the land of Egypt: for they shall cry unto the Lord because of the oppressors, and he shall send them a savior, and a great one, and he shall deliver them. And the Lord shall be known to Egypt, and the Egyptians shall know the Lord in that day.

  What a glorious prophecy. Christ in the millennial kingdom will include in it also the children of Ishmael—the Arab world. They will trust in the Lord.

- God has a purpose and a design for those people but what of us? I am not a child of Ishmael, nor of Isaac, nor of Jacob. But in Isaiah 49:6–8, we read:

  And he said, It is a light thing that thou shouldest be my servant to raise up the tribes of Jacob, and to restore the preserved of Israel: I will also give thee for a light to the Gentiles, that thou mayest be my salvation unto the end of the earth. Thus saith the Lord, the Redeemer of Israel, and His Holy One, to him whom man despiseth, to him whom the nation abhorreth, to a servant of rulers, Kings shall see and arise, princes also shall worship, because of the Lord that is faithful and the Holy One of Israel, and he shall choose thee. Thus saith the Lord, In an acceptable time have I heard thee, and in a day of salvation have I helped thee: and I will preserve thee, and give thee for a covenant of the people, to establish the earth, to cause to inherit the desolate heritages.

- Thus, the covenant of the Lord is for us in this dispensation:

  In that day shall Israel be the third with Egypt and with Assyria, even a blessing in the midst of the land: whom the Lord of hosts shall bless, saying, Blessed be Egypt my people, and Assyria the work of my hands, and Israel mine inheritance. (Isaiah 19:24–25)

CHAPTER 20

This brief chapter continues the burden of Egypt. The last chapter closed on the high note of future blessing for Egypt in the millennial kingdom. Now we see that there is a danger in Israel looking to Egypt for help in a crisis as Assyria in the north came against them. Isaiah was to make it clear to God's people that there was no real assistance to be expected from Egypt, as she likewise would be at the mercy of Assyria.

Egyptians were to suffer at the hands of Assyria and were to be carried into captivity as well as Ephraim (Samaria, which is the ten northern tribes of Israel). This was to take place in three years. The last chapter closed with the far-reaching view—the millennial view. This chapter opens and closes with a near immediate view. This chapter could be called "current events," which proves the reliability of Isaiah as a prophet of God. This chapter puts the microscope down on the very days in which Isaiah lived.

Another feature about this chapter is the reference in verse 1 to Sargon. This is the only place that he occurs in the Bible. Up to comparatively recent times, he was unknown in secular history. Now Sargon's name and record have been found in the monuments and he is established in secular history. He succeeded Shalmaneser but was not his son. He was the father of Sennacherib. It is consoling to have archeology establish the authenticity of Scripture and especially of a man mentioned only once in Scripture and nowhere in literature up until recent times. The reverent student of the Word of God does not need this confirmation to establish the accuracy of Scripture. Rather, Scripture establishes the accuracy of archeology and history. Faith does not nor can it rest upon the inspiration of the pick and shovel. Nonetheless, most people expect the stones to cry out to satisfy their own curiosity.

1. VERSE 1
   + This name *"Tartan"* was a general in the Assyrian army. (See 2 Kings 18:17.) *"Ashdod"* was a city in Samaria (the ten northern tribes).

2. VERSE 2
   + Isaiah was to become a walking parable to Israel as a warning not to become confederate with Egypt. Isaiah was not asked to go in the nude. Clothing was and is essential to the customs of the east and nudeness is so revolting that it is obvious that this was not intended. Isaiah was to lay aside his outward tunic of mourning. This would attract immediate and startling attention to the prophet. It would enable Isaiah to make his point publicly. The outer garment was always worn by men and especially by a prophet, so what Isaiah was therefore directed to do was simply opposed to common custom and not to moral decency.

3. VERSE 3
   + Isaiah did go three years without his outer garment and in three years, this would happen to Egypt. Ethiopia is included in this parable.

4. VERSE 4
   + Egypt could not protect herself nor could Ethiopia. She would not be a reliable ally for Israel. Both Egypt and Ethiopia were invaded by Sargon and there came this shame upon Egypt.

5. VERSES 5–6
   + In their desperation, the Israelites would recognize their helplessness and cry out for help. That help will be the deliverer—yet to be revealed in the coming day of the Lord.

CHAPTER 21

In this chapter we have three burdens—Babylon (the desert of the sea), Edom (Dumah), and Arabia.

The three burdens in this chapter are set forth by expressive symbols. These represent certain nations and apparently were as clear to the people of Isaiah's day as the stars and stripes are to us. These insignia in this chapter are not quite as clear to us and as a result, there has been some disagreement among Bible students. Each one will be considered separately as we go through the chapter. These three, Babylon, Edom, and Arabia, were enemies or were potential enemies of Israel.

1. VERSE 1
   + *"The desert of the sea"* is a strange expression. It is like saying, "the dryness of the water." However, that may not be too peculiar since today we are producers of "dry ice" and "cold heat."

- This verse alone does not identify the nation, but verse 9 does identify it. Before Babylon became a world power, her doom was predicted. The first burden in chapters 13 and 14 was against Babylon. Babylon became so frightful, powerful, and represented so much in Scripture that we have this further word concerning its doom here in this chapter. It was the first place of united rebellion against God called Babel, and it represents the last stronghold of rebellion against God in Revelation 17 and 18.

- *"Desert of the sea"* is a paradoxical phrase. Babylon was geographically located on a great desert plain. It was irrigated by canals from the Euphrates River. The desert and the sea form a weird amalgamation in this chapter. The same thing is referred to by John in Revelation 17:1–3.

2. VERSE 2

- God commands the twofold nation of Media-Persia to destroy and spoil the city when He says, *"Go up, O Elam [Persia]: besiege, O Media."*

3. VERSES 3–4

- Here, the prophet Isaiah is moved with great feeling and emotion when he learns of the coming devastation. This is the heart of God desiring to show mercy even during times of judgment.

4. VERSES 5–10

- It gave Isaiah no pleasure to be able to predict the awful suffering to which Israel's enemies were to be exposed. His tender heart grieved deeply over the desolation and destruction that their idolatry and corruption were to bring down upon them.

- He speaks almost as an eyewitness of the scene of revelry and in few but lucid words he speaks the word of the Lord. The watchman brought word to the King of Babylon that it had fallen: *"Babylon is fallen, is fallen; and all the graven images of her gods he hath broken unto the ground"* (verse 10). This is a sigh of sorrow as well as relief. Babylon was a source of all idolatry.

5. VERSE 11

- Here we see the second burden in this chapter and it is the burden of Dumah, or Edom. Dumah means "silence." Our word "dumb" is close to the intent of Isaiah. *"Seir"* means "rough or hairy." Esau was the first one who could be called by the description in Genesis 25:25. Esau dwelt in Mt. Seir. (See Genesis 36:8.) It also was a land swept with storms. Seir also means storms. What a play upon words, "silence and storm."

- Here is another paradox. Out of the land of silence and storm comes this inquiry that is twice repeated, *"Watchman, what of the night?"* In other words, how much of the night is gone? How long will it be before God's glory will be revealed when the Son of righteousness will arise?

6. VERSE 12

- The watchman said that both morning and night were coming. What will be the glory of some will be the doom of others. What will be the light for Israel will be the night for Edom.

7. VERSE 13

- Here we have the third burden in this chapter and it is the burden upon Arabia. Arabia was the land of the Ishmaelites—the Bedouin tribes of the desert—the modern Arab.

8. VERSES 14–17

- Whether or not we are able to follow each detail here recorded, it is evident that Arabia was to suffer at the hand of the Assyrians in a very definite manner. For the time at least, the pride of the Ishmaelite tribes was to be humbled and their cities spoiled, yet there is no hint of their eventual destruction—for Arabia is still to be blessed in the coming day because throughout the centuries, God has preserved the descendants of Abraham's son born after the flesh.

How Much Do You Remember?

1. What is the chief target of God's condemnation toward the nation of Egypt in chapter 19?
2. What are the three burdens found in chapter 21?
3. Describe Isaiah's countenance as he delivered the prophecy of desolation and destruction in chapter 21.
4. In chapter 21 verse 12, what is meant by the phrase, *"The morning cometh, and also the night"*?

Your Assignment for Next Week:

1. Review your notes from this lesson.
2. Read Isaiah chapters 22–24.
3. Underline your Bible.

Lesson 8 Notes

_____

_____

_____

_____

_____

_____

_____

_____

_____

_____

_____

_____

_____

_____

_____

_____

_____

_____

_____

_____

_____

Lesson 9
CHAPTERS 22, 23, AND 24

CHAPTER 22

The prophet now turns to deliver a message from the Lord to the people of Jerusalem at a time when it was in danger of being destroyed by the Assyrians and their allies from Elam and Kir. Elam, as we know, is Persia and had been for centuries an enemy of Assyria, but at this very time, it had become cooperative to a certain degree with Sennacherib in an attempt to conquer the land of Judah. This burden refers to Jerusalem as we will point out through the chapter. The burdens began way off at a distance in Babylon and they have continued to come closer and nearer to Jerusalem as we have studied them chapter after chapter. Now the storm breaks in all of its fury upon Jerusalem. Just what siege and what enemy is in the mind of the prophet Isaiah? Persia is mentioned by name, but Jerusalem was in ruins while Persia was in power. Apparently, all the enemies who have come up against Jerusalem are before us here in this chapter—from the Assyrian who laid waste the land but did not enter the city—to the last enemy from the north who will threaten the city but will not enter. The interval between these two has seen this city captured more than any other. This is the total burden of Jerusalem.

1. VERSE 1
   + *"Valley of vision"* refers to Jerusalem as is implied in verses 4, 8, 9, and 10. The expression *"valley of vision"* is another of Isaiah's paradoxical statements. "The mountain of vision" would be understood because the mountain is the place of the far-off view. Moses stood on Mt. Nebo to view the land of promise. Our Lord looked over Jerusalem from the Mount of Olives. The valley, in Scripture, is always the place of sorrow, humbleness, and death. Valley of salt, slaughter, and death are scriptural expressions. The saying "how pleasant is my valley" is secular. The vision here is one of sorrow and coming battle. The valley is the proper place for this vision.

2. VERSES 2–8
   + These verses apply in a definite way to the siege of Jerusalem by the Assyrians. In Isaiah's day, that destruction was deferred because of the faithfulness of King Hezekiah and later of Josiah, but nevertheless, the prophet recognized the fact that the holy city was eventually to become the prey and the victim many times of covetous Gentile nations.

3. VERSES 9–11
   + All of this took place during the reign of Hezekiah and this can be documented historically out of the archives in Jerusalem. All of this described in this chapter is history.
   + Hezekiah actually took precautions as described here in these verses in defending Jerusalem.
   + As you read these verses and this chapter, you must realize that it was divine intervention alone that destroyed the Assyrian army and delivered Jerusalem. There was, on Hezekiah's part, a sincere turning to the Lord while the masses of people would not turn to the Lord.

4. VERSES 12–14
   + *"In that day"* refers to the future and the word *"did"* refers to the past and to history. It is both historical and prophetic.
   + God gave His people feast days to come before Him with joy. Their sin made it imperative to substitute fasting for feasting and weeping for joy. Then people complained in the days they should have rejoiced. In their desperate plight, when they should have mourned, they adopted the materialistic

philosophy of a God-rejecting people. They adopted the philosophy of "eat and drink for tomorrow we shall die" and this is fatalistic.

5. VERSES 15–19

- *"Shebna"* was secretary of the treasury and a cheap politician under Hezekiah. Apparently, he was misappropriating funds and you will find references to this in 2 Kings 18:18–19:2 and in Isaiah 36:3 and 37:2. Shebna was building a tomb to perpetuate his name. It was ironical as he was to die and be buried in a foreign land as you read in verses 17 and 18.

6. VERSES 20–24

- Eliakim was a trustworthy man, a true statesman, and a loyal servant of King Hezekiah. He was a statesman and not a mere politician. He was motivated by sincere love for his country and for God. He was to take the office that was vacated by Shebna.

- To him was to be committed the key of David, that is, the key to the royal treasury, over which he was given authority to open and close as he saw fit. In this we see a very clear type of our blessed Lord, who uses the very expressions that we have here when He addresses the church at Philadelphia in Revelation 3:7: *"These things saith he that is holy, he that is true, he that hath the key of David, he that openeth, and no man shutteth; and shutteth, and no man openeth."*

- To those who look up to Him as their divinely given guide and protector, He opens the treasure house of divine truth, revealing to them the precious things that God has stored away in His Word.

- Eliakim was to be as a nail, fastened in place. Upon Eliakim would depend the means of refreshment and comfort that God had provided for His people. We see in this illustration a security for those who have put their trust in Christ for salvation. He is, indeed, a nail fastened in a sure place, and upon Him may be hung the glory of His Father's house and the vessels both large and small. Their safe keeping consists not in their own ability to cling to the nail, but in the fact that they are hung upon the nail that remains securely. Shebna pictures the anti-Christ while Eliakim pictures Christ.

7. VERSE 25

- This verse refers back to Shebna and he is a picture of the anti-Christ. The statement is prophetic as the phrase *"in that day"* clearly indicates.

CHAPTER 23

This is the eleventh and last burden against the nations—and this is the burden of Tyre. Each one of these great nations represents or symbolizes some great principle, philosophy, or system that God must judge:

1. Babylon: represents false religions and idolatry.
2. Palestine: represents true religions, which became apostate.
3. Moab: represents a formal religion, a form of godliness but denying the power thereof.
4. Damascus: represents compromise.
5. Ethiopia: represents missions.
6. Egypt: represents the world.
7. Persia: represents luxury.
8. Edom: represents the flesh.
9. Arabia: represents war.
10. Valley of Vision (Jerusalem): represents politics.
11. Tyre: represents commercialism or big business.

Tyre and Sidon were the two great cities of the ancient Phoenicians—Sidon, the mother city, was surpassed by her counterpart. The ships of the Phoenicians entered all ports of the Mediterranean Sea and their ships penetrated the uncharted oceans of that day. Their vessels brought tin from Great Britain. The Phoenicians were aggressive and progressive peoples. Carthage in North Africa was settled by them. Cypress owed its prosperity to trading with Tyre. This was true of other centers. It is of interest that the Phoenicians invented the alphabet.

Ezekiel 26 contains a remarkable prophecy concerning Tyre that has had an exact fulfillment. Tyre was destroyed by Babylon and was taken into captivity for the same seventy years as was Judea. The city was partially recovered, but later Alexander the Great scraped the ancient site of Tyre to make a causeway into the new city. The old city is never to be rebuilt until the millennium, as is indicated in the last verse of this chapter.

1. VERSE 1

    + *"Tarshish"* was a distant land referred to in Isaiah 66:19. Jonah fled there. It was evidently in the south of Spain, where a colony from Tyre was established and given the name of Tartessus. It was near Gibraltar and is obviously the place mentioned in this verse. Imports of silver, iron, tin, and lead were brought to Tyre from Tartessus.

    + *"Chittim"* was the island of Cypress.

    + This burden opens with the ships of Tyre returning from far away Tarshish and they hear of the destruction of Tyre. All the houses are torn down and the harbor is blocked. This news spreads to the island of Cypress, where Tyre carried on an extensive business.

2. VERSE 2

    + Tyre was partially built on an island. Tyre and Sidon go together like pork and beans. They were the two leading cities of the Phoenicians. The prominent sea merchants of Sidon had made Tyre the great city that it was.

3. VERSE 3

    + Sihor means "black" and refers to the Upper Nile, which overflows and floods Egypt and makes it fertile. The wealth of Egypt had flowed through the port of Tyre.

4. VERSE 4

    + This verse suggests that Tyre is the daughter of Sidon. Historically, this is correct.

5. VERSES 5–6

    + The destruction of Tyre ruins the commerce of Egypt. The fall of Tyre causes universal mourning. This is similar to the fall of Babylon at the end of the great tribulation. Some escape to Tarshish.

6. VERSE 7

    + The people of Tyre were urged to flee as far as possible. This is the city of antiquity—it was formerly the joyous city.

7. VERSE 8

    + *"The crowning city"* means the "giver of crowns." The wonder of Tyre originated the present-day popular practice of giving the name of "queen" to every known growing thing. That is, the potato queen, the orange queen, the cotton queen, and the rose queen. Colonies from the city of Tyre had established kingdoms within the cities. These were the crowns. The question asked in this verse is answered in verse 9.

8. VERSE 9

    + It was the Lord of Hosts who had determined the destruction of Tyre. He offers no apologies for making the arrangements.

9. VERSE 10
   - The river referred to here is the Nile. As she overflowed her banks, this colony of Tarshish is now free to do as she pleases. The phrase *"there is no more strength"* means that nothing binds them.

10. VERSE 11
    - Tyre is given a threefold description:
        a. In verse 7, it is called a joyous city.
        b. In verse 8, it is called a crowning city.
        c. Here in verse 11, it is called a merchant city.

11. VERSE 12
    - What was suggested in verse 4 is plainly declared here. Tyre is the daughter of Sidon. Sidon was the older city and rich merchants from there had founded Tyre and given her prestige. The joy of prosperity was to disappear. Some thought by fleeing to Cypress that they might make a fresh beginning. In this they were to be disappointed.

12. VERSE 13
    - Attention is drawn to the future conqueror of both Tyre and Judah. The Babylonians were to be the human instrument.

13. VERSE 14
    - This verse is a repetition of verse 1 and completes this section.

14. VERSE 15
    - Tyre was to go into captivity for the same seventy years that Judah did and by the same enemy—Babylon.

15. VERSES 16–17
    - At the end of seventy years, Tyre was to return and begin again her world commerce. The prophet compares Tyre to a harlot in her unholy trade.

16. VERSE 18
    - There is an interval between verses 17 and 18. At the end of verse 17 we see Tyre assuming her ancient position. This continued until she was destroyed by Alexander the Great. Other centers since then have been the centers of big business. However, verse 18 makes it clear that Tyre will enter the millennium. This lapse of time between verses is not unusual and it is simply one of the elements of prophecy. This is confirmed in Psalm 45:12 where we see Israel once more as the wife of Jehovah and Tyre among those who rejoice in her blessing and bring their gifts to the king.

We have now finished the book of burdens. You will remember that the book of Isaiah is broken up into different sections and we have studied the book of Immanuel and also the book of Burdens. All of these burdens—all eleven of them—makes us sensitive to the fact that He is the Lord of all the nations of the world. The same Lord God who guided the life and future of Israel is the same as the Lord who guides the nations of the world.

Look at the word *"burden"* that God uses so often. Isaiah 22:25 is a good definition of that. The word means "to lift up a heavy load and to carry it." From that meaning came the meaning that the delivery of the judgment of God was weighty—heavy—it is a burden—something God placed upon some of us at some time. You see that in the message of God to the nations. The Word of God is weighty, heavy, and sometimes hard to take. It is a sharp, two-edged sword. God applies those burdens and those judgments as He pleases and He wills. God is a judge and He is a consuming fire. In our age, there is not a person nor a nation anywhere in the world where God is not speaking or has spoken in times past with heavy burdens—judgments.

Now we have finished the book of burdens and we look at the next ten chapters in which we see a study of the great tribulation and of the kingdom age—the millennial reign of Christ and the regathering of Israel.

CHAPTER 24

From chapters 13 through 23, we saw God's judgment upon the surrounding nations and upon Israel itself, and much of this judgment has been fulfilled in the past, but now we come to a new section of Scripture beginning with chapter 24 and continuing through chapter 35. These chapters are entirely in the future and these chapters are often labeled "the little apocalypse."

The particular judgments that we have been following in the preceding chapters, called "burdens," all flow into this last judgment called the great tribulation. The judgments that we have studied in chapters 13 through 23 come together in chapter 24 as a mighty, moving flood and the entire earth is involved in this judgment.

The word "earth" or its equivalent occurs eighteen times in this chapter. The word translated "land" is the same word as that translated for the earth. Some expositors take the position that the earth in this chapter refers to the land of Israel only, while others take the position that the whole world is involved. I think there is an element of truth in both because it seems to me that it involved the whole world, but it centers in the land of Israel. I get that connotation just from reading the chapter and comparing the events of this chapter with that of the book of Revelation. Even though this chapter is all judgment and it looks toward the great tribulation, there is a little ray of light that breaks into the chapter as we see a company who are preserved through the great tribulation.

1. VERSE 1
   + *"The Lord maketh the earth empty, and maketh it waste, and turneth it upside down, and scattereth abroad the inhabitants thereof."* The word *"earth"* means "the whole world." The words *"empty"* and *"waste"* remind us of a former judgment in Genesis 1:2 that says *"without form, and void."* The first judgment in Genesis 1:2 had nothing to do with the sins of man, but this future judgment has everything to do with man and his disregard for God. (See Isaiah 45:18 and Jeremiah 4:23.)

2. VERSE 2
   + The judgment reaches every class and condition of society. There is nothing in the past that can possibly be considered as anything like a fulfillment of this prophecy and so, according to the short and easy method of infidelity, called modernism, it is calmly swept aside as being spurious and therefore not written by Isaiah at all.
   + In this way, practically all of prophecy can be disposed of. To us, there is not the slightest difficulty in recognizing that this holy man of God called Isaiah is here being moved to speak as the Spirit of God directs him and he depicts the terrors of that day in which God will judge the world. It is true that from a human standpoint, it was far off in that day that Isaiah wrote, but it has come so very near to us now.

3. VERSE 3
   + The judgment is from God and it is worldwide in extent. The whole world is like a vessel turned upside down, emptied, and all classes and conditions are involved in one sweeping judgment.

4. VERSE 4
   + It is the entire earth that is coming under divine judgment. As you will notice here in this verse, we have the word *"earth"* twice and the word *"world"* once.

5. VERSE 5
   + *"The laws"* are not confined to the Ten Commandments in this verse. *"The everlasting covenant"* should be carefully examined. What is that *"everlasting covenant"* that the inhabitants of the earth

are charged with breaking? In Genesis 9:8–17 we have exactly a sevenfold recurrence of that word *"covenant,"* which is in itself a mark of divine importance. Among the terms applied to that covenant that God then made with the earth, there is the term *"everlasting covenant"* in verse 16. Here then we clearly have the answer to the question. At that time the rainbow was the token that God gave to man.

+ What was the basic principle of that covenant that made it everlasting? It could be nothing but grace, well-founded on absolute justice. The covenant that God made was with *"all flesh that is upon the earth"* as stated in Genesis 9:17. This is totally a covenant of grace and the nations of the earth have spurned and rejected it.

6. VERSE 6

+ God promised Noah that He would never destroy the earth again with a flood. Note here in this verse that the judgment is fire with the word used *"burned."* (See 2 Peter 3:6–7.)

7. VERSES 7–9

+ Wine is the source of joy but all joy is gone. Music is the expression of joy, but all joy is gone. Wine, women, and song are not the pastimes in the great tribulation.

8. VERSE 10

+ The *"city of confusion"* means the same as *"city without form"* and it is commonly connected with Babel.

9. VERSES 11–12

+ This is a picture of the stark reality of tribulation.

10. VERSES 13–15

+ Here we see again that remnant preserved by divine grace as long as there is one single true Israelite living—not merely an outward Jew, but an inward Israelite, neither the flesh nor the earth can be utterly destroyed.

+ Precisely in the same way and for the same reason—as long as there is one single member of the body of Christ on earth, one single true Christian, the great tribulation of which our chapter speaks cannot possibly come, for the church, composed of all these, will still be here and dwelling upon the earth with the Holy Spirit dwelling within them, therefore they become the hinderer of the work of Satan.

+ The remnant, though small, will lift their voices in praise to God for His deliverance. So few will be preserved it will be as though a few olives are left after the harvest and as the gleaning of grapes—the leftovers.

+ Now as we look at this chapter from the standpoint of prophecy, you ask yourself, "How do I know that this is the great tribulation and how does it parallel with the Scripture?" Refer to Revelation 6, which takes place after the rapture of the church and after Christ has been declared *"worthy to take the book, and to open the seals thereof"* (Revelation 5:9). Then in chapter 6, we begin with the first seal and on through the sixth seal and then there is a parenthesis and in chapter 7, we see the remnant and those who are saved during the tribulation, not only Jews but also a great number of Gentiles that no one could number. And then in chapter 8, we see again resumed the seventh seal and then the seven trumpets, which are worse judgments than the first and then following the trumpets are the seven vials, which are worse than the trumpets, and all the tribulation continues until chapter 19 of Revelation. So, when you parallel that with this chapter in Isaiah, we see chapter 24 beginning with the great tribulation over all the earth and then there is a parenthesis of the remnant—small though it might be in ratio to the total inhabitants of the earth—there is still a remnant. And there is resumed the great tribulation in verses 16–22.

11. VERSE 16
   * The songs are drowned out now because of the wailing brought about by the intensity of the suffering. When Isaiah sees the awful character of the destruction of the great tribulation, he cries out *"my leanness,"* which means "my misery, my misery."

12. VERSE 17
   * Three dangers are upon the inhabitants of the earth:
     1. Fear—there is no freedom from fear.
     2. Pit—is danger of death.
     3. Snare—is deception.

13. VERSE 18
   * This verse is merely an explanation of verse 17.

14. VERSES 19–20
   * Everything that man has considered stable and lasting will be shaken to pieces so that the land will seem to reel to and fro like a drunken man. This suggests the great earthquakes, which will add to the terror of those days of grief and sorrow.

15. VERSES 21–23
   * Not only will the misguided rulers of the nations be dealt with in judgment, but God will deal with those unseen principalities and powers that have sought to dominate the hearts and minds of men in authority so that they are also described in Ephesians 6:12 as *"the rulers of the darkness of this world."*
   * The *"host of the high ones that are on high"* (verse 21) refers to those wicked spirits in the heavenly who attempt to control the minds of men in such a way as to set them in opposition to God and in the vain endeavor to thwart His unchanging plans.
   * We learn that the fallen star called Satan is the leading actor and his hosts of spirits that are with him are described here by the prophet as a defeated army from which the prisoners are confined in a pit to prevent escape and for their final dispensation they are to be visited later.
   * We find no hint here of a church and no New Jerusalem coming down from God out of heaven.
   * Verse 23 does refer to the fact that when the Lord arises to shake the earth then these signs—mentioned in verse 23 and to which Christ referred—will be apparent when the Lord of Hosts will come again and descend to take over the government of this world and to bring the long awaited age of righteousness.

How Much Do You Remember?

1. Describe why the phrase *"valley of vision"* from chapter 22 verse 1 is paradoxical.
2. Recall as outlined in the chapter 23 notes the symbolism or representation of the judgments of God against each nation.
3. Describe the burden of Tyre and recall Tyre's threefold description.
4. Who will be affected in chapter 24 as the judgments come together as a mighty, moving flood?

Your Assignment for Next Week:

1. Review your notes from this lesson.
2. Read Isaiah chapters 25–27.
3. Underline your Bible.

Lesson 9 Notes

Lesson 10
CHAPTERS 25, 26, AND 27

CHAPTER 25

This chapter brings us into the Kingdom Age. The clouds of the great tribulation have rolled away and the sun of righteousness is shining. This chapter is a song of deliverance. It is the Hallelujah Chorus and the shout of victory. This is the first chapter we have considered in a long time that is pure, undiluted joy. The kingdom is a literal reign of Christ upon the earth as king for one thousand years. There can be no kingdom without a king. Wherever you are, as a group of believers, you become part of a nucleus, like all other bodies of believers everywhere. We become part of the kingdom of heaven and we are automatically heirs to that kingdom, which, in turn, makes us heirs to the kingdom of God that is everlasting.

At the close of the last chapter, the moon was confounded and the sun ashamed, which tells us that He is come. Long hidden, as was the high priest on the Day of Atonement, He has been revealed at last in all His glory, and the holy angels with Him. (See Matthew 25:31.)

1. VERSE 1
   + This is a song or a praise of sheer delight and worship. This comes from a heart full to overflowing because the worshipper has come into a new knowledge of who God is and what God has done.

2. VERSE 2
   + It seems strange that these citizens of the kingdom would rejoice over ruined cities and destroyed civilization, but remember that "the city of confusion" was the enemy of God and it is here that God's people rejoice.

3. VERSE 3
   + Does this mean worldwide conversion? Indeed it does, for this is the millennium.

4. VERSE 4
   + As we look back over their long past, they begin to reminisce because it is now over.

5. VERSE 5
   + They recall the awful blasphemy of the last days, personified in one of whom it is written *"Who opposeth and exalteth himself above all that is called God, or that is worshipped: so that he as God sitteth in the temple of God, shewing himself that he is God"* (2 Thessalonians 2:4).

6. VERSE 6
   + Here, the Lord spreads a table loaded with a feast. The things are literal yet there is a spiritual meaning of these "*fat things*" and "*wines.*" They stand for some real corresponding feast in which we will have a part.
   + At this table, we can sit and those "*fat things full of marrow*" speak of the rich blessings we have in Christ of which we can feed. Thus they become as much a part of our spirit as literal food to our body.
   + No one can feed upon Christ without corresponding joy, which is figured in the word "*wines.*" The one single word in Hebrew for the words "*wines on the lees*" is from a root that means "to keep or to preserve." It means the wines that have been kept on those dregs and is improved in strength, color, and bouquet. The clear wine is not drawn at once but is kept and preserved on the dregs. Then the "*wines on the lees well-refined,*" which is the last few words of verse 6, tells us that the clear liquid has been drawn off, well-refined.

- Who could resist the conviction that there is a spiritual teaching here? Jehovah has been dealing with His elect nation Israel, a representative of the whole race, and in those dealings, we can trace what is taking place and has taken place, not only among the Jews but also among the Gentiles. He leaves the dregs of the old Adamic nature within us. The life that we have in Christ is indeed joy-filled and all of us have that life by the new birth. But this life is still *on the lees* of the old nature of Adam. In other words, the dregs of sin are still there, and from those very dregs, the Lord works in us to increase the strength of joy and add fragrance to our life so that in that day when even the dregs, or lees, having done their work, we will become *well-refined.* Does this not give a worthy reason for our present condition and explain to some degree the old nature within us?

7. VERSE 7
   - All spiritual darkness will be removed and those who have had a veil put over their eyes by Satan will have it removed to behold the manifold display of new spiritual truths.

8. VERSE 8
   - This verse is quoted by Paul in 1 Corinthians 15:54. The reference is to the rapture, the great truth will then *be brought to pass.*
   - All tears will be wiped away. What an occasion for rejoicing. *Rebuke,* or reproach, will be removed. Sin is no longer present to condemn man. *The Lord hath spoken it* and the trusting soul needs no future assurance.

9. VERSE 9
   - Attention is drawn to the person of God. Do we know Him, love Him, serve Him? God and His salvation are vital to men.

10. VERSE 10
    - Why is Moab introduced here? This is difficult to say. When Moab is up, God is down. When God is up, Moab is down. So, the main question here is, Who is the subject: Jehovah or Moab?
    - Here we are in the kingdom and in the mind of the spirit of prophecy, that which is best pictured as the sphere of this earth is the word *Moab.*

11. VERSE 11
    - Once again, who is the subject—the swimmer—Jehovah or Moab? The structure of the sentence leaves it unclear. Most believe it is Moab vainly struggling in the deep waters of calamity.
    - In the second clause, there is no reason for doubt. It is Jehovah who *shall bring down their pride* as a guilty nation.

12. VERSE 12
    - Man cannot be exalted without bringing God down. The pride of man is his undoing. Man is debased when man is exalted, but man is exalted when God is exalted.

CHAPTER 26

In chapters 25 and 26, we have what might be termed "the tale of two cities"—one representing that proud city that man has built contemptuously, called in Isaiah 24:10 *the city of confusion,* and the other city built by the Lord God Himself. The last verse of chapter 25 told us of the great world city represented by Moab, brought down to dust, but here, in contrast therewith, Israel, brought through the time of trouble, cries out, *We have a strong city.* The meaning here is that the walls were not of thick stone but of a different kind of protection called "Jehovah's salvation."

It is well for us to keep in mind that the blessings spoken of in this chapter are for those who enter the kingdom—the millennium—for Israel in particular, and for the Gentiles in general. Certainly, believers today can and do rejoice in those blessings promised to Israel in particular. There are great spiritual principles in this chapter that are applicable for God's people in all ages. This chapter continues to set forth the same subject and praise as does chapter 25.

1. VERSE 1

    - The language here precludes the possibility that this is a literal city. This is God's metropolis, where He protects His own. The walls are God's salvation. This is the city prepared for the earthly people. (See Isaiah 60:18.)

2. VERSE 2

    - *"The righteous nation"* is Israel in the kingdom. Of Israel, in that day, God has said their iniquities will be purged and their hearts cleansed by the washing of the water of the Word, according to the promise given in Ezekiel 36:25–26:

      Then will I sprinkle clean water upon you, and ye shall be clean: from all your filthiness, and from all your idols, will I cleanse you. A new heart also will I give you, and a new spirit will I put within you: and I will take away the stony heart out of your flesh, and I will give you an heart of flesh.

    - The veil taken away from their eyes, they will then be delivered from unbelief and will find an all-sufficient Savior in their once rejected Messiah.

3. VERSE 3

    - Here is a good example of a great spiritual principle that is applicable to all ages. The word for *"mind"* here means "that which is formed." The heart is the womb of thought and the brain merely carries that thought as a telephone does a message. When all of our thinking is positioned upon God in Christ today, perfect peace is our portion.

    - This same thought or idea is suggested by Paul in Philippians 4:6–7, which says, *"Be careful for nothing: but in every thing by prayer and supplication with thanksgiving let your requests be made known unto God. And the peace of God, which passeth all understanding, shall keep your hearts and minds through Christ Jesus."*

4. VERSE 4

    - Here we have a significant statement in the words *"Lord Jehovah is everlasting strength."* We must remember the meaning of the name *Jehovah*. It is a divine word because, like Him of whom it speaks, it is impossible for our minds to fully understand its significance. Its most simple English equivalent would be "he who is," answering precisely to Exodus 3:14: *"I am that I am"*—that is, He who is ever-existent, ever-present, who, if He enters into any covenant, will surely maintain it and keep it forever.

    - But this being true, the name must cover all tenses. "He who is," is always the "I Am." He must ever have been and ever will be. Thus, we have in the one sacred name, the full equivalent of *"the same yesterday, and to day, and for ever"* (Hebrews 13:8), or basically, it means the same as Revelation 1:8: *"I am the alpha and omega, the beginning and the ending, saith the Lord, which is, and which was, and which is to come, the Almighty."*

    - In the day when restored Israel has learned again how to sing, she is not content with the one name Jehovah but must intensify her delight in the covenant-keeping faithfulness expressed by duplicating the meaning in the words *"Lord Jehovah"*—the word *"Lord"* speaking of personality, of what He is Himself, and *"Jehovah"* speaking of His relation with men and especially with Israel.

    - In Christ, we have a far dearer name, a relationship—that name being Savior, Redeemer, and a score of other names that could be added. The words *"everlasting strength"* can be interpreted as meaning "Rock of Ages."

5. VERSE 5

+ Another city is brought before us here. This is man's city—the city of confusion. We will see here man's city versus God's city. The eternal versus the temporary. Man's city is to be destroyed so that God's city might be exalted.

6. VERSES 6–8

+ The city seems to carry its own destruction. It destroys itself.

+ In verse 7, we find another grand spiritual principle. It literally means that God levels out the path of the just. He does not weigh our deeds in the sense of a balance scale. This path of the just is made up of successive steps. The word *"uprightness"* should be *"uprightnesses,"* which means that we take a step at a time and we only take a step as we can see the next step. Then God makes it clear for us to take another step. Distress, poverty, sickness, bereavement, extreme need, and even death are no evidences of the path being a wrong one; very far from it, it is in all these things that we are more than conquerors through Jesus Christ. (See Romans 8:37.) We are to walk by faith because the Bible says, *"This is the way: walk ye in it"* (Isaiah 30:21).

+ In verse 8, Israel was to wait for her Messiah coming in judgment of her enemies. It is always judgment before blessing—the night before the dawn. For the believer, the judgment is in the past, at the cross.

7. VERSE 9

+ Through the long night, the righteous and patient soul waits for God. The Jew never looks for divine intervention on his behalf by being caught up to meet his Messiah in the air but he does wait for the Messiah to return in judgment for his oppressors on the earth. Dear to their thoughts, through the dark night of their own sorrow, has been the name of Jehovah, for their salvation, they believe, is embedded in that name, as ours is embedded in the same God but under the name of Jesus. Remember that we, as Christians, are not the children of the night but of the day. Nevertheless, we need to alert ourselves and not sleep in the night of sin. Paul describes this in Romans 13:11–13:

> *And that, knowing the time, that now it is high time to awake out of sleep: for now is our salvation nearer than when we believed. The night is far spent, the day is at hand: let us therefore cast off the works of darkness, and let us put on the armour of light.*

8. VERSES 10–15

+ God's grace is extended to the wicked, but they spurn and reject it. Since the wicked will not have the grace of God, they must, according to verse 11, inevitably have His judgment. The redeemed remnant will confess their part in the sin of the nation as they examine their own lives in the light of His presence and they will come in confession of sins.

+ Now specifically in verse 14, we must interpret that in its context. Who are these dead who will never revive? To say that they were individuals who will have no personal resurrection would contradict the plainest Scriptures that there will be *"a resurrection…both of the just and the unjust"* (Acts 24:15). Who then can these be? They can only be those "lords" who have had dominion over Israel—the Gentile world powers that have successively lorded it over Israel. These will pass away and never return. Nations die, empires crumble, and others take their place, but they never recover. This is the fate of the dominate world powers, here referred to as *"lords"* in verses 13 and 14. But in strongest contrast here is a little nation, long dead and buried in the dust of the earth (that is, long scattered among other people)—now revived and restored to their home land. It is growing fast, and its borders need enlarging. That national resurrection will speak of Jehovah's work as we see in verse 15.

9.   VERSE 16

*   The prophet goes back in his memory and lingers over that time of sorrow and suffering through which Israel has been brought, and in which that penitent little remnant expressed their repentance in whispering appeals to God. The prophet goes back in retrospect to those difficult days.

10.   VERSE 17

*   Here we find the prophet still thinking and he likens that time of anguish to the birth pangs of a mother because their suffering was so great. Isaiah is now looking back over that period that is yet future. He saw it from the other side of the river of time. The birth pangs spoken of here speak well of that great tribulation yet to come.

11.   VERSE 18

*   The suffering never produced any fruitful results. This time of travail is evidently the great tribulation and this period will not change the heart of the real wicked. They will continue to blaspheme the God of heaven.

12.   VERSE 19

*   Here, the voice of the prophet is lost in what Jehovah Himself cried: *"Thy dead men shall live."* Whose dead? There can be no other answer to this than Israel, with which the whole chapter is primarily occupied. It is in this reviving that she is in contrast with all other powers of the earth. *"Thy dead men shall live."* It is to this little people identified with Christ that the final victory of this earth will go because it will not go to Babylon, Rome, or any other modern nation or league of nations. These dead are now invited and included in the words *"awake and sing."*

13.   VERSES 20–21

*   Isaiah moves back to the scene of the great tribulation as he describes it as the *"indignation."* God counsels His people to come, as in the days of Noah, into the ark and be protected while the storm of indignation sweeps over the earth. Jehovah Himself is to be their protector as we see in Psalm 27:5: *"For in the time of trouble he shall hide me in his pavilion: in the secret of his tabernacle shall he hide me; he shall set me upon a rock."*

CHAPTER 27

As we enter this chapter, let's remember that we are still talking about the coming kingdom. This is the closing chapter of this section and, omitting verse 1, we it beginning with the song of the vineyard is Israel.

1.   VERSE 1

*   Let's begin though with verse 1, which should be a part of chapter 26. *"In that day"* occurs three times in this chapter—verses 1, 2, and 12. This familiar expression is a technical one, as we have seen, and covers that period beginning with the great tribulation and extending through the millennium. In this chapter, it can be pinpointed in each instance as the time of the coming of Christ to set up His kingdom.

*   The word *"leviathan"* means "Satan." Other names for him are used such as "the old serpent," or "the dragon," but here, we find another name added and that name is *leviathan*. This strange word must surely have some significance worthy of its being found in a divine revelation. It is a compound word made up of the word "levi," which means "joined" and then you add the word "than," which means "a dragon" or "serpent." So, the whole word would be "the joined dragon." That is not very intelligible so we must seek another description of what "the joined dragon" means. When you turn to Job 41:15–17: *"His scales are his pride, shut up together as with a close seal. One is so near to another, that no air can come between them. They are joined one to another, they stick together, that they cannot be sundered."*

- His scales are his protection and he thinks he is invulnerable. This leads to the pride of Satan. Then, in 41:34, we find the close of this description: *"he is a king over all the children of pride."* When we turn back again to Isaiah, we see who it is that the Spirit of God designates by the word *"leviathan."* That it is used symbolically cannot be questioned, for Jehovah does not contend with literal crocodiles, as described in Job 41. What does it describe? Most commentaries describe it this way: the piercing serpent or swift flowing serpent is Assyria represented by the swift Tigress River. That crooked serpent is Babylon, represented by the winding Euphrates, and "the dragon in the sea" is Egypt, surrounded by the Nile, which is always termed a sea, as was any expanse of water. So, we have the word *leviathan*, which refers to all the things uniting them together, for this leviathan is both a swift and crooked serpent.

- All of these things express to us that Satan, the devil, this dragon, expresses and instills antagonism toward Christ and His church and he tries to conquer man's heart. It is this leviathan who is behind modernism that denies every foundation of the truths of the Word of God. Don't forget, "in that day" the Lord will punish and, with a strong sword, fight all the pride, antagonism, sin brought by the leviathan, which means the "joined dragon."

- The best way I could express it would be: take all the names you can remember that are applied to the devil, join them together, and seek out the meaning of each one. Then compound that and realize that this is Satan personified at full strength and with complete power. Isn't it great to know that "in that day," the Lord will take care of the joined dragon?

2. VERSE 2
- We begin now the song of the vineyard, which reminds us of Isaiah 5. The vineyard is Israel in both chapters, here and in chapter 5. All is in contrast, however. There was failure and judgment in chapter 5. Here, there is abundance, blessing, and satisfaction on the part of the Lord. In chapter 5, the Lord looked for grapes and found only wild grapes. This speaks of the past. In this chapter, the Lord finds it is a vineyard of red wine and this speaks of the future. The subject here in verse 2 is altogether different from verse 1. A vineyard of red wine speaks of abundance, fruitfulness, bounty, and joy.

3. VERSE 3
- The Lord will be the husbandman here. Never again will He let it be kept by others. He is the husbandman who keeps an eye continually upon the vineyard Israel. He watches it day and night that no enemy will hurt it. Here, we must realize that with leviathan being slain, or as the New Testament tells us, the devil being shut up in the bottomless pit, we naturally have a song of joy. Here it is, the Lord Himself, who sings and celebrates the attractions He now finds in His vine called Israel.

4. VERSES 4–5
- If briars or thorns appeared again, He would burn them out.
- The enemy can make peace with God even in the kingdom, for God never ceased to be merciful. This is the only place in Scripture where it is even suggested that man can make peace with God. Of course, here, it has to do with obedience to the King and not the acceptance of a Savior. Man cannot make peace with God about the sin question. God has already done that. He made peace by the blood of His cross. Today, we have peace, as Paul says in Romans 5:1: *"Therefore being justified by faith, we have peace with God through our Lord Jesus Christ."*

5. VERSE 6
- The song of the vineyard concludes with Israel fulfilling her God-intended mission at last. She fills *"the face of the world with fruit."* Jehovah is satisfied. Israel will blossom and bud, as she is doing even today. (See Isaiah 35:1.)

6. VERSE 7
    - This verse opens with a question that has been partially answered already in the book of Isaiah. Light creates responsibility. In view of the fact that Israel had more light, her sin was blacker. Her punishment has been greater. She has received more punishment than the nations who have tried to strangle her. But through all the punishment, God did not destroy Israel as He did some of the other nations. But since they are His people and His covenant was with them, He will ever preserve them. Psalm 118:18 says, *"The LORD hath chastened me sore: but he hath not given me over unto death."*

7. VERSES 8–9
    - It was not the suffering for sin that atoned for Israel's sin. The sin of the nation is expiated by the blood of Christ.

8. VERSES 10–11
    - Still, the cities that Israel built are to be destroyed, like any city that man, apart from God, might build.

9. VERSES 12–13
    - This section reveals that God definitely intends to restore the nation Israel to the Promised Land. They will be returned, personally and individually. Nothing could be clearer than that. Assyria, Egypt, Israel, and Jerusalem are all literal and language means what it says. The logical conclusion is that God will regather Israel. Since this has never been fulfilled in the past, it is yet in the future.

How Much Do You Remember?

1. What is the Kingdom Age that we read of beginning with chapter 25?
2. Why can Israel claim to be *"a strong city"* in chapter 26 verse 1?
3. What two cities are referred to in chapter 26?
4. Contrast the vineyard spoken of in Isaiah chapter 5 with the vineyard in this section found in chapter 27.

Your Assignment for Next Week:

1. Review your notes from this lesson.
2. Read Isaiah chapters 28–30.
3. Underline your Bible.

Lesson 10 Notes

_____

_____

_____

_____

_____

_____

_____

_____

_____

Lesson 11
CHAPTERS 28, 29, AND 30

CHAPTER 28

This chapter brings us to an entirely new section. The prophecies that are totally future are included in chapters 24 through 27, which we have just finished. From chapter 28 thtrough chapter 35, we have prophecies that have an immediate fulfillment as well as prophecies that reach into the future and cover the same period as in the previous section (chapters 24–27).

This section we are entering into now is identified as "the six woes." The six woes are found in Isaiah 28:1, 29:1, 29:15, 30:1, 31:1, and 33:1. This section culminates in the Battle of Armageddon found in chapter 34, followed by the millennial glories brought to the earth in chapter 35.

Chapter 28 is a fine illustration of the culmination of the near and distant future prophecies. It gives in detail the past and the future events—the local and the immediate; the general and the far distant.

The Northern Kingdom of Israel, designated here by the term Ephraim, was soon to go into Assyrian captivity. This was a preview of the coming future day, but it was to be a warning to the Southern Kingdom of Judah as well. The first part of this chapter was fulfilled in 721 B.C. when Shalmaneser, King of Assyria, invaded Ephraim and overthrew what is known as Israel, or the Northern Kingdom.

As we approach the verse-by-verse study of this chapter, we must remember that in the past, what seemed impenetrably obscure has glowed with light as we pondered over it and studied it—therefore, we are confident that the same goodness of the Holy Spirit will guide us as we enter this section of Scripture known as the six woes.

1. VERSE 1
   + Ephraim and Israel are synonymous terms for the ten northern tribes, also called Samaria. The picture here of drunkards is both literal and spiritual. They were in a stupor as far as spiritual understanding was concerned.
   + The woe is on Ephraim. When Isaiah wrote, all was fair enough to outward appearance, but a deeper insight, given alone by the Spirit of God, discerned that the moral condition of that kingdom was crying aloud for divine intervention. Its prime was past. It was still a flower…but a fading flower.
   + The people of Ephraim, or the Northern Kingdom, were so given up to worldly luxury and fleshly pleasures that, in the spiritual paralysis that these always produce, they can only be likened to drunkards who are lying prostrate in their shame.
   + It is always the characteristic mark of the last days; so today, under cover of a formal religion, the mass of Christian professors are *"lovers of pleasure, more than lovers of God"* (2 Timothy 3:4). The doom, or the woe, mentioned here in verse 1 has long been fulfilled because Assyria longed for that land. Therefore, Shalmaneser captured it in 721 B.C. and the people were led away into captivity. (See 2 Kings 17.) But this does not complete the prophecy in its deeper meaning.

2. VERSE 2
   + The Assyrian is designated here as a strong one, a destroying storm and a flood of mighty waters.

3. VERSE 3
   + Here the prophet picks up the figure of the drunkards. A high level of civilization had been developed in the Northern Kingdom with its comforts and outward beauty expressed in homes, gardens, and trees.

4. VERSE 4

    ♦   Verse 4 is again referring to the fading flower of Ephraim.

5. VERSES 5–6

    ♦   Here the prophet shifts to the far-off day in the future with the expression *"in that day."* How do we know that it is future? Seven years after the fall of Ephraim, the Assyrian armies invaded Judah and threatened Jerusalem, but Hezekiah, who was then reigning, placed the matter unreservedly in the hand of the Lord God with the result that the city was completely delivered. (See 2 Kings 19.) But this cannot even be considered the final settlement—for after Hezekiah's death, the true condition of the people was again evidenced and judgment again overhung Jerusalem. This has not had a satisfactory fulfillment in the past—it can be found nowhere in history, and we must still look to the future for the final fulfillment of these verses.

6. VERSES 7–8

    ♦   These verses refer to Judah, where the people have walked in the same path of uncontrolled pleasure, termed drunkenness, as in Ephraim, and with even more disastrous results, for their privileges have been greater.

    ♦   The depth of the fall is always determined by the height of the privilege and this was true as far as Judah was concerned. But even the priests and prophets are swallowed up by the red wine that they have swallowed. This we may interpret as an intoxication with the falsehood that they preach. They are as repulsive in their senseless pride, in their ill-timed pleasures, as drunkards that vomit on the table. This reminds us of how the Lord gets sick at the lukewarm, self-complacency of people as He says in Revelation 3:16: *"I will spue thee out of my mouth."*

7. VERSES 9–10

    ♦   This is one of my favorite parts of Scripture because it deals with teaching and with learning. This is the compassionate dealing of God with His people and here we learn how God teaches. Notice—

        Whom shall he teach knowledge? and whom shall he make to understand doctrine? them that are weaned from the milk, and drawn from the breasts. For precept must be upon precept, precept upon precept; line upon line, line upon line; here a little, and there a little.

    ♦   The prophet, on the part of Jehovah, asks, "To whom shall the knowledge of His ways be imparted?" It will be so simple that even infants with nothing but the ability to listen will be able to understand it; yet that very simplicity will stumble the wise and the prudent who in their own pride will be blind to its perfections.

    ♦   Patiently will the Lord work, with precept added to precept, line added to line, giving a little here and then a little there, until the words become so familiar as to be monotonous. But if this is revealed to babes, it is hidden from the leaders of the nation who conceive of themselves as being the wise and the prudent.

8. VERSES 11–13

    ♦   Notice in this section that the Lord comes back with the same thing over and over and over again and here we find in this section that He will speak to them and it will give them rest. The burden of the speech that they heard was "rest for the weary," a tender message of grace. Someone has said that Isaiah is the prophet of the commonplace. Teaching is slow, patient, and continuous work. This is the way that even spiritual truth is imparted. God does not impart it in a flash to the lazy and the lethargic soul.

    ♦   As the people lapse into apostasy, it becomes increasingly difficult to teach and impart spiritual truth. These verses, though, remind you perfectly of what our Lord said in Matthew 11:28: *"Come unto me, all ye that labour and are heavy laden, and I will give you rest."* In close connection with this blessed invitation to rest, we immediately hear those scornful men in Isaiah's day who were rulers claiming to have perfect ability to attain rest for themselves and for their people in their keeping of laws. In order for us to find that rest, we must depend wholly upon the Lord Jesus and we must let the light of 1 Corinthians 14:20 fall upon this Scripture, for it is the same reference to children and to babes as we have here.

9. VERSE 14
    + The judgment coming to Israel in the north should be a warning to Judah in the south. Ephraim speaks to Jerusalem.

10. VERSE 15
    + The covenant with death and hell refers to the future covenant of Israel with the anti-Christ. (See Daniel 9:27.)

11. VERSE 16
    + Christ is *"a chief corner stone"* (1 Peter 2:6). The Lord had come to Israel in lowly grace only to be rejected, but as Psalm 118:22 tells us: *"the stone which the builders refused is become the head stone of the corner."*
    + All blessing for Israel and Judah, as well as for the Gentile world, is bound up with Him. To refuse God's testimony regarding His Son is to deliberately choose everlasting judgment. To receive Him means everlasting life and blessing. Israel has been blinded for so long and because of their failure to receive their king when He came in grace, they have had to endure such incredible sufferings throughout the long centuries of their wanderings. Even after they have returned to their land will they still have great sufferings in store for them until at last they look upon Him whom they have pierced and mourn for Him who mourns for His only son. (See Zechariah 12:10.)

12. VERSE 17
    + When that day of trouble comes, those who refuse allegiance to the beast and the anti-Christ will wait in faith for the manifestation of this "living stone," which is to fall upon the feet of the great image of the Gentile supremacy and grind it to powder. It will be their portion to wait quietly, realizing the truth that *"he that believeth shall not make haste"* (verse 16). God's plan will be fulfilled in His own time.

13. VERSES 18–19
    + The Lord's appearance will destroy the refuge of lies and annul the covenant with death and the agreement with hell. Judgment will be the portion of all those who accept the mark of the beast and the number of his name, but those who put their trust in the Lord God will be vindicated and given their place in the coming glorious kingdom when it is set up on the earth in visible power.
    + Until that day, those who turn away from the Lord will trust in their own plans for deliverance and will find themselves like the uncoverable sleeper described in the next verse.

14. VERSES 20–22
    + These verses speak of the utter inadequacy of all human schemes when God intervenes. The apostates had made a comfortable bed for themselves, as they assumed—but, it is too short to permit them to stretch themselves out upon it. They also provided a covering that should have given more comfort, but it was too narrow. Here we see that God is active in His strange work. It is His work, necessary and inevitable, but He does it. In verses 21–22, you see the judgment of God is coming in the immediate future and the people are urged to believe and not scoff, as this merely intensified the weight of judgment.

15. VERSE 23–29

- Beginning with verse 23, we find Jehovah speaking and teaching here through parables. This is similar to the parable of the wheat and tares. (See Matthew 13:24–30.) The picture here is of a good sower who breaks up the earth with the plow and sows the different kinds of grain. There are soft and hard grains. Different methods must be employed in harvesting them. The soft grain must not be beaten with the same intensity as the hard ones or else they will be destroyed. Thus, God judges. The individual or nation actually determines the character of the judgment that is to fall upon them. This section throws added light on the following passages in Matthew:

> *Let both grow together until harvest: and in the time of harvest I will say to the reapers, Gather ye together first the tares, and bind them in bundles to burn them: but gather the wheat into my barn.* (Matthew 13:30)

> *The Son of man shall send forth his angels, and they shall gather out of his kingdom all things that offend, and them which do iniquity; and shall cast them into a furnace of fire: there shall be wailing and gnashing of teeth. Then shall the righteous shine forth as the sun in the kingdom of their father. Who hath ears to hear, let him hear.* (Matthew 13:41–43)

- The meaning here is that God prepares the heart of man by conviction, sorrow, and trouble, as well as spiritual concern. Then the good seed falls and the fruit follows.

CHAPTER 29

The prophecies are confined to Jerusalem, but they extend into the future from the invasion of Sennacherib—through the time when Jerusalem will be trodden down by the Gentiles and until the last invader (see Zecharaiah 14:1–7) will have destroyed Jerusalem and finally to the establishment of the kingdom when the Messiah will come and His feet will touch the Mount of Olives.

It is necessary to establish the fact that Jerusalem is the city designated under the title of Ariel. Isaiah delights in a play upon words as we have observed in our study. Ariel means "lion-like." The word occurs in 2 Samuel 23:20, where we find the words *"lionlike men."* A "lion-like man" is an Ariel man. The word means "the lion of God." The word could mean "altar of God." Both designations are a fitting title for the city of Jerusalem. It is further identified as *"the city where David dwelt."* The lion is the insignia of this family. Our Lord is called *"the Lion of the tribe of Judah"* (Revelation 5:5). Likewise, Jerusalem was the place where the temple of God was and the altar of course was there.

1. VERSE 1

- The second woe is pronounced here upon Jerusalem under the name of Ariel. It corresponds to a great sign of concern that comes from a heart welling up with emotion. It reminds us of our Lord's lament over Jerusalem,

> *O Jerusalem, Jerusalem, thou that killest the prophets, and stonest them which are sent unto thee, how often would I have gathered thy children together, even as a hen gathereth her chickens under her wings, and ye would not! Behold, your house is left unto you desolate.* (Matthew 23:37–38)

- These words come from a Man who was weeping and He longed to extend mercy. He was reluctant to display His judgment.

2. VERSE 2

- In verse 2, you find here the judgment upon Jerusalem (don't forget the word *"Ariel"* means "Jerusalem").

3. VERSES 3–5
   - Jerusalem has been besieged and captured by the enemy more often than any other city. The Gentiles have marched through her streets and still do so until this very moment. The passage refers specifically to the siege of Sennacherib, recorded further on in this book in chapters 36 and 37. There, the angel of the Lord lifted the siege by destroying the Assyrian hordes.
   - It begins with "the times of the Gentiles" in 606 B.C. and continues through the entire time when *"Jerusalem shall be trodden down of the Gentiles"* (Luke 21:24). It will culminate in the final siege, which is the worst of all (see Zecharaiah 14).

4. VERSES 6–8
   - This final attack upon Jerusalem is a judgment of God, but He will intervene at last to deliver His people from extermination. These dreams of the enemies of God to bring in their own kingdom will be frustrated, and attempts to build a kingdom are merely strange visions.

5. VERSES 9–10
   - Even the prophets and princes did not anticipate this deliverance from God. They were as blinded to the future as the enemies of God. They were as men who were dead drunk.

6. VERSES 11–12
   - The attitude of the people, including God's people, before their final deliverance by God, was, and is, that prophecy is too obscure to be understood, that it was a sealed subject about which they could know nothing.

7. VERSES 13–14
   - People are judged for taking the attitude that we cannot know God's sure word of prophecy. But we can, because we know in the New Testament there are many passages that guarantee us that we can rest in the fact that *"all scripture...is profitable"* (2 Timothy 3:16).
   - The prophet likens it to a mouth religion but not a heartfelt religion (verse 13).

8. VERSE 15
   - This chapter contains two woes because first, they act as if God does not see or know, and second, they act as if they are getting away with it as indicated here in this verse.

9. VERSE 16
   - The confusion produced by this topsy-turvy turning of things causes God to do the same thing socially, economically, and politically. This false spirituality denies that God created man and indulges in the blasphemy of questioning God's wisdom and actions.

10. VERSES 17–21
    - We leave the evening of man's day and now we enter the morning of God's day. This is a picture of the kingdom that is coming. Fruitfulness returns to the earth, and the spiritual blindness is lifted.

11. VERSES 22–24
    - These final words look into the future for their total fulfillment. There has been nothing in the past that compares to this; therefore, it is future.

CHAPTER 30

This is the fourth woe. There is no record that the Southern Kingdom of Judah brought their doom by uniting with Egypt. On the other hand, the Northern Kingdom of Israel did in 2 Kings 17:4. Obviously, this prophecy concerns the Southern Kingdom of Judah as indicated in verse 19, where we find the term *"Zion at Jerusalem."* This seems to be a warning in the form of a prophecy yet to be fulfilled. Will Israel turn to Egypt as a wall against a future enemy? At the moment, it seems very unlikely. We do know from other prophecies that Israel will turn for help to an outside source against the king of the north. Some commentators say that Egypt could be a representative power to which the total nation of Israel will turn for help in the future day. The use of the nation Egypt could be explained because the danger in Isaiah's day was in turning to Egypt. This chapter has much instruction given to Israel to turn to the Lord for help. This is especially impressive in view of the future blessing God has in store for His people. In accord with the chapters previously taught, this chapter refers to the same false confidence that is found in chapter 28, which is termed "The Covenant with Death."

1. VERSES 1–2

   + This is a woe because it is a warning. The prophecy that the nation of Israel will turn to Egypt in the future with dire results is a red signal for the present day. Surely there is an analogy here for the Christian who has been delivered from the world. He is still in the world, but is not of the world. There is always the ever-present danger of turning back into the world, living like the world, and leaning upon the supports of the world.

2. VERSE 3

   + God warns Judah that Egypt is no real strength or ally for them. It is merely a mirage on the desert of adversity.

3. VERSE 4

   + This is a picture of ambassadors advancing on Egypt for assistance.

   + The word "Zoan" is actually now called "Tanis—along the delta of the Nile River."

   + The word "Hanes" is Heracleopolis, which is a place farther up the Nile.

   + Let's look at those two words for just a moment. The names Zoan and Hanes surely must have some teaching for us either in their meaning or in something that other Scriptures may tell us. Zoan is significant enough for it comes from a root meaning "to strike tent," as the Nomadic tribes do even to this day. This tells of the opposite of the permanent rest or abode as Jerusalem will be in the future. Egypt and Zoan are in strict correspondence. The old Hebrew names give a clear suggestion of a very precious truth; for of Hebron, it is written that it *was built seven years before Zoan in Egypt* (Numbers 13:22). Why would that be important? To Jewish ears, these names would tell a very great truth and so, they may be meaningful to us. We learn that Hebron is the very opposite of Zoan, and means "communion"—which means affection, harmony, and sentiment, combined with perfect intimacy. Joseph was sent by his father out of *the veil of Hebron* (Genesis 37:14) to serve his brethren, a picture of our Lord sent by His Father away from the joys and intimacies of the bosom of that Father to His brethren who refused Him. In 1 John 1:3, our Lord is bringing us back with Him to that "veil of Hebron" for *our fellowship is with the Father, and with his Son Jesus Christ.* We dwell in Hebron.

   + Now, with these meanings in view, is it not something far more refreshing than merely saying, "Which was the most ancient of two old cities?" when we read "Hebron was built seven years before Zoan in Egypt?" The first would serve us little but that "seven years," which is a symbol of completeness, means that this place of rest and refuge was seven years before this restless, homeless scene of removals—Zoan—was built. The purpose of God was to have all of His redeemed home with Him; or in other words, in total grace, we will be raptured and that will be seven years of rest with the Lord—seven years before the coming of Christ with us in judgment. We are in Hebron and thank God, Hebron was built before Zoan.

   + These "messengers" of foolish Judah go to Zoan. Then they are seen having made still further progress onto Hanes. It is a compound word of "Han," which means "grace" and "nes," which means "to flee," which is at least suggestive of the path the messengers were taking away from that grace that should have been Judah's surest confidence. The word "Hanes" means then, "to flee from grace." Isn't it amazing how God includes certain words for our instruction?

4. VERSE 5

   + The mission of the ambassadors seems to be futile.

5. VERSE 6

   + This is an apt description of the wild animals of Africa.

6. VERSE 7

   + The prophet continues to warn against an alliance with Egypt. The Egyptians will not help. All of their suggestions and endeavors will be in vain. The phrase *"their strength is to sit still"* is interpreted in some translations as "boaster."

   + We find another name for Egypt over in Isaiah 51:9 and that name is "Rahab." This is a play on words, for in Job 26:12, Rahab stands for "the proud." Thus, the one word covers double meaning of Egypt and pride—they are synonymous.

7. VERSE 8

   + Isaiah is told, *"Now go, write it before them in a table, and note it in a book, that it may be for the time to come for ever and ever."* Here we see that the only One who could see from afar is the real Author of the Scriptures. The Jew of 2,700 years ago and the professing Christian of today are alike. He would rather be comfortable, deceived, and listening to a soothing lie than to be rendered uncomfortable by truth. As we look around us even today, another man of God, speaking by the same Spirit, wrote, *"For the time will come when they will not endure sound doctrine; but after their own lusts shall they heap to themselves teachers, having itching ears; and they shall turn away their ears from the truth, and shall be turned unto fables"* (2 Timothy 4:3–4).

8. VERSE 9

   + He describes the attitudes of the people in that day. They would not hear; they were rebellious; they were lying.

9. VERSE 10

   + They even said, *"to the seers, See not; and to the prophets, Prophesy not unto us right things, speak unto us smooth things, prophesy deceits."*

10. VERSE 11

    + They invited the Holy One of Israel to get out of their way, to get from in front of them.

11. VERSES 12–14

    + The Lord gives His answer and His judgment, and He says, *"Because ye despise this word,"* their iniquity would be like a high wall that suddenly crashes upon them and this is found in verses 13 and 14.

12. VERSE 15

    + This is another one of the great spiritual principles with which Isaiah abounds. This is a good exhortation for any age. Here we find the Lord God, the Holy One of Israel, talking loud and clear. Instead of departure from God, He suggests a return to God. Instead of a weary labor, He suggests rest. But still, this is ever too humbling; men will not return.

13. VERSES 16–17

    + Far more manly would be to get on the horse and ride away and escape. They will indeed flee, says the Lord, but the ones who pursue them will be swifter.

14. VERSES 18–22

    + No dispensational distinction affects the heart of God. He is always swift to hear the cry of repentance, He always runs to meet the returning prodigal son, and He always waits for the first word of confession to show His love and mercy.

- Verse 18 is the pivot on which the spirit of prophecy turns from threatening to consolation. Babylon will never be rebuilt (chapter 13); Nineveh will be a desolation (see Zephaniah 2); the city of the nations is no city (chapter 25); yet the Jew will have in Zion, even in Jerusalem, an everlasting dwelling.

- Note in verse 18 the phrase *"the Lord is a God of judgment: blessed are all they that wait for him."*

- The place and the people are identified in verse 19 and this, of course, is the millennial reign.

- In verse 20, Jehovah lets His people know that He has been neither ignorant of, nor indifferent to the sorrow through which they have passed. He has indeed fed them with the bread of affliction—but now that chastisement has done its work and their teachers will not be hidden anymore. Up to that time, He had been teaching them, in a veiled way, and by sorrow and adversity. But from this point on, He says He will guide in a very different way and that they will see.

- They will also hear and they will be guided by the word that is spoken unto them, *"This is the way, walk ye in it"* (verse 21).

- The genuineness of Israel's conversion is indicated in verse 22—what they had honored and loved they now loathed—as once they had almost despised the divine Word. Such a complete reversal of loves and hates always accompanies a divine work in the soul of man.

15. VERSES 23–26

- Here we have to make a judgment as to the literal interpretation of this passage. For instance, if our sun was to shine with a sevenfold intensity, we would perish and that alone would render life support as a destroyer rather than a provider. If the moon were to literally shine as bright as the sun, we would soon mourn the loss of sleep and cry out for darkness. These verses simply make a perfect picture of abundance below and an increase of every gracious provision that God has made, which is provided by these heavenly bodies. From a spiritual sense, it could also mean that truth, corresponding to the light, will flood the scene.

16. VERSES 27–28

- These two verses give Jehovah's intervention for Israel. Note, He does not say that He Himself comes, but it is His name that comes; for that name, Jehovah, embodies in itself all that He is, in His relationship to Israel. The imagery of verses 27 and 28 tells us that Judah is making an alliance with Egypt when she should be making a step toward God because His judgments upon the world will be a terrible thunder, turning streams into rushing water that will be neck-deep. He will sift the nations in their own sieve of vanity and put His bridle into the jaws of the people.

17. VERSES 29–33

- The Assyrian here is the final enemy of God in the great tribulation. Assyria, including Babylon, is present-day Iraq and Saudi Arabia. Tophet was a place in the valley of Hinnom where the most abominable idolatries were practiced. Historically, this name belongs to a place in the Valley of Hinnom where human sacrifices were offered. The word means "place of fire." The symbolic reference is to the Lake of Fire and to the doom of the beast. Gehenna is a compound word made of up "geh" meaning "valley" and "henna" the Greek form of Hinnom, so the whole word means "the valley of Hinnom."

- The fire of Tophet will be started by the breath of the Lord (verse 33). His breath will be like a stream of brimstone.

To summarize this chapter, you will find first a warning to Judah not to seek an alliance with Egypt in verses 1–14. Second, an encouragement to look to Jehovah for He is willing to deliver them (verses 15–26). Third, a statement that God will deal with the Assyrian (verses 27–33).

How Much Do You Remember?

1. Recall the parable of the good sower found in chapter 28, verses 23–29. How does this apply to judgment?
2. Define the word *"Ariel"* and describe its meaning for Jerusalem.
3. What was the attitude of the people before the final deliverance of God (chapter 29:11–12) and what does the prophet liken it to in verses 13–14?
4. Recall the two woes found in chapter 29.
5. To whom is the fourth woe directed in chapter 30?
6. Define the words *"Zoan," "Hanes,"* and *"Hebron."* What significance do these definitions add in understanding the text? (verse 4)
7. Summarize chapter 30 into its three distinct sections.

Your Assignment for Next Week:

1. Review your notes from this lesson.
2. Read Isaiah chapters 31–35.
3. Underline your Bible.

Lesson 11 Notes

_____

_____

_____

_____

_____

_____

_____

_____

_____

_____

_____

_____

_____

_____

_____

_____

_____

_____

_____

CHAPTERS 31, 32, 33, 34, 35

CHAPTER 31

So deep-seated in every heart is the tendency to false confidence that in this short chapter, we have a strong reiteration of the warning in the form of a "woe" pronounced in chapter 30 and again in this chapter. Each one of us has a little bit of "Egypt" in us and we have the danger of false confidence in us. In this chapter, it is not primarily against Egypt itself that the woe is pronounced but against the Hebrew for depending on Egypt. You should always remember that the road to Egypt is always going down; it is a descent, a lowering of moral standing and dignity, for man's place of trust should be in the Lord God as revealed in His beloved Son, Jesus Christ. When and if we leave that standard, we always go down, never up.

The prophet in this chapter warns God's people not to look to Egypt for help, but to look to the Lord because He will defend Jerusalem. The danger was prevalent and it was so evident that the Israelites would turn to Egypt that the prophet continued to warn Judah of the futility of such a measure. Egypt is the menace of this chapter and Assyria only mentioned. This is a very practical chapter for all Christians today, for most of us are inclined to lean on some material or physical support rather than rest upon the spiritual resources that God has provided.

1. VERSE 1
    *   This is the fifth woe and it is pronounced upon those who go down to Egypt for help. Observe that the movement is always down, never up. Observe also that the woe is not upon Egypt but upon those who turn to Egypt. Egypt did have chariots and horsemen and their forces were strong and many. A materialistic philosophy says that it is smart to look to Egypt. The real source of difficulty was that God's people did not seek Him or look to Him. Since they did not trust the Lord, they turned frantically to some outside, physical display of power rather than saying with the psalmist: *"Some trust in chariots, and some in horses: but we will remember the name of the* Lord *our God"* (Psalm 20:7).

2. VERSE 2
    *   This is a bit of irony here. After all, the Lord is as wise as those who turn to Egypt think they are. God is against those who turn to Egypt. God is opposed to all forms of apostasy.

3. VERSES 3–4
    *   In verse 4, we see a young lion growling over its food or its prey and a company of shepherds are approaching with the evident purpose of taking away that food. Neither the number nor the noise frightens him. It appears sure that the fearless lion pictures Jehovah Himself, who has come down to contend with some foe. The question then is raised: against whom does Jehovah fight? And that is explained in verse 3. Never does Jehovah fight against faith, nor against the penitent remnant of His people, but here He fights against "the helpers and those that helped."

4. VERSE 5
    *   Here, the figure changes and the Lord God is likened to birds flying. If the figure of Jehovah as a young lion is suitable in view of Jerusalem's enemy, then that of a bird guarding her nest with fluttering wings fits His action toward the city of Jerusalem, His beloved city. This contrast of stern strength with tender gentleness is a lovely picture. The mothering bird gives a beautiful figure of care.

5. VERSE 6
   - The plea is made to turn to the Lord, since it is His intention to protect His people; they can safely trust Him. However, they are in a state of revolt.

6. VERSE 7
   - Here the prophet looks on to the day when they will turn from their idols to God.

7. VERSE 8
   - Although the Assyrian is the immediate danger to the holy city, the emphasis here in this chapter has been upon the danger of turning to Egypt for help and not the danger of an attack from Assyria. The Lord had already determined that the Assyrian would fail and fall in his attack upon Egypt, therefore the real danger was in turning to Egypt.

8. VERSE 9
   - The Lord will deal with the Assyrian. This chapter closes with the assurance that it is Jehovah who speaks and He has taken His place in Zion with burning wrath against her foes in Jerusalem.

CHAPTER 32

This chapter is a bright note between the fifth and sixth woes and a ray of light to God's people in a dark place. It has been some time since the person of the King has been before us, but we find Him introduced again at this point, for there can be no millennial blessing without Him.

The setting here is the tribulation and the kingdom blessing (millennial blessing) to follow.

1. VERSE 1
   - This verse projects us on into the kingdom. The King is none other than the Lord Jesus Christ. The character of His reign is righteousness (compare this to chapter 11).

2. VERSE 2
   - He is not only King, He is Savior. He bore the judgment of sins for us. He is also a rock for protection.

3. VERSES 3–4
   - There will be spiritual understanding given to all of God's people. First Corinthians 13:12 says, *"Now we see through a glass, darkly; but then face to face."* True spiritual values will then be ascertained and made obvious.

4. VERSES 5–8
   - Everything will be seen in its true value and its true colors in that day. Every man will be seen for what he is. There will be no "putting on a front" or assuming what we are not. The mark of hypocrisy will be removed. You will note the word *"liberal"* in verses 5 and 8. The word *"churl"* means "a rude or coarse person."

5. VERSES 9–14
   - The woman who lives in pleasure in that day will not sense the coming judgment. Ordinarily, women are the first to be alarmed and are sensitive to danger. Here, they continue in pleasure and frivolity because they are insensitive to the serious condition. They are dead even while they live in pleasure. The judgment comes upon the land, and the land is made desolate. This has a bifocal fulfillment, both near and far. It was partially fulfilled under Sennacherib but it looks ahead to the day of the great tribulation.

6. VERSE 15
   - As the land of Israel flourished under a twofold blessing of rain—the early and the latter rain (see Hosea 6:3; Jeremiah 5:24; Deuteronomy 11:14)—so there will be a corresponding twofold pouring out of the Holy Spirit upon the people of Israel.

- The first, or the early rain, fell at Pentecost. A distinction must be observed between the "last days," when the prediction relates to the church. The last days as related to the church began with the advent of Christ but have special reference to the time at the end of this age. The last days as related to Israel are the days of Israel's exaltation and blessing.

- Now turn to Joel 2:28–29:

    And it shall come to pass afterward, that I will pour out my spirit upon all flesh; and your sons and your daughters shall prophesy, your old men shall dream dreams, your young men shall see visions: and also, upon the servants and upon the handmaids in those days will I pour out my spirit.

Notice the word *"afterward"* meaning "the last days." Peter used the same words and quoted Joel in Acts 2:16–21. The early rain at Pentecost resulted in three thousand souls turning to the Lord, but the representatives of the nation were far from doing the same, and so, *"wrath is come upon them to the uttermost"* (1 Thessalonians 2:16). This still awaits its climax when they have returned to the land; it shall cease with the outpouring of the Spirit as the latter rain. During that long time, the land is desolate just like its people. Israel awaits that latter rain and they alone are its object. God, the Holy Spirit, came to this earth at Pentecost, and that event has never been repeated. There can, therefore, be no second outpouring during this dispensation for He is already here. The Spirit cannot be poured out on Israel as long as He is here in this dispensation (and I mean the Holy Spirit). He cannot be poured out upon Israel while they are scattered. When Israel is restored to her land, then will there be the second effusion of the Spirit as told here in Joel, Acts, and Zecharaiah 12:10.

7. VERSE 17
- This is another great spiritual principle that is for men of all ages. The work of righteousness is always peace and the effect of righteousness is always quietness and blessed assurance.

8. VERSE 20
- This last verse is so constantly used as the sowing of the Word of the gospel that it is difficult to admit any other thought. Yet the Jewish readers would understand a sowing in the land as literal as the land itself in which the literal sowing would take place. The animals that do the work for them will be allowed to stray into cultivated fields because of the abundance of the harvest. Everything they sow will bring forth abundance and so they have no real care about a little damage to the fields. But the thing we should remember is that we should sow the Word of the Lord—teach it and study it every day.

CHAPTER 33

This chapter records the sixth and last woe of this section of Scripture. It begins a movement that is projected into the kingdom blessings of chapter 35. At chapter 35, we are brought to the end of the first major division of Isaiah. This chapter in particular pronounces a judgment on those who seek to destroy God's people and lay waste to His land. It refers to the Assyrian in the immediate future of Isaiah's day but it extends on to the final enemy of Israel in the last days. This chapter depicts the land as the thing of primary importance.

1. VERSE 1
- The spoiler here is Sennacherib, who came against Jerusalem during the reign of Hezekiah. (See Isaiah 36 and 37.) This is the unanimous conclusion of all scholars. However, it does not limit this chapter to the Assyrian only but it is the beginning of a wider and more complete fulfillment, as this chapter clearly indicates. This will be consummated finally in the anti-Christ and the restored

Roman Empire. The reference here is primarily to the king of the north who will come down like the Assyrian in the last days. (See Ezekiel 38 and 39.)

2. VERSE 2

+ This is the prayer of the godly remnant of Israel, then and also in the future.

3. VERSE 3

+ Notice the word *"nations"* is plural. The enemy here is more than the Assyrian. The Lord heard the prayer then and He will hear it in the future.

4. VERSES 4–6

+ A great transformation will take place in God's people in that day. They will turn from the material to the spiritual. This will be in the day when the kingdom is established here on the earth, that is— the millennium. This applies to Israel and the nations here on the earth in that day. The reference is *not* to the church.

5. VERSES 7–9

+ Here we hear the cries of the ambassadors who had tried to make an agreement with Sennacherib but were unsuccessful and, as a result, the highways become desolate, without a passenger. The very land itself reflects the misery of the people—the cedars of Lebanon droop as if they are weeping, the flowers of Sharon wither in shame, and the falling leaves of Carmel and Bashan are in accord with the falling tears of the people. This is but a picture of the last days when another ruler will break his covenant with Israel in the midst of the seventieth week of Daniel.

6. VERSES 10–12

+ Notice the word *"now"* repeated three times. The time is come and it is not one moment behind the time that was appointed by Jehovah. Always, He comes just as His people reach their extremity.

+ Notice the progression of these three "now's." First, like a sleeper awakened; then he takes his place in the tumult and it is a commanding role; finally, he alone is exalted above all.

+ This description of Israel's case is not far from the condition of the church now and at the moment of His coming in glory. Her glories are lying waste; her walls of separation from the world are broken down; shame and confusion exist. But when He comes and that happy moment arrives, things will be different. Until then, all we can do is hold fast and depend upon the Lord as the Holy and true One who keeps and sustains.

+ Note in verse 11 the cutting sarcasm when the enemy will be but chaff. They can bring forth nothing but stubble, which is adapted for burning and for nothing else. The enemy's own hot breath of wrath will start the flame.

+ This is judgment from God.

7. VERSE 13

+ Two groups of people are addressed here—*"ye that are far off,"* the Gentiles, and *"ye that are near,"* which is Israel.

8. VERSE 14

+ *"Sinners in Zion"* are those of Israel who are not Israel. There are godless Israelites as well as godless Gentiles.

+ *"The devouring fire"* does not refer to the Lake of Fire but rather to the fact that our God is an all-consuming fire. It is not a reference to hell, but to the holiness of God.

9. VERSE 15

+ The questions of verse 14 are answered here. (See also Psalm 15.) This is in accord with the whole tenor of Scripture. The one who has been declared righteous by his faith in Christ is called to walk in righteousness. What will we say then? Will we continue in sin, that grace may abound? (See Romans 6:1; Ephesians 2:8–10.)

10. VERSES 16–17

- This is the happy anticipation of those who have put their trust in the Lord.

11. VERSE 18

- Paul quotes this verse in 1 Corinthians 1:20: "*Where is the wise? where is the scribe? where is the disputer of this world? hath not God made foolish the wisdom of this world?*" The quotation here is more precisely interpreted like this—the word "*wise*" is substituted for "scribe," the word "*scribe*" is substituted for "collector," and "*disputer of this world*" is substituted for "*he that counted the towers.*"

12. VERSES 19–24

- This is the glorious prospect that is held out for Jerusalem. The eye of faith looks beyond the immediate hard circumstances to the glorious prospects of the future. This is the day when the King will be in Jerusalem. The Prince of Peace will then bring peace to the earth. Babylon could boast of the Euphrates. Assyria could boast of the Tigress. Egypt could boast of the Nile. In that day, Jerusalem, a landlocked city, can boast of the Lord as the source of her strength and life. The important item is that sin will be removed.

CHAPTER 34

Just as the burdens that affected various nations in chapters 12–23 were followed by a general crash in chapter 24 that, in turn, was succeeded by the joyous chapter of 25, here, we have various nations threatened by woe after woe until both Gentile and Jew were apostate. Now again comes the crash in divine judgment upon all the earth here in chapter 34. This chapter will be followed, just as we saw before, by the sweet strains of promise to be found in chapter 35.

Man looks to the future as a time when he will improve the world by his own efforts and his own "good deeds" that he will establish and bring in the millennium himself. This will never happen and that theory is of Satan. The Bible, however, looks to the millennium and a better day. Before the kingdom, or millennium, is established, everything that man has built, apart from God, is coming under terrific judgment. All of man's work is contrary to God and must come into a final conflict. That conflict is set before us here in this chapter under the title of "The Battle of Armageddon." The "sin of man" will finally be headed up in the "man of sin," and he and Christ must come to grips with each other. Light and darkness, good and evil, cannot coexist.

Many of the passages of Scripture record this event, such as Isaiah 61:2, Isaiah 63:1–6, Zechariah 14:1–3, and Revelation 19:11–19.

This chapter looks entirely to the future. First, we look at the indignation of the Lord poured out on all the nations and this is found in verses 1–4.

1. VERSE 1

- In Isaiah 1:2, God called heaven and earth to witness His judgment upon His people, Israel. In this chapter, God calls only the nations of the earth to witness His final judgment upon the nations.

2. VERSE 2

- Observe carefully the words chosen to depict this judgment: "*indignation,*" "*fury,*" "*utterly destroyed,*" "*delivered...to the slaughter.*" They are the strongest possible expressions that could be used. The judgment is universal and it is severe. It is not only the "*time of Jacob's trouble*" (Jeremiah 30:7), it is the time of the earth's travail. Our Lord spoke of this as a time unparalleled in the history of the world. The seals, trumpets, and vials of Revelation all intensify and confirm this truth.

3. VERSE 3
   + This is repulsive and terrible beyond description (read Revelation 19:17–19).
4. VERSE 4
   + This is to be taken literally, as it is repeated in Matthew 24:29. For other references, see Psalm 102:26 and compare that with Hebrews 1:11 and also Revelation 6:12–14.
5. VERSES 5–7
   + Now we see the target and the figure of all of God's enemies described in verses 5–7 under the name of Idumea (known as Edom).
   + In verse 5, Edom is representative of all in Adam that are rebellious against God and God's people. (See Malachi 1:4.) God will judge Edom. (See Obadiah 1:4–8.)
   + Verse 6 is a figure of a *"sword…filled with blood."* It is bathed in heaven, for sin began there and will be judged there. The sword is the instrument of judgment.
   + In verse 7, the sacrifice of animals is not enough. The blood of bulls and goats will not take away sin.
6. VERSE 8
   + This is the day of the Lord's vengeance.
7. VERSES 9–10
   + This seems to be confined to the land of Edom, but it could be taken as the judgment on the old earth before the new earth comes into existence.
8. VERSE 11
   + *"Confusion"* and *"emptiness"* are the Hebrew words for *"without form and void"* found in Genesis 1:2. There was a pre-Adamic judgment of the earth and there will be a post-Adamic judgment of the earth.
9. VERSES 12–15
   + This is a picture of Edom today, but it looks on to the future judgment in the future upon the earth.
10. VERSES 16–17
   + God's Word never fails. It is always true. Not one word will pass away until all these things are fulfilled. We can put our confidence in it.

CHAPTER 35

We come now to the millennium, a picture of the kingdom of the Lord Jesus. This chapter is a gem. The fires of judgment have now been burned out, the evening of trouble on the earth is ended, and the morning of millennial delight has come. God's method has always been through suffering to peace—through the night to dawn, through judgment to salvation. This chapter is in contrast to the storms of judgment of the last few chapters.

First, we will see the curse of sin lifted and the material earth restored.

1. VERSE 1
   + We are informed that the deserts of the world are being enlarged each year. Drought and soil erosion are hastening this process. All of this will be reversed in the millennium. This familiar and beautiful statement *"the desert shall rejoice, and blossom as the rose"* is an apt and happy picture of the earth's future. Those who are familiar with the great desert area of our country will be impressed with this statement.

2. VERSE 2
   - This is a picture of the curse being removed from the earth and it is in direct opposition to the conditions of today. Paul says, creation is groaning and travailing in pain today (see Romans 8:22), but in the millennium, all creation will rejoice.
   - An important note to remember is that all Scripture agrees that the millennial day is not the eternal day, not the perfect day. The millennium is not "the rest of God," the final Sabbath, the seventh day, but it is the sixth day in which the government of the earth is in the hand of Christ, the second man, the last Adam with his bride, with all evil kept under control, although present. Just as in our personal regeneration, there is still the old nature within us that must not be permitted to reign (see Romans 6:12), so in that time called the millennium, the old nature—sin—will not reign.

3. VERSES 3–4
   - We see that men will be renewed and their bodies strengthened. In the midst of the storm of judgment, God's people can rejoice because they will know that God will come and the strength of His coming will give strength to the fainting heart and it is the hope of His coming that will strengthen and does strengthen the faint heart of the Christian. The church has the added hope and joy of never experiencing this vengeance because we will not go through the great tribulation.

4. VERSES 5–6
   - During the millennium, sickness, disease, and all affliction will be lifted and bodies will be restored from their illness. Our Lord sent these credentials of Himself to John the Baptist in Matthew 11:2–6.

5. VERSES 7–9
   - Here Isaiah returns to the benefits that will come upon the earth. "The way of holiness" (verse 8) has been mentioned before in Isaiah 19:23.

6. VERSE 10
   - This not only includes Israel but it will include the redeemed who entered the millennium. Notice the words "the ransomed of the Lord." For Israel this is the end of a long journey. Like Jacob, they have wandered far but here they are at last back again at Bethel, the very house of God, and in that house, they will dwell forever. This brings us to the end of the first main division of the book of Isaiah.

7. ADDITIONAL NOTES ON THE MILLENNIUM
   - There are more than three hundred references in the Old Testament dealing with the second coming of Christ. In the New Testament, there are more than three hundred fifty references.
   - The Bible divides human history into seven unequaled periods called ages, or dispensations:
     a. First Dispensation—innocence—Genesis 1:26–3:24
     b. Second Dispensation—conscience—Genesis 4:1–7:24
     c. Third Dispensation—human government—Genesis 8:1–11:32
     d. Fourth Dispensation—promise—Genesis 12:1–Exodus 18:27
     e. Fifth Dispensation—law—Exodus 19:1–Acts 1:26
     f. Sixth Dispensation—grace—church age—Acts 2:1–Revelation 3:22
     g. Seventh Dispensation—millennial—1,000 years—Revelation 20:1–15
        (After these dispensations there will be eternity.)
   - No one will enter the millennium unless they are saved. (See Matthew 25:31–46.)

- The millennium is prophesied more in the Old Testament than any other place. Revelation merely gives us a definite period of time—1,000 years. John doesn't give us many details about the millennium. It is the Old Testament prophets who paint the picture that has whetted the appetite of all of us about that glorious age when Christ will be King in His kingdom.

- The Old Testament prophets tell us of a kingdom of peace and tranquility where men *"shall beat their swords into plowshares, and their spears into pruninghooks…neither shall they learn war any more"* (Isaiah 2:4). Then in Isaiah, the wolf will lie down with the lamb (11:6) and a man will be a child when he is a hundred years old (65:20).

- In Revelation 20:1–3, Satan is bound for the 1,000 years so he can't deceive the nations any longer. Even with Satan not active, there will still be a certain amount of sin during the millennium.

- The resurrections—Revelation 20:4–6. The first resurrection: there are four phrases (see 1 Corinthians 15:20–25):

  a. Christ is the first fruits—the first one to be raised—never to see death or decay.

  b. *"They that are Christ's at his coming"* (verse 23)—the rapture.

  c. Old Testament believers and the martyred saints of the tribulation are raised after the tribulation. (See Daniel 12:1–3).

  d. Mortal believers in the millennium will receive eternal bodies with no death.

How Much Do You Remember?

1. Who was the woe of chapter 31 directed toward?
2. Who is the menace, or danger, of chapter 31?
3. Describe the twofold pouring out of the Holy Spirit found in chapter 32.
4. Upon whom is the last judgment pronounced in chapter 33?
5. Describe the transformation that will take place in God's people in chapter 33.
6. What is the major event that takes place in chapter 34?
7. After the judgment of chapter 34, what follows in chapter 35?
8. Describe the various phases of renewal found in chapter 35.

Your Assignment for Next Week:

1. Review your notes from this lesson.
2. Read Isaiah chapters 36–39.
3. Underline your Bible.

Lesson 12 Notes

Lesson 13
CHAPTERS 36, 37, 38, 39

In chapters 36 through 39, we now come to the historic interlude forming a clearly marked second main division in the book of Isaiah, radically different in form from the chapters we have studied thus far, and quite different from the chapters we will study hereafter. Chapters 36–39 will not detain us long but we must not dishonor them by indifference or neglect. Divine history is never merely history, never a simple account of events. If we are enabled to profit by the moral lessons that we can learn from it, we have not exhausted our time. There are deep truths of a spiritual character that are only spiritually discerned, and for that discernment, we are dependent on the Holy Spirit. Recognizing these chapters as a division of the book of Isaiah serves to make the whole book a trilogy—that is, it gives the book the significance of the number three, which speaks of the full manifestation of God.

A comparison of these four chapters with 2 Kings 18–19 gives every evidence that either both accounts are taken from some common source or from one another.

We are dealing with a country the size of Rhode Island. Most historians would categorize a nation of that size of little worth historically, yet the destiny of man is far more dependent upon the Jew than any other nationality.

This section of Scripture leaves the high plateau of prophecy and drops down to the record of history. Even the form of language is different. Why are these four chapters of a historical character wedged between the two major divisions of the book of Isaiah? This is a reasonable question that requires investigation and rewards the honest student. There are several significant factors that are worthy of mention.

First, sacred and secular history are not the same. Dr. F. C. Jennings, in his book *Studies in Isaiah*, states, "Divine history is never *merely* history, never simply a true account of past events."[1] There are great spiritual truths couched in sacred history that are seen only by the eye of faith. The Holy Spirit must teach us the divine purpose in recording scriptural history. Let us note several suggestive reasons:

1. These incidents might seem trite to the average historian who records great world movements but events that concern God's people were important according to the standard of heaven.

2. Actually, these chapters note the transfer of power from Assyria to Babylon. Babylon was the real menace to God's people and was to begin the period designated by our Lord as "the times of the Gentiles."

3. This section is a record of a son of David, who was beset by enemies and who went down to the verge of death but was delivered and continued to reign. In this, he foreshadows the "great Son of David" who was beset by enemies, delivered to death, was raised from the dead, and is coming again—that one being Jesus Christ. Hezekiah was only a man who walked in the ways of David, another weak man. Our Lord was greater than David and as the crucified Son of God is made unto us *"wisdom, and righteousness, and sanctification, and redemption"* (1 Corinthians 1:30). There are other great spiritual truths and principles that we will note in our outline.

The second significant factor in this historical section is that these particular events are recorded three times in Scripture: 2 Kings 18–19, 2 Chronicles 29–30, and again, here in Isaiah. The fact that the Holy Spirit saw fit to record them three times is in itself a matter of great importance. These records are not identical but similar. Some scholars think Isaiah is the author of all three passages, or at least the passage in 2 Kings. Surely the Spirit of God has some special truth for us here that should cause us not to hurry over these events as if they were of no great moment.

Third, three significant and stupendous miracles are recorded in this brief section:

1. The angel slays 185,000 Assyrians (chapter 37:36–38).
2. The sun retreats ten degrees on the sun dial of Ahaz (chapter 38:7–8).
3. God heals Hezekiah and extends his life fifteen years (chapter 38:1–5).

Fourth, this section opens with Assyria and closes with Babylon. There are two important letters that Hezekiah received. The first was from Assyria, which Hezekiah took directly to God in prayer and God delivered his people (chapter 37:14). The second letter was from the king of Babylon and flattered Hezekiah, which he did not take to the Lord in prayer. As a result, it led to the undoing of Judah (chapter 39:1–8).

CHAPTER 36

Sennacherib, king of Assyria, had come down like a flood from the north, taking everything in his path. He either captured every nation and city that stood in his path or they capitulated to him. Proud with victory, he appears with the Assyrian host before the walls of Jerusalem. He is surprised and puzzled that Hezekiah would attempt to resist him. He seeks for some explanation, as Hezekiah must have some secret weapon. Rabshakeh, his representative, ridicules all known possibilities of help. Arrogantly, he demands unconditional surrender. This chapter closes with the terms and threats reported to Hezekiah.

This is a pathetic picture of a coming day when the enemy will have surrounded Jerusalem again. No human help can deliver them, as the enemy has come from the north, east, south, and west.

1. VERSE 1
   - Hezekiah was actually one of the five good kings of Judah who promoted revival. The record in 2 Chronicles gives him a clean bill of spiritual health. (See 2 Chronicles 29:1–11.) Nevertheless, he was a man and he became a weak king. He attempted to stave off the invasion of Jerusalem by bribing Sennacherib. (See 2 Kings 18:13–16.)
   - Hezekiah had stripped the gold and silver from the temple to meet the exorbitance of the king of Assyria. It was to no avail as the army of Assyria was outside the gates of Jerusalem.

2. VERSE 2
   - Sennacherib did not condescend to come personally, but sent an army under Rabshakeh. Note where he stood: *the conduit of the upper pool in the highway of the fuller's field.* This is the exact spot in which Isaiah had previously stood to encourage the heart of Ahaz, the father of Hezekiah, and to prophesy the virgin birth of Jesus (see notes on Isaiah 7:3).

3. VERSE 3
   - Hezekiah sent forth an embassy of three to receive the terms offered by Sennacherib.

4. VERSE 4
   - Rabshakeh arrogantly expresses surprise that Hezekiah would dare to resist. He wants to know the secret weapon in which Hezekiah trusts.

5. VERSE 5
   - Rabshakeh begins to deal with the possibilities that may have caused Hezekiah to resist and dismisses them as foolhardy. He mentions four possibilities that have given Hezekiah a false hope.

6. VERSE 6
   - The first possibility is the notion that Hezekiah might be looking to Egypt as a strong ally. Actually, the Assyrian host was then on the way to Egypt to capture that kingdom and was incensed that Jerusalem blocked the way.
   - The facts were that Hezekiah hoped for some help from Egypt, even as Ahaz, his father, before him. The Assyrian calls Egypt a *broken reed,* which was true, as succeeding events proved and Isaiah had warned.

7. VERSE 7

- The second source of help that Rabshakeh mentioned was the Lord. Here is where his spiritual discernment gave him a wrong cue. The high places that Hezekiah had removed were immoral places of idolatry. There was only one place to worship—the temple in Jerusalem. There was only one approach to God—the altar on which the blood sacrifice was made.

- The man of the world today says that all churches are good and it does not make any difference what you believe, as long as you are sincere. This contradicts the words of our Lord when He says in John 14:6, *"I am the way, the truth, and the life: no man cometh unto the Father, but by me."*

8. VERSES 8–9

- The third possibility suggested by Rabshakeh reveals the haughty attitude of the Assyrians. There was the bare possibility that Hezekiah was depending on his own resources and manpower to defend the city. This was so absurd that the Assyrian offered to furnish horses for two thousand men if they could be found to mount the horses for battle. Equipment from Egypt, even if it arrived, would have been of little help.

9. VERSE 10

- The fourth reason is the most subtle of all. Rabshakeh suggests that Jehovah of Israel has sent the Assyrian against Jerusalem, and He, Jehovah, is therefore on the side of the Assyrian.

10. VERSE 11

- All this time, Rabshakeh has been speaking loudly in the Hebrew language so the soldiers on the walls of Jerusalem could hear him. This was done to the annoyance of the representatives of Hezekiah, who suggest that he speak in the Assyrian tongue, which they understood.

11. VERSE 12

- Haughty Rabshakeh declines to do so for he is definitely trying to destroy the morale of the army in Jerusalem.

12. VERSE 13

- Now he turns to the people on the walls and addresses them in a proud and disdainful fashion.

13. VERSES 14–15

- He urges them not to trust in the Lord. His words are pragmatic and, on the surface, are intended to cause fear.

14. VERSE 16

- He now attempts to show them that if they surrender without resisting, the king of Assyria is prepared to show mercy. His mercy is a cruel thing.

15. VERSE 17

- The method of Assyria was to uproot a people, move them far from their homeland, and colonize them there. This was a great morale destroyer.

16. VERSES 18–20

- Arrogantly, he boasts that none of the gods of other nations have delivered them. Why should they expect Jehovah to deliver Jerusalem? He places Jehovah on a par with heathen idols.

17. VERSE 21

- The representatives of Hezekiah do not answer but hold their peace. They were instructed to proceed after this fashion *"and answered him not a word."* It is the best answer when the enemy seeks to make you liable.

18. VERSE 22

+   The messengers return to report these doleful words to Hezekiah. Clothes speak of the dignity and glory of man. The grass is clothed with the flower and Solomon in all of his glory was not arrayed as one of these. (See Matthew 6:28–30.) But the rending clothing speaks of humiliation and shame. This chapter closes on a dark and doleful note but all the record is not in this one chapter.

CHAPTER 37

Before I start the verse-by-verse study of this chapter, let me give you a broad outline, since it is lengthy.

First, we find a reaction of Hezekiah to the messenger's report (verses 1–4).

Second, there is a word of encouragement to Hezekiah from the Lord through Isaiah (verses 5–7).

Third, Rabshakeh's temporary withdrawal from Jerusalem and his letter to Hezekiah (verses 8–13).

Fourth, Hezekiah receives the letter and then Hezekiah's prayer (verses 14–20).

Fifth, God's answer to Hezekiah's prayer by Isaiah (verses 21–35).

Sixth, the record of the destruction of 185,000 Assyrians by the angel of the Lord (verses 36–38).

1. VERSE 1

+   Hezekiah's reaction to the report of his messengers reveals a man of great piety. In his extremity, he turns to God and to the house of the Lord.

2. VERSE 2

+   He now sends his messengers to Isaiah, the prophet. This is another act of faith.

3. VERSE 3

+   The message to Isaiah was surely ominous and black. It was a day of trouble, rebuke, and blasphemy.

4. VERSE 4

+   Here, Hezekiah reveals an aberration of faith on his part. He speaks of the Lord as *"thy God"* and not as "our God." Note that he corrected this prayer in verse 20.

5. VERSES 5–6

+   God gives assurance to Hezekiah that the blasphemy of the Assyrian has not escaped His attention. Likewise, God cannot ignore it, nor will He.

6. VERSE 7

+   God declares the destruction of the Assyrian. This had a literal fulfillment, as we shall see.

7. VERSES 8–9

+   A rumor came that the main force of the Assyrian army was being attacked by the Egyptian army. Rabshakeh withdrew temporarily to assist the main force of the Assyrian army, but to save face, he dispatched a letter from Sennacherib to Hezekiah.

8. VERSE 10

+   This is the way Satan works. He tries to destroy the faith that any person might have in the Lord.

9. VERSES 11–12

+   Here, Rabshakeh goes beyond the former word and boasts that no gods of any nation had delivered their people out of the hand of the Assyrian.

10. VERSE 13

+   He quotes historical facts that were difficult to answer. He asks, "Where are all the kings?"

11. VERSE 14

+   When Hezekiah received the letter, he went to God directly and spread the letter before Him. Then follows one of the truly great prayers of Scripture.

12. VERSES 16–20

- No instructed Israelite believed that God was a local deity who occupied a house in Jerusalem, but Hezekiah recognized that the Shekinah presence, or glory of God, abode between the cherubim. He acknowledged that man can only approach God by sacrifice. He approached God upon the mercy seat. He acknowledged that God is the Creator of all and is over all.

- In verse 17, Hezekiah shows God the letter and calls attention to the fact that it is directly against God.

- He acknowledges the truth of the letter in verses 18–19. There was no need to deny or ignore it. When we deal with God, it is wise to tell Him the truth, especially about ourselves. Do not conceal anything.

- Verse 20 is a simple appeal to God to save Judah for His name's sake. This is prayer.

13. VERSE 21

- God always answers.

14. VERSES 22–28

- Here, we see that the Assyrian has blasphemed God. God will do something about it. The pride of the Assyrian caused him to boast. His success deceived him but God humbled him.

15. VERSE 29

- God had heard the blasphemy of the Assyrian and had taken note of it (see verse 4).

16. VERSE 30

- The primary thought is that the children of Judah would continue on in the land a little longer. Difficult days were in the future but God would use them to strengthen His people. The Lord addresses Israel directly, beginning here in verse 30.

17. VERSE 31

- This all leads to the vine producing fruit. Note this lovely expression: *"take root downward, and bear fruit upward,"* which is applicable to all of God's children, of all ages.

18. VERSE 32

- It is always the remnant, small as it is, that is true to God.

19. VERSE 33

- Note the boldness of this prophecy. If one of the 185,000 Assyrians had accidentally shot an arrow over the walls of Jerusalem, God's Word would be inaccurate. How wonderful are the promises of God!

20. VERSE 34

- This prophecy is specific, and also was literally fulfilled.

21. VERSE 35

- God promises to defend His city for His sake and for David's sake. Has God promised to defend His own? Of course He has throughout the ages, and also in this dispensation. (See John 17:11.)

22. VERSE 36

- Judgment was promised and came to pass, just as it will come to pass in the future. God has a way of bringing about His own judgment, and here we see Him taking swift action and destroying 185,000 Assyrians.

23. VERSES 37–38

- Secular history records that this actually happened. Sennacherib was slain by his sons. Now we are ready to look at another side of the personal life of Hezekiah, and here, another miracle is recorded.

CHAPTER 38

King Hezekiah reigned over Judah for twenty-nine years, and it was fifteen years prior to his death that he became critically ill. (See 2 Kings 18:2.) This sickness was in the fourteenth year of his reign. (See Isaiah 36:1.) All of this happened in the same year—the sickness of Hezekiah and the siege of Jerusalem by the Assyrians.

1. VERSE 1
   - The sentence of death is delivered to Hezekiah by Isaiah. It is true that this sentence of death rests upon each one of us, although we do not know the day nor the hour. The instruction Isaiah received from the Lord was that Hezekiah should put his house in order.

2. VERSE 2
   - This scene takes place in the sick room in which Hezekiah lies prostrate with a malignant boil or ulcer. Hezekiah turned his face to the wall and began to pray.

3. VERSE 3
   - This is the ground on which the Old Testament saint prayed, which is confirmed in 2 Kings 18:4–7. This is especially evident in verse 5: "*He trusted in the Lord God of Israel; so that after him was none like him among all the kings of Judah, nor any that were before him.*"

4. VERSES 4–5
   - God heard the prayer and answered immediately. Notice in the answer of the Lord that not much is said about Hezekiah's perfect heart, but the Lord God identified Himself as "*the God of David thy father.*" Our prayers are heard for the sake of David's great Son—the Lord Jesus Christ. Fifteen years are to be added to the king's life, a period of time as long again as he had already reigned, but the answer goes beyond the petition as we see in verse 6.

5. VERSE 6
   - Not only does God grant Hezekiah fifteen additional years but He also declares that the threatened city will not be captured. In other words, God ties in the deliverance of Jerusalem from the Assyrian with Hezekiah's deliverance from death. His answer to one request will encourage the believer's heart that He will answer other requests.

6. VERSES 7–8
   - Jehovah gives the sign that Hezekiah had asked for. (You will note this in 2 Kings 20:8–10 and also in Isaiah 38:22.) Let me paraphrase verse 8 into a literal reading: "Behold, I will cause the shadow of the steps to return, which is gone down on the steps of Ahaz with the sun, backward ten steps. And the sun returns ten steps by the steps that it had gone down." The most difficult word is the one rendered as "steps." Here, in this literal translation we are compelled to see a form of literal steps, the form of a sundial. Hence, the word is rendered "*the sun dial of Ahaz.*"
   - We can now take ourselves back to Hezekiah's palace and into his chamber. There lies the king, still prone on his couch, his face no longer turned to the wall. Now joy and hope brighten his eyes as he looks out of his window to the garden. In full view stands a column with a series of steps leading up to it. At least ten of them are lying in the shadow over that number of steps. As one looks again, the once darkened steps are now in clear sunlight. This is the sign for which the king had asked.
   - Commentators have written page after page discussing how the recession of the shadow was affected but, seemingly, they have all been vain and unsatisfactory. Of three things, however, we are quite sure:
     a. First, it was a supernatural intervention of God, controlling His own laws as He sees fit.

b. Second, it was a sign that necessitated Hezekiah being able to see what had taken place, for unless a sign appeals in some way to the senses, it would be an extra strain on faith rather than an aid to faith. So, the sundial was visible from the sick chamber of Hezekiah.

c. Third, it was not a meaningless sign but a supernatural act on the part of God.

+ We may be assured that the king would ponder the meaning of the sunlight on those steps that had once been in shadow, and it would cause him to remember the steps in which Ahaz had walked. (See Isaiah 7:10–13.) Ahaz was the father of Hezekiah, and Hezekiah's sickbed was in the palace of the king. He saw the columns and steps of his father's porch.

+ Now the conditions are reversed and we find that the Assyrian is not threatening the son of Ahaz but the son of David. The sign taught him, and it should teach us, that *"if we walk in the light, as he is in the light, we have fellowship one with another"* (1 John 1:7).

+ For extra study, the word for *sundial* literally means "to go up." It is translated as *"steps"* in Exodus 20:26, and it is translated as *"degrees"* in the Song of Degrees from Psalms 120 and 134.

7. VERSES 9–22

+ The writing of Hezekiah is significant and the following verses are a fine thesis on death by one who had almost experienced it. And this thesis is found beginning with verse 10 through the end of the chapter. Don't forget that this is Hezekiah's writing.

+ Note in verse 20 that this thesis suddenly was set to music. The question arises at this juncture whether Hezekiah should have died at the appointed time. The account in 2 Chronicles has an interesting verse in this connotation after the illness of Hezekiah: *"But Hezekiah rendered not again according to the benefit done unto him; for his heart was lifted up: therefore there was wrath upon him, and upon Judah and Jerusalem"* (2 Chronicles 32:25). We will find in the next chapter that Hezekiah played the fool after his recovery.

+ It might be interesting to note that during this recovery and afterward, Manasseh was born. Manasseh was Hezekiah's son who began to reign when he was only twelve years of age, which means that Manasseh was born after Hezekiah's sickness.

+ Note that Hezekiah writes that Isaiah instructed them, *"Take a lump of figs"* (2 Kings 20:7). Actually, the healing of Hezekiah was of the Lord but it was aided by a poultice of figs. Hezekiah's sickness was a "boil," which in the Hebrew means "to be hot." Elsewhere, it is referred to as *"the botch of Egypt"* (Deuteronomy 28:27). It was Job's disease.

CHAPTER 39

There is a transfer from Assyria in this chapter, as the enemy of Judah is one of the outstanding figures of this section. At this time, Babylon was a struggling city on the banks of the Euphrates, unable to overcome Assyria. However, Babylon was to become the great head of gold in the times of the Gentiles (see Daniel 2:37–38), and that makes this chapter significant. This chapter reveals the great blunder of Hezekiah's life. After his sickness, he obviously attempted to please God. This chapter reveals his human frailty and weakness. It is after the hour of great spiritual triumph that our worst defeats come.

1. VERSE 1

+ Merodachbaladan is a meaningless king to us but his name is full of meaning. Dr. F. C. Jennings calls attention to the fact that the consonants that form the first part of the name are the same letters used in Nimrod—M-R-D. The word means "the rebel." Baladan means "not lord." His full name then means "the rebel, not lord." Behind this king, along with Nimrod, stands Satan, the arch rebel. He is the god of this world. He came with flattery and a show of interest in Hezekiah. Merodachbaladan sent letters by messengers with a present for Hezekiah. These were sent under the assumption that it was to be a congratulations and well-wishing for Hezekiah's recovery.

Hezekiah had taken the letter of the Assyrian and spread it before the Lord. Here, he does not, as he feels no necessity. This was the most dangerous letter of all.

2. VERSE 2
   * Hezekiah made the mistake of showing his silver and gold, for he was immensely wealthy. The attention of Merodachbaladan made Hezekiah glad and so he just opened up all of the things among his treasures and the messengers made note of it. Later, when a king of Babylon needed gold and silver, he knew where to go.

3. VERSE 3
   * Isaiah sensed the danger and came immediately to Hezekiah to find out how far he had gone with them. Hezekiah had no discernment of the coming danger. Now you see, dramatically, the role of a prophet.

4. VERSE 4
   * Isaiah immediately asked: "What have you shown them?" and Hezekiah, bragging, said, "Everything."

5. VERSES 5–7
   * This is a prophecy that Isaiah spoke from the Lord that was fulfilled. (See 2 Kings 24–25; Daniel 1).
   * History tells of the fulfillment of this prophecy, for after the capture of Jerusalem by Nebuchadnezzar, the city has been trodden down by the Gentiles and will continue to be so until the times of the Gentiles be fulfilled. The captivity by Babylon then is really the beginning of that series of four monarchies that followed, one after the other, replacing Babylon with Medo-Persia, then with Greece, and then with Rome.
   * There is a truth here that all of us should learn. Hasn't God given to all of us precious things in the way of "truths"? Have we not looked upon these truths as ours and kept them? Have we not personally too often become friendly with a Babylonian-type spirit that governs the day? Have we not said, "I am rich and increased with goods?"

6. VERSE 8
   * This seems a strange statement for Hezekiah to make. He was grateful that these things would not come to pass in his day, but what about his children and great grandchildren?
   * This concludes the historic section.

How Much Do You Remember?

1. What is this section of Isaiah considered to be (chapters 36–39)?
2. Describe the character of King Hezekiah.
3. Recall Hezekiah's two different reactions to the two letters he received.
4. How does God respond to Hezekiah's prayer in chapter 38?
5. What human weakness does Hezekiah display in the last chapter?

Your Assignment for Next Week:

1. Review your notes from this lesson.
2. Read Isaiah chapter 40.
3. Underline your Bible.

Lesson 13 Notes

Lesson 14
INTRODUCTION TO THE THIRD SECTION OF ISAIAH AND CHAPTER 40

We cannot approach this last part of the book of Isaiah, which speaks so clearly and directly of our Lord—both as to His sufferings and the glory that will follow—without fearing that we have failed to discern the intention of the Spirit of God as He speaks through His prophet, Isaiah. We know that we are about to enter a department of the divine Word of God in which we will find treasures of gold, silver, and precious truth, but without the light and the leadership of the Holy Spirit, we will fail to find those truths.

With this in view, I find little necessity in showing the unity of the whole book as being the authorship of Isaiah in both parts. For two thousand years and more, there was not a whisper of a "second Isaiah," but you will find in a great many of our modern-day commentaries that when you come to chapter 40, there is mention of a "second Isaiah."

In the eighteenth century, there arose a school of theologians, mostly from Germany, comprising names that have since become notorious rather than famous among all who love and revere the Bible. Names such as Eichorn, Paulus, Hitzig, Nobel, and others, whom we can classify among those who constantly cause a world of confusion to the average lay person and even to some theologians. Just before the time of their appearance, there arose such men as Wesley, Whitfield, Watts, and a host of other kindred evangelists who had been commissioned of the Lord to go over all the earth with the gospel of Christ. Immediately after these evangelists had caused a worldwide attention upon the name of Jesus, these men were sent out with their poison, marked with such evidence of Satan, fighting back, as is the case when revival is experienced. Their claim of superior insight and a higher degree of knowledge generally unwrapped the package that is called today "higher criticism."

We must be fair to those German scholars who are led by the Holy Spirit and have done a great work—among them, you will find men like Keil, Delitzsch, and others.

For us, the clear testimony of the prophets, apostles, and inspired writers of the New Testament will be all that we need. John the Baptist testified of himself in Matthew 3:3 by saying, *"For this is he that was spoken of by the prophet Esaias* [Isaiah], *saying, The voice of one crying in the wilderness."* That, to me, is not a "second Isaiah" or "the great unknown," but the well-known Isaiah, the same as wrote the first thirty-nine chapters, and we find that quote here in chapter 40.

Jesus Himself distinctly confirmed the genuineness of the book of Isaiah when He quoted from Isaiah in Luke 4:17–21. We find other references in Matthew 8:17 and John 12:37–41. We also find a well-known passage of Scripture in Acts 8:26–40. If these words in the book of Acts that the eunuch read are not Isaiah's and if they do not really predict the sufferings of the Lord Jesus, and if they are the words of a nameless writer, then we must conclude that the eunuch would have been deceived and taught a falsehood by a conspiracy of at least three parties: the evangelist Philip, the angel of the Lord, and the Holy Spirit of God. Paul adds his voice to the sure truth of Isaiah in his letter to the Romans 10:16–21. We will thus assert that Isaiah is the one and only author of the book by his name. Isaiah is the only name among men that, by its very significance, fits the contents of this second part of the book of Isaiah. The name *Isaiah* means "the salvation of Jehovah." These chapters, 40–66, could be entitled "The Salvation of Jehovah," and in these chapters, salvation is more clearly set forth than in any other part of the Old Testament.

The discovery of the complete scroll of the prophecy of Isaiah in Qumran Cave 1 presents us with a text almost identical with the translation of the book that we hold in our hand.

The historical setting of these chapters can be remembered from a study of the book of Daniel. The setting is about the middle of the sixth century B.C., and the Persian king, Cyrus, was the great figure on the horizon of world politics (Isaiah 44). Babylon had been the dominate world power, but now was about to fall (chapter 47). The captive people of Israel were shortly to be released from exile by Cyrus and permitted to go back to Palestine (chapter 45). You will recall in Daniel chapters 2 and 7, we have the order of the empires. First, there was Babylon. (See Daniel 2:37–38, 7:1–4.) Second was the empire of Medo-Persia. (See Daniel 7:5.) Third was the empire of Greece. (See Daniel 2:39, 7:6.) Fourth, the world empire of Rome. (See Daniel 2:40–43, 7:7.)

The Assyrian Empire weakened and fell in the last part of the seventh century. Nineveh, its capital, was destroyed by the Medes and the Babylonians in 612 B.C. The Babylonians, also called Chaldeans, rapidly took over the Assyrian Empire and destroyed Jerusalem and Judah in 587 B.C. With the death of Nebuchadnezzar, Babylon's great king, in 561 B.C., their empire rapidly weakened. Meanwhile, the Persian king, Cyrus, united Media and Persia (modern Iran), moved into Armenia and Asia Minor, and defeated the Babylonian army headed by Belshazzar. Cyrus was then welcomed in Babylon by its people. Among his first acts were decrees permitting the people who had been dislodged from their homes to return to them. The Hebrew version of the decree for the release of the Judeans is given in Ezra 1 and another decree permitting the rebuilding of the temple at Jerusalem is quoted in Ezra 6. The rebuilding of the temple was completed between 520 and 515 B.C. by a governor named Zerubbabel, a descendent of David. (See Matthew 1:12–13.)

Now you have the historical setting. Maybe this will help you to understand some of the characters we will study in this section of Scripture. We are here in the historical setting of Cyrus—Medo-Persia.

This is the second and last major division of Isaiah. It is in contrast to the first major division in the first section, where we had judgment and the righteous government of God. In this section, we have the grace of God, the suffering, and glory to follow. The opening statement of *"Comfort ye…"* sets the mood and tempo. The message is now one of comfort and God reveals Himself as Creator, Savior, and Sustainer.

In this last section, Isaiah is mentioned by name many times, but in this passage, he is not mentioned, as if it is one continual discourse. Just as in Revelation, John is transported by the Holy Spirit to scenes in the future, so here, the prophet is transported by the same Spirit to the future of Israel and the coming of the Messiah, including His death and plan of redemption. John is the counterpart of Isaiah. *Isaiah* means "the salvation of Jehovah" and *John* means "the grace of Jehovah." So set your mind to think as though you were studying Revelation—all prophecy.

CHAPTER 40

Now let us take a look at the verse-by-verse study, beginning with chapter 40. The first chapters of Isaiah were made up of God's judgments and woes. Now we find the people of Israel in exile, their nation destroyed, and the temple of Solomon is in ruins. They seem completely defeated as they sit by the river of Babylon and cry. In the midst of that suffering and sadness, the prophet Isaiah is sent by the Lord with a message of hope and assurance. In these chapters, 40 through 66, there are three main themes. In chapters 40–48, we find the promise of deliverance. From chapters 49–57, there is the revelation of the One who is coming to deliver us. Third, in chapters 58–66, is the picture of a delivered people after they have passed through the refining fires of their chastening God.

1. VERSE 1
   + As the people of Israel realize their condition—their land is lost, their temple of worship has been destroyed, and they seem in total despair—God comes through the prophet Isaiah and says, *"Comfort ye, comfort ye my people."* This is a wonderful message of consolation and care.
   + Notice the Lord says, *"my people."* There is a great deal of significance in that statement because God cannot possibly leave those whom He owns, for He is their God, their all.

2. VERSE 2

+ Here we find a word of forgiveness: *"Speak ye comfortably to Jerusalem, and cry unto her, that her warfare is accomplished, that her iniquity is pardoned: for she hath received of the Lord's hand double for all her sins."* This is a heart-to-heart talk between God and Israel.

+ Notice that statement *"she hath received of the Lord's hand double for all her sins."* Does this mean that the Lord is being so severe with her that He is punishing her twice? Of course not. The Bible is an Eastern book and the illustrations, therefore, are taken from the Eastern way of life. In those times, if a man was hopelessly in debt and unable to make payment, it was the custom for a creditor to write out a statement of his indebtedness that would be nailed to the door of the debtor's house. All who passed that way would know that this was a man who was bankrupt. The extent of the debt was there for all to see, for it was written on parchment. But if the debtor had a wealthy friend, or someone who would come to pay the debt for him, he would go to the creditor and say, "I am prepared to accept responsibility for this man's indebtedness and pay you fully." Immediately, the creditor would go to the house of the debtor and cancel the amount of debt on the parchment by folding it over and sealing it on the door. The parchment was folded over *double* and sealed. That is the meaning of *"received of the Lord's hand double for all her sins."*

+ Immediately this great evangelical prophet introduces us to the idea of the cross of Calvary, where the Lord Jesus Christ was made sin for us for *"God was in Christ, reconciling the world unto himself"* (2 Corinthians 5:19). Note here an important truth. The people were told by Isaiah *"that her iniquity is pardoned,"* but the natural consequences of sin remain. The punishment had to be taken. A man reaps what he sows. David was forgiven for the tragedy of the affair with Bathsheba. To his dying day, he knew forgiveness and the cleansing and pardon of God, but for the rest of his life, he bore the consequences of his sinfulness.

3. VERSE 3

+ The voice of forgiveness is immediately followed by the voice of deliverance. The writers of all four of the Gospels refer to Isaiah 40:3 as related to John the Baptist, the one who is to come to prepare a highway for our God.

4. VERSES 4–5

+ Here is the word of deliverance.

> *Every valley shall be exalted, and every mountain and hill shall be made low: and the crooked shall be made straight, and the rough places plain: and the glory of the Lord shall be revealed, and all flesh shall see it together: for the mouth of the Lord hath spoken it.*

+ When God speaks to the heart a word of forgiveness, it is only the prelude to an experience of His deliverance. Forgiveness is not the end of the Christian experience; but only the beginning. Our Savior's name was called Jesus, not that He might save us *in* our sins but that He might save us *from* our sins.

+ The way back from Babylon to Judah was about a thirty-day journey through the desert, over mountains and through valleys. The journey would have seemed impossible but when God takes a hand and steps in to deliver, the message of the prophet is that every mountain and hill will be made low and the crooked will be made straight and the rough places plain. This was to be a highway for our God. It has a more significant meaning than just the return of Israel to Judah because in verse 5, the glory of the Lord will be revealed and all flesh will see that manifestation together. It was a similar situation when the young baby Jesus lay in Bethlehem's manger. The glory was there but it was so veiled that all flesh did not see it—only a few could pierce that veil and see and discern *"(...the glory as of the only begotten of the Father,) full of grace and truth*" (John 1:14). But today, if one suddenly appeared with radiant glory and with the hosts coming with Him, could people look anywhere else?

5.   VERSES 6–8

+   Here, we hear a second voice with authority and this is the voice of God and the voice says, "*Cry.*" Then Isaiah answers, "*What shall I cry?*" Then comes a portion of Scripture that is so meaningful to all of us. Notice in verse 6: "*All flesh is grass.*" Then, in verse 8: "*The grass withereth, the flower fadeth: but the word of our God shall stand for ever.*" The grass, mentioned twice, is a fitting emblem of the frailty of man. At his best, he is but as a blade of grass, or a flower that withers and fades, as compared to the Word of God that abides and stands forever. We hold in our hand that which abides forever and ever. Peter emphasizes this in 1 Peter 1:24–25. Therefore, here in verses 6–8, Isaiah gave to the people a word of assurance. God is not dependent upon man or methods, and one word of all His good promise has never failed. The authority of the Word of God is something you can rest your heart upon in absolute assurance and confidence.

+   After the word of forgiveness, which is always followed by a word of deliverance, followed by the word of assurance—which is the bedrock of Scripture—we find a word of testimony.

6.   VERSE 9

+   This word of testimony has been heard many times in musical presentations. The thrust of this word to the heart of God's people was not for them simply to listen to what God had to say, but to believe it, appropriate it, and do something about it. They were to shout with their voices and be not afraid. And what were they to shout? We find it here: "*Behold your God!*" There was no apology for the message. There was to be no concern about popular opinion. They were only to be concerned with lifting their voice and being unafraid.

+   So often, Christians lose confidence in their message. To many people, it can seem that Christianity is fighting a losing battle. We find in America the soft pedaling of the Word of God because the message of the gospel is often not real and vital to the lives of those who profess to be Christians. Lift up your voice, speak to the people, don't be ashamed of your message, teach it, and preach it. And what are we to preach?

7.   VERSE 10

+   We saw a part of what we are to preach and what Israel was to proclaim in the last part of verse 9, and it finishes here in verse 10. They—and we—are to brilliantly and vibrantly say to all people, "*Behold, the Lord God will come with strong hand, and his arm shall rule for him: behold, his reward is with him, and his work before him.*"

+   Picture this message getting into the country of Babylon, to a people suffering from the chastening of God because of their sins. Then they are told these words. But it has a far more significant meaning for us. This is a picture of the coming of the Lord a second time. Isaiah not only saw the near future, but also the far distant future, even to the point of describing the word of John the Baptist.

8.   VERSE 11

+   "*He shall feed his flock like a shepherd: he shall gather the lambs with his arm, and carry them in his bosom, and shall gently lead those that are with young.*" Compare this to Psalm 23. The coming One is Emmanuel—"God with us."

+   Here, His character is given as the tender shepherd. When the Lord Jesus actually came, He took the various phrases spoken by Isaiah. He said, "*I am the good shepherd: the good shepherd giveth his life for the sheep*" (John 10:11, see also 1 Peter 2:25).

+   And so, as the tender shepherd, He is pictured here in the good news that God brings to Israel—the shepherd carrying the lambs in His bosom and gently leading the flock. This One who comes so tenderly as the Good Shepherd—a real man, a man in absolute holiness, compassionate and loving—is the almighty, omnipotent God. The message in these verses of Isaiah point to a Man upon a cross and to the blood that streamed from His hands and His side, and the message says, *"Behold your God!"*

+ If in your life, there is a desperate sense of failure in spite of all your professions of Christ, of faith, and of various religions, there comes to you this word of forgiveness. Then all of the mountains in your life will be made low, every valley should be raised, all the crooked places made straight, and the rough places plain. He will do this for you.

9. VERSE 12

+ This verse introduces the section that speaks of the greatness of God as Creator. Notice first, His omnipotence. I don't think that there has ever been written such majestic language as we find here. Here is God answering a people under the burden of guilt and a sense of oppression, and look at what He says to them: *"Who hath measured the waters in the hollow of his hand, and meted out heaven with the span* [three fingers]*, and comprehended the dust of the earth in a measure, and weighed the mountains in scales, and the hills in a balance?"*

+ The vastness of the reach of the hand of the almighty God is an amazing thing. He makes us see that the great mountain ranges such as we know in this country are but toys. He can pick them up and weigh them as a storekeeper can weigh food in a scale. We see here the vastness of the reach of God, which stretches around this globe we call the earth, can hold the ocean in the hollow of His hand and the mountains in His scales.

10. VERSES 13–14

+ Now he speaks to us about the greatness of His wisdom.

> *Who hath directed the Spirit of the LORD, or being his counselor hath taught him? With whom took he counsel, and who instructed him, and taught him in the path of judgment, and taught him knowledge, and shewed to him the way of understanding?*

+ He takes our tiny, miserable, complaining experience that grumbles against Him and, holding us in His presence, we hear Him say, "Who do you think taught me to make this great universe?" When we look at the wisdom, the power, and the glory of God, somehow, our complaints seem to make us blush and our grumbling over little things makes us want to hide our faces from Him.

11. VERSE 15

+ Not only does He remind us of the vastness of His reach and the greatness of His wisdom, but He also reminds us of the insignificance of the nations, when He says, *"Behold, the nations are as a drop of a bucket, and are counted as the small dust of the balance: behold, he taketh up the isles as a very little thing."*

+ The greatest of nations, the most powerful, the most idolatress, and the most wicked are simply nations that are as a drop in a bucket.

12. VERSES 16–17

+ The nations of the earth may think they have insurmountable problems, but they present no problem to God. Note that the entire forest of Lebanon would not make a fire for a burnt offering even if all of the animals of the world were offered to God. All would be totally inadequate. Only in the sacrifice of Jesus Christ can God find satisfaction.

13. VERSE 18

+ Here, the prophet contrasts God to idols. No image of God was permissible in the second commandment. Why does he ask such a question as we find in verse 18?

14. VERSE 19

   + The answer to the question in verse 18 is found in verse 19. This people, in times of sin and disobedience, when they experience the chastening hand of God, instead of heart-searching and repentance, what did they do? They manufactured a god of their own, as we find in verse 19: *"The workman melteth a graven image, and the goldsmith spreadeth it over with gold, and casteth silver chains."* In other words, he did the best job he could. He polished it to shine. Inside that graven image was not gold but something that would tarnish, rot, and wear out.

15. VERSE 20

   + Some people were so poor that they could not afford the luxury of one of these finer images, so they cut down a tree and found a cunning workman to prepare what the Bible calls *"a graven image,"* one that would last as long as humanly possible. Thus, they substituted idols for deity, death for life, and religion for the living God.

16. VERSE 21

   + God begins to speak to them about this idol worship by asking questions. Notice the profound questions He asks the people of Israel because they had been given instruction they knew, they heard, and they should have understood.

17. VERSE 22

   + Here we find Scripture that tells us the earth is round—*"the circle of the earth."* Nothing is new under the sun, even though many of our ancestors thought that the earth was flat and square. God's throne is far beyond the penetration of the most powerful telescopes because man is as a grasshopper.

18. VERSES 23–24

   + We see here what happens to images or idols that have been worshipped in the place of our living God. This is what happens when we get into the whirlwind of life and death to find that every substitute that is put in place of God is an absolute sham. When God strikes in the time of whirlwind, all is found to be as chaff.

19. VERSES 25–30

   + Here, He asks questions again about His holiness and His greatness. Part of the answer is found in verses 28–30. We find some light on this matter of complaining. Do you notice the contrast? The everlasting God faints not, He is not weary; but we faint and become weary, not merely physically and mentally but spiritually. We know absolute exhaustion that brings upon our lips the unworthy argument with God. We all grow faint and weary and baffled, and then we cry out, "Lord, why is there no deliverance?" But God is never weary and never faints. We should see here then some light upon the problem of our lack of guidance and deliverance. When we sever the connection between God and our daily life, we become utterly weary.

20. VERSE 31

   + The Lord God never becomes weary, and after reading this verse, can it be that He wants to make us like Him? Yes, He does. The whole purpose of redemption is to change our nature and to help us begin to grow into the image of the Lord Jesus Christ. There seems to be a strange order of events in this verse.

   + *"They shall mount up with wings…they shall run…they shall walk."* This order is opposite of how we learn to move, progressing from walking to running and then, someday, the body of Christ will indulge in some wonderful space travel when Jesus comes again. Walk, run, faint—no! Walk, run, mount—no! God said that they will first mount up with wings, then they will run, and they will walk and never faint. That is heaven's order. Why? They that wait upon the Lord will mount up into heavenly places in Jesus Christ and take the place where God has put them, with their hearts in heaven and their feet on the ground.

+ Some have likened this verse to the three stages of Christian growth that we find in 1 John 2:12–14, which are:

    a. The young Christian will mount as an eagle.

    b. The adult Christian will run.

    c. The mature Christian will walk.

+ The ways of guidance and deliverance are open to us if we are prepared to stop arguing with God and turn to Him with all of our heart.

+ Don't forget, all of this chapter is spoken to a people in exile—God's people, Israel—but it has a profound meaning for us because Isaiah could see the immediate future for Israel and, I am sure, our far-distant future, wherein these words affect our lives, day by day.

How Much Do You Remember?

1. What are these chapters (40–66) entitled?
2. Recall the historical setting of this next section of Scripture.
3. What is the state of the people of Israel in chapter 40?

Your Assignment for Next Week:

1. Review your notes from this lesson.
2. Read Isaiah chapters 41, 42, and 43.
3. Underline your Bible.

Lesson 14 Notes

_____

_____

_____

_____

_____

_____

_____

_____

_____

_____

_____

_____

_____

_____

Lesson 15
CHAPTERS 41, 42, AND 43

CHAPTER 41

This chapter is the great I WILL chapter of the Bible. No fewer than fourteen times in the scope of these verses does God reinforce His authority with this promise, "I will."

Let us take a brief look first at these "I will's." Let us feast upon them and ask that God may make them real to each of us personally. Notice them carefully:

- Verse 10: *"I will strengthen thee…I will help thee…I will uphold thee."*
- Verse 13: *"I…will hold thy right hand…I will help thee."*
- Verse 14: *"I will help thee."*
- Verse 15: *"I will make thee."*
- Verse 17: *"I…will hear them,…I…will not forsake them."*
- Verse 18: *"I will open rivers in high places…I will make the wilderness a pool of water."*
- Verse 19: *"I will plant in the wilderness a cedar…I will set in the desert the fir tree."*
- Verse 27: *"I will give to Jerusalem one that bringeth good tidings."*

When God says, *"I will,"* He says it with all authority and omnipotence. He has foreseen every difficulty and every obstacle that may come. He has anticipated every possible contingency. He knows the weakness of the one to whom He makes His promise, and yet, He says, *"I will."*

No wonder, therefore, that three times in this chapter, there is a further word of encouragement in verses 10, 13, and 14: *"Fear thou not,"* and *"Fear not."*

During the study of this chapter, we will not take it in consecutive order as we have in the past chapters. We will teach a verse and then see if other verses in the chapter shed light on it. Therefore, you must read the entire lesson in order to understand God's meaning of chapter 41.

1. VERSE 1
   - Here, the almighty God calls to the uttermost ends of the earth for a consultation to settle an issue finally, and the test that is proposed is very simple. The gods of heathen nations are invited to predict events in the future, or to show that they had any understanding of events of former days.
   - We find this spelled out in detail in verses 21–22:

     Produce your cause, saith the Lord; *bring forth your strong reasons, saith the King of Jacob. Let them bring them forth, and shew us what shall happen: let them shew the former things, what they be, that we may consider them, and know the latter end of them; or declare us things for to come.*

     Here is the challenge of One who claims to be omnipotent directed against all who claim to be worthy of the worship of another, and He says, in essence, "Very well then, come before Me."

2. VERSE 2
   - There is one referred to in this verse but basically you will notice that Jehovah demonstrates His ability to do the very things that He challenges other gods to do.
   - As to the past, He has raised up one from the east whom He called in righteousness. Most writers will refer to Cyrus but this one here in verse 2 does not fit the description of Cyrus at all. This reference is to Abraham. He *"called him to his foot…and made him rule over kings."*

- As to the future, in verse 25, it says He would raise up one from the North who would lead His people from captivity. This is a reference to Cyrus, king of Persia.
- Thus, God demonstrated His ability to explain the past and predict the future, and He is not afraid to face the whole world and challenge every idol to do the same. God is still on the throne.

3. VERSES 5–7

- The result of this challenge was a great commotion. Fear struck the people as they drew near, and since God was to judge right and wrong, you will find a graphic picture of the reactions of people in verse 7.
- In the emergency, many resorted to making a temporary idol following their refusal to look to the Lord. They industriously polished up their dilapidated gods and made new ones, determined to put the best show upon their idol worship that they could. But when they faced the Lord God, the idols were dumb—not one of them could speak. Not one of them had a word to say concerning the subject submitted to them.
- As the Lord looked upon them in verses 28–29, He declared that there was no counselor who could answer a word: *"Behold, they are all vanity; their works are nothing: their molten images are wind and confusion"* (verse 29). They had no answer to the challenge of omnipotence.
- This speaks not merely of Jewish history but also of contemporary Christianity, in which the church stands in the midst of a tremendous battlefield. The spiritual conflict experienced today is exactly of the same nature and the same character as you find depicted here in chapter 41. The issue is still unsettled in the minds of people, though it is settled eternally in the mind of God. The world is making every effort to put the best possible show upon its worship of the creature rather than the Creator. Its worship is more the patronizing of the shell of religion than bowing in submission before an empty cross, an occupied throne, and the King of Kings in glory.
- This tremendous spiritual battle between God and those who would challenge His authority is rapidly coming to a climax in which He will demonstrate His authority once and for all, and the whole world will be on its face before the throne of God in acknowledgement that He is the King of Kings.
- Here then, in these people, the church, God is to manifest His glory to every idol, every heathen, every individual, and will reveal to them that He is in fact omnipotent and His interest is in His people. If this be so, what do I expect to find concerning His people? They must be invested with a great deal of power to stand such days as these and, presumably, we are going to find them in high and influential places. We would expect to find them in possession of great ability and talent, possibly possessed with quite an amount of earthly goods, men who are able to meet men on their intellectual level and answer back. In short, men of some prominence. Do I find God's people there? I do not.
- Isaiah 41:17 describes them as poor and needy. They seek water and there is none. The heights are bare, and the valleys without pasture. Their journey takes them through the wilderness. They are as powerless as a weak, wiggling worm (verse 14). It is among people like this that God finds His own, not among the wise or the prudent, but among the babes. Not among the high and the mighty, but among the lowly and the obscure, the nobodies. This is how the apostle Paul described Christians in 1 Corinthians 1:26–29:

  > *For ye see your calling, brethren, how that not many wise men after the flesh, not many mighty, not many noble, are called: but God hath chosen the foolish things of the world to confound the wise; and God hath chosen the weak things of the world to confound the things which are mighty; and base things of the world, and things which are despised, hath God chosen, yea, and things which are not, to bring to nought things that are: that no flesh should glory in his presence.*

- It is people like this in whom God is interested, and it is such people through whom He works. The greatest blessing to the Lord is the man who is poor in spirit, persecuted, emptied, suffering, and starving for God. To such a man, God says, *"Fear thou not; for I am with thee."* He comes nearer to him and says, *"I will strengthen thee."* And then He comes still nearer, and says, *"I will help thee,"* until He puts His arm around him and says, *"I will uphold thee with the right hand of my righteousness"* (verse 10).

- All of us at one time or another feels as though we have suffered far more than is due. Listen to the voice of our loving Lord as He speaks with all authority: *"I am with thee."* He knew what would happen; He foresaw it and permitted it, for nothing has ever happened in the lives of His people but that it has first passed through His presence. The Good Shepherd goes before His sheep.

4. VERSES 14–15

- He is with us not only in identity and in sympathy, but He is also with us in transforming power.

- In verse 14, the Lord speaks to the *"worm Jacob."* Then, in verse 15, He says, *"I will make thee a new sharp threshing instrument having teeth."* I don't know of anyone other than the Creator Himself who can take a weak worm and make it sharp with teeth. God can do that.

5. VERSES 18–20

- We must remember that in the words of Paul, we have been made a spectacle to the world, a gazing stock of men. (See 1 Corinthians 4:9.) This is how God deals with His people for it to be a testimony, so that they can show His greatness and His love.

- Yes, He makes us like this and puts us through it all but what seems to be a desert in the minds of an onlooker has become the garden of the Lord in the soul.

So, in this chapter, we find God dealing with individuals in verses 1–6, and then dealing with Israel in verses 7–20, and then overturning and overthrowing the idols in verses 21–29.

Confusion is the end result of idolatry, or any philosophy that is anti-God or atheistic. It does not have an answer to the problems of life. Man-made systems cannot satisfy the human heart. The answer is found in the *"one that bringeth good tidings"* (verse 27).

CHAPTER 42

It seems imperative that we discover and distinguish the two separate servants mentioned in this chapter.

The Messiah, Jesus, is definitely in view in verses 1–7. In Matthew 12:17–21, there is an application of this prophecy to Jesus Christ. In Mark 1:1–13, we see the beginning of the gospel that goes back to Isaiah 40. You will remember that in Isaiah 40, there is a forerunner introduced who, in turn, introduces the Messiah. In Mark, He is God's servant. (See Mark 10:45.) Since Mark emphasizes the humanity of Jesus, it seems that the servant character of the Messiah is given in order to set forth Jesus, the man. He identified Himself with the nation Israel that He might become the representative of that nation as a servant. It is said of Jesus that He *"took upon him the form of a servant, and was made in the likeness of men"* (Philippians 2:7). It is well to emphasize again that when Jesus became a man, He not only identified Himself with all humanity, but He also specifically identified Himself with the nation Israel, *"of whom as concerning the flesh Christ came"* (Romans 9:5). As the servant of Jehovah, He was obedient to the Father's will. He did not obey men.

In this chapter, you will find a broad outline such as this:

- The servant of Jehovah – Jesus – verses 1–7

- The denunciation of idols – verses 8–17

- The other servant in this chapter – the nation Israel – verses 18–25

Before we begin, let us identify some of the words at the beginning of this chapter over in the New Testament. Turn to Matthew 12:14–21. We have no problem relating the One referred to here with the first verses of Isaiah 42. It all centers around our blessed Lord.

1. VERSE 1
    + The word *"behold"* is a bugle call to arrest our attention and fix our eyes on Jesus. It reminds us of Hebrews 3:1: *"Consider the Apostle and High Priest of our profession, Christ Jesus."* Consider Jesus as the theme of this section. It is "looking unto Jesus" that will keep us from all modern forms of idolatry.
    + *"My servant"* is the descriptive title that gives the tone of this new section of Isaiah. The servant character of Christ becomes dominate and prominent in this last section of Isaiah. Here, we see Christ in the role of a servant.
    + You recall that the previous chapter painted a vivid picture of the conflict that goes on constantly and is continuing between the forces of righteousness and the forces of evil. That chapter concluded with a statement of absolute helplessness on the part of men: *"Behold, they are all vanity; their works are nothing: their molten images are wind and confusion"* (Isaiah 41:29).
    + By contrast we see, *"Behold my servant."* When all else fails, that is the time to look up and behold the Lamb of God.
    + Notice in this first verse what is said about Christ: *"My servant, whom I uphold."* It seems as though we are introduced, for a moment, into the sacred councils of the Godhead, where we hear the Father saying of the Son, "My servant—behold Him whom I uphold." This verse also tells us that He is One upon whom the Spirit of God dwells in all fullness. Therefore this God, who is trusted, upheld, loved, and anointed in heaven, is the one who cannot fail. He will bring forth judgment to the coasts (isles) and to the ends of the earth.

2. VERSE 2
    + We are always in a hurry whereas God is never in haste. We are often so noisy while He is quiet and still. *"He shall not cry, nor lift up, nor cause his voice to be heard in the street."* The Lord does not need fanfare, pomp, or splendor, neither talent nor special learning. He works in silence. We should see that our Lord is a perfect gentleman and that He never forces His will or attention upon those who resist it.

3. VERSE 3
    + This verse is quoted in Matthew 12:20. The servant of Jehovah, Jesus Christ, is great in mercy toward His people. In Matthew 12, we find that the Lord Jesus was being assaulted by the scribes and Pharisees but refused to enter into controversy with them. They were merely bruised reeds and smoking flax. Had He chosen to do so, He could have broken them to pieces, but He did not come to drive out sin by argument or force but rather to expel it by putting truth and righteousness in its place.
    + Notice Matthew 12:20: *"A bruised reed shall he not break, and smoking flax shall he not quench, till he send forth judgment unto victory."* In other words, when He does send forth judgment unto victory, that will be the end of every bruised reed and every smoking flax—for the hypocrite, the Pharisee, the formalist, and all other enemies will then be finished. That is the primary meaning of these words, and from them, we might do well to learn that the greatest way to fight what is wrong is to display truth. If you see a crooked stick in front of you, there is no need to start demonstrating to other people just how crooked it is; they can see that. Place a straight one alongside the crooked one and the straightness of the one will rebuke the crookedness of the other. If you want to stand against sin, live Christ; if you want to rebuke error, live the truth. This is the lesson to be learned from the Lord's words.

- ◆ There is another meaning here, however. A bruised reed is something that has suffered an injury. It is not entirely broken or beyond repair; it is bruised. A smoking flax is something that is almost but not quite dying out. There is a spark somewhere, for it is still smoking. In the case of the smoking flax, if it is allowed to continue, it will burst into flames.

- ◆ What is a bruised reed? Was it a small plant under the heel of a man? Or a flute made out of a stock? The analogy is something like that. When a life is crushed and stepped on, the Lord Jesus picks up that life and puts it back together. Then that life can make a sound of joy and praise.

- ◆ The smoking flax is a dimly lighted wick, barely a flame. Have you ever seen a man or woman with almost no hope left in their life? Maybe just a spark of hope and then the Lord stands beside that person and pours in the oil of the Holy Spirit. That person becomes not a dimly lighted wick any longer but a raging fire because the Lord has added new life and meaning.

4. VERSE 4

- ◆ This verse applies to our Lord: *"He shall not fail nor be discouraged."* This verse can again be compared with Matthew 12:20.

5. VERSE 5

- ◆ God rests His authority upon the fact that He is the Creator.

6. VERSE 6

- ◆ Jesus is the Light of the world. Specifically, He is the light for the Gentiles. Notice in verse 1, that He will bring forth judgment to the Gentiles, and then, in verse 6, He is a light for the Gentiles. The prophets connected the Gentiles with Christ in a threefold way:

    a. First, as the Light, He brings salvation to the Gentiles. (See Luke 2:32; Acts 13:47.)

    b. Second, as *"a root of Jesse"* (Romans 15:12), Christ is to reign over the Gentiles in His millennial kingdom. (See Isaiah 11:10.) The salvation of the Gentiles is the distinctive feature of this present age. (See Ephesians 2:11–12.)

    c. Third, believing Gentiles during this Church Age—together with the believing Jews—constitute *"the church, which is his body"* (Ephesians 1:22–23).

- ◆ Remember that the prophets did not understand the great predictions of the suffering Messiah— the meaning of His death, the institution of the church—because all of that was hidden in the heart and mind of God. They merely caught a glimpse of what was to be, but they did not know the full meaning of it.

7. VERSE 7

- ◆ Christ was to open the eyes and release the prisoners and to bring light to those in darkness. He did these things when He came the first time.

8. VERSE 8

- ◆ Here, we begin the section of the Scripture where the Lord God talks to Israel about who He is and instructs them, once again, in reference to idols. God never shares His essential glory with any other creature. There is a glory that He gives to us in His church, which is found in John 17:22: *"And the glory which thou gavest me I have given them; that they may be one, even as we are one."* God never permits any creature to take His place as God in the affections and devotions of His creatures.

- ◆ In verse 8, He declares who He is, then He says, *"My glory will I not give to another, neither my praise to graven images."*

9. VERSE 9

- ◆ The *"former things"* of verse 9 are a reference to Isaiah's prediction of Sennacherib's invasion and its results, described in Isaiah 10 and also in Isaiah 37. Since the former things had come about, the

Lord also said that new things He would declare before they came to pass. Only God can predict the future accurately.

10. VERSES 10–12

+ Isaiah calls for the praise of the people toward the Lord God, and He does not leave out any segment of society. He even declares that all people in the wilderness, like the villages of Kedar, a desert city, and even those who live in the mountains, should sing and give glory to the Lord.

+ You will notice in verse 12 the word *"islands."* Verses 4 and 10 refer to "isles." This literally means "the sea-washed shores" and refers to the continents where all the Gentiles dwell,

11. VERSES 13–20

+ Here, we begin a passage describing the chastening of Israel. In the proper setting, this is the Lord dealing with Israel through His servant, Jesus Christ. Notice in verse 13 that He will cry, He will roar, and He will prevail.

+ Then, in verse 14, we have the words of the Lord God Himself, and this continues through verse 20. This is self-explanatory with one exception that we should look at in verse 19.

+ In verse 19, we find the other servant of this chapter—Israel. After the chastening words of the Lord, He sums it up by saying, *"Who is blind, but my servant? or deaf, as my messenger that I sent? who is blind as he that is perfect, and blind as the Lord's servant?"* In other words, who is more blind than those who should not be blind, such as My servant who knows me—Israel. They have seen and heard many things, and yet they have not seen nor heard at all, according to verse 20.

12. VERSES 21–25

+ As a continuation of what the Lord God has said, Isaiah says that the Lord will magnify the law and make it honorable.

+ In verse 24, who gave Jacob or Israel for a spoil—did not the Lord? Isaiah continues with his judgmental remarks toward the nation of Israel through the end of chapter 42, but the scene changes as we enter into chapter 43.

CHAPTER 43

In this chapter, we will see the chosen nation redeemed and restored. We will see God's faithfulness to Israel. Sections in Scripture such as this make it tantamount to unbelief to deny that God has no further purpose with the nation Israel. There is no greater sorrow than the tendency to identify Israel with the church and the church with Israel. Such an interpretation of the Bible brings a student to a conclusion like the liberal who says the book is full of confusion.

1. VERSES 1–7

+ God's faithfulness to Israel is one of the paramount promises in Scripture that we can depend on. This is shown in verses 1–7.

+ The sovereign purpose of God for Israel is His unconditional promise that He made with Abraham, and which He reemphasizes throughout the Old Testament.

2. VERSES 8–10

+ God as Creator operates in His dealings with His people by grace. They are blind and deaf, although they have eyes and ears. God can make them see and hear. If all the nations are gathered together, and if they have gods that they think are superior, bring them forth and see if they can predict the future—of course they cannot. God never recognizes an idol or anyone who thinks they are equal with Him because He alone is God.

3. VERSE 11

- Likewise, He recognizes no one in the saving business. If there is no other savior than God, and if Jesus is that Savior, then Jesus is God.

4. VERSE 12

- When God's people eliminate idolatry, then God will move and save. Israel was a witness to the whole world in a world of many gods. They were to bear witness to the unity of the Godhead. The church is to bear witness to the trinity of the Godhead.

5. VERSE 13

- The word *"let"* means "to hinder." God is before all creation. Time is a "created thing." No creature can slip out of the hand of God or escape His reach.

6. VERSES 14–15

- The ultimate destruction of Babylon is foretold, and you find that in the word *"Chaldeans."* Surely it is inescapable that the nation Israel is in view. God takes responsibility for bringing them into existence.

- Every anti-Semitic group or person should ponder this statement *"the creator of Israel."*

7. VERSES 16–19

- First, we find a reference to the crossing of the Red Sea in verses 16–17.

- Then, in verses 18–19, we find that the reason for forgetting was because the new thing would so outshine the former that it would become insignificant. The little candle makes a noticeable light in the midnight darkness but the sun at midday, essentially, puts it out, even though it is still burning. The new thing mentioned here is the miraculous manner in which God will regather Israel.

8. VERSES 20–22

- This speaks of the manner in which God will preserve and restore Israel into their own land, and it also speaks of God's eternal purpose with the nation Israel. They have, and they had, forgotten God, but their present condition is no barometer for what God will do for them in the future.

9. VERSES 23–24

- They had failed to bring the sacrifices that looked forward to the sacrifice of Christ upon the cross. They were tempting God to fellowship with them as undiluted sinners who failed to recognize their sins. All of this caused God to be *"wearied."*

10. VERSE 25

- Their neglect to offer that which was typical of Christ's death would not deter God from sending Him to die so that sin might be blotted out for those who accept Him.

11. VERSE 26

- This verse reminds us of Isaiah 1:18.

12. VERSE 27

- This is a reference to Abraham. Surely Scripture records his failures and his sins. We have only to mention the matter of his lying to Pharaoh about Sarah, his wife. The term *"thy teachers"* means "interpreters." Those who interpreted God to the people had faults and sins, such as Samson, Samuel, and David.

13. VERSE 28

- Their present condition is a judgment from God but it is not the final state for Israel.

How Much Do You Remember?

1. Following their refusal to look to the Lord, how did the people respond in an emergency, as noted in chapter 41?
2. What three groups is God dealing with in chapter 41?
3. How is Christ portrayed in the beginning of chapter 42?
4. What can we glean from Christ's example in chapter 42:3 about fighting what is wrong?
5. Who is the other servant in chapter 42?

Your Assignment for Next Week:

1. Review your notes from this lesson.
2. Read Isaiah chapters 44, 45, 46, 47, and 48.
3. Underline your Bible.

Lesson 15 Notes

_____

_____

_____

_____

_____

_____

_____

_____

_____

_____

_____

_____

_____

_____

_____

_____

_____

_____

_____

_____

_____

_____

Lesson 16
CHAPTERS 44, 45, 46, 47, AND 48

CHAPTER 44

This chapter continues the theme of the last chapter; however, the last chapter closes with the dire mention of a coming judgment. This chapter moves directly into the light of the coming kingdom. That is the time when the Holy Spirit will be poured out upon all flesh. This chapter includes a brilliant and bitter satire against idolatry. This is the recurring theme of this section of Scripture. The human heart has a way of turning from God to various idols. Today, we do not go after graven images but anything to which a person gives himself, instead of to the true God, is an idol. I have mentioned these idols in previous chapters but to reemphasize, we can make an idol out of money, fame, pleasure, sex, alcohol, self-adoration, and even business and family.

The high point of the prophet's controversy or argument against idolatry will come in chapter 46. There, we will have occasion to consider this subject further and to examine the real distinction between God and idols.

The last verse of chapter 44 obviously belongs in chapter 45, and again, it is a good example of the mistakes that were made in chapter divisions. The chapter divisions have nothing to do with the inspiration of the Scriptures. Here, we will see that the last verse is concerning Cyrus and it rightfully belongs in chapter 45.

1. VERSE 1
   - The nation Israel is still designated as a servant, as you will see here, as well as in verses 2 and 21 of this chapter. We learned this also back in Isaiah 42:18–25.
   - Note also here in verse 1 the twofold name given to the nation—Jacob and Israel.

2. VERSE 2
   - Here the Lord God adds another name to Israel and Jacob and that name is *Jesurun*, which means "the upright." This name corresponds to Israel but is in contrast to *Jacob*, which means "the crooked." Jesurun occurs first in Deuteronomy 32:15 and 33:5, 26—and apparently is a synonym for Israel.

3. VERSE 3
   - Here we have the promise of God to pour out His Spirit upon Israel. That has not taken place yet and is not to be confused with the Day of Pentecost. This passage in Isaiah 44:3 corresponds to Joel 2:28–32:

     And it shall come to pass afterward, that I will pour out my spirit upon all flesh; and your sons and your daughters shall prophesy, your old men shall dream dreams, your young men shall see visions: and also upon the servants and upon the handmaids in those days will I pour out my spirit. And I will shew wonders in the heavens and in the earth, blood, and fire, and pillars of smoke. The sun shall be turned into darkness, and the moon into blood, before the great and terrible day of the LORD come. And it shall come to pass, that whosoever shall call on the name of the LORD shall be delivered: for in mount Zion and in Jerusalem shall be deliverance, as the LORD hath said, and in the remnant whom the LORD shall call.

   - Obviously, all of these things were not fulfilled at Pentecost. In fact, none of these things were fulfilled. All that Peter said was that it was similar to what Joel had promised (Joel's context is all in the future):

But this is that which was spoken by the prophet Joel; And it shall come to pass in the last days, saith God, I will pour out of my Spirit upon all flesh: and your sons and your daughters shall prophesy, and your young men shall see visions, and your old men shall dream dreams: and on my servants and on my handmaidens I will pour out in those days of my Spirit; and they shall prophesy: and I will shew wonders in heaven above, and signs in the earth beneath; blood, and fire, and vapour of smoke: The sun shall be turned into darkness, and the moon into blood, before the great and notable day of the Lord come: and it shall come to pass, that whosoever shall call on the name of the Lord shall be saved. (Acts 2:16–21)

+ The Spirit was not poured out on *all flesh* at Pentecost. After two thousand years, it is still not *"all."* It will be in the kingdom of which both Joel and Isaiah spoke. You will find this spelled out in detail in my notes on Isaiah 32:15.

4. VERSE 4
+ This speaks of 100 percent fruit-bearing in the kingdom of Christ.

5. VERSE 5
+ The nation Israel will confess that they belong to Jehovah in that day. He will not be ashamed of the lowly name of Jacob, and some will even appropriate the lofty name of Israel.

6. VERSE 6
+ This is an assertion concerning monotheism. Notice the title that God claims in relation to His people: *"King of Israel," "Redeemer," "Lord of hosts," "the first, and…the last."* He concludes by stating, *"Beside me there is no God."*

7. VERSE 7
+ Here, the Lord God does what He has done so many times in the past in Isaiah. He says, in essence, "If there is another god, let him come forward and declare the future." This is the real test.

8. VERSE 8
+ Israel is a witness to the oneness of God. They were to bear witness to monotheism. If there were another god, surely the omniscient God would have at least heard of him.

9. VERSE 9
+ Here begins the brilliant satire against idolatry. Those who make images are witnesses to the senseless character of their gods. An image does not even have the five senses of the human being. An image cannot see or hear.

10. VERSE 10
+ The people create their gods instead of the gods creating the people. This is a vain and unprofitable business.

11. VERSE 11
+ God makers—idol makers—should be ashamed.

12. VERSE 12
+ First of all, the one who works with metals works hard to forge a god, but this labor weakens him and reveals that he is but a man. It is ironic that a poor, frail man could make a god that will not be strong enough to help the poor, frail man.

13. VERSE 13
+ The carpenter now contributes his talent and labor to make the false god. First of all, the god is put on a drawing board and is measured. Imagine measuring the infinite God. When the carpenter finishes, the image looks like a man, not God. What irony.

14. VERSE 14

    + The origin of a man-made god begins in the forest. It is first a tree, which the real God has created. Those idols made from wood do not create the tree but vice versa.

15. VERSE 15

    + The chips and scraps from the production of a wooden god are used to kindle a fire for the man to warm himself and to bake bread. This is the only practical and helpful contribution that comes from the making of a false god. In fact, the scraps are more helpful than the image.

16. VERSE 16

    + So the only value of the wooden idol comes from the scraps that warm the body and cook the food; therefore, the scraps do more for the man than the idol can do.

17. VERSE 17

    + This is a biting satire. Actually, the idol of wood and metal constitutes the scraps that a man sets up and bows before as his god.

18. VERSE 18

    + Men proved themselves to be as senseless as the idol they worshipped by this procedure.

19. VERSE 19

    + They do not realize that the warming of the body and the cooking of the meal with the wood is a good thing, and that when part of the wood is worshipped, it becomes an abomination.

20. VERSE 20

    + Idolatry is self-deception.

21. VERSE 21

    + In verses 21–27, we find God prompting Israel to remember Jehovah.

    + Israel is urged to turn from such atrocious acts. They are to remember that God formed them and He will not forget them.

22. VERSE 22

    + God has done something no idol can do: He has redeemed Israel.

23. VERSE 23

    + All creation is to join in praising God because He is Israel's Redeemer—even the forests are to praise God.

24. VERSE 24

    + God is both Redeemer and Creator.

25. VERSE 25

    + God will bring confusion to the worldly wise who deny Him.

26. VERSE 26

    + Again, God makes it clear that Jerusalem and the cities of Judah are still in His program for the future.

27. VERSE 27

    + Here we see a reference to the Red Sea crossing and a look into their coming deliverance.

28. VERSE 28

    + This is a remarkable prophecy concerning Cyrus. He is named here about two hundred years before he was born. He is designated as *"my shepherd."* This is the only instance in which a pagan potentate is given such a title. He is one of the unusual pictures of Christ, which we will develop further in the next chapter.

CHAPTER 45

It is rather unfortunate that the last verse of chapter 44 is not the first verse of this chapter. It is indeed remarkable that Cyrus would be named and identified two hundred years before he was born. This unusual prophecy has caused liberal critics to construct, out of the web of imagination, the figment of "the great unknown" or "the second Isaiah." The fact that Isaiah could name a man two centuries before he appears is too strong a tonic for the weak faith of an unbeliever. Don't forget that Isaiah also named Christ many times and depicted parts of His life as well as His death. This chapter is filled with prophecy and, at the same time, it takes our minds back to the creation of the universe.

1. VERSE 1
    + Cyrus is named and identified before he is born. About two hundred years elapsed between this prophecy and the appearance of Cyrus. It would be humanly impossible to perform this feat outside of the leadership of the Spirit of God.
    + Jesus was named and identified two thousand years before He came. (See Genesis 49:10.)
    + Cyrus is given titles of dignity that make him a Gentile figure of Christ. He is called *"shepherd"* in the last verse of chapter 44, a title that prefigures Christ.
    + He is also given the title of *"anointed."* This is quite remarkable. Doubtless, Cyrus was given this title because he delivered them from captivity and permitted them to return to the Land of Promise. He also encouraged those who remained to send rich gifts of gold, silver, and precious things with those returned. In this respect, he was a Gentile messiah of Israel and a vague foreshadowing of the One who was to come.
    + *"The two leaved gates"* is a reference to the numerous gates of Babylon that kept Israel from returning to Palestine.
    + Cyrus, the Persian, was the nephew of the king of Media. Media and Persia were, as a rule, closely related. They sprang from the same stock and it was these kingdoms, united together, that eventually conquered Chaldea. Babylon became one of the chief cities of the Persian Empire until its destruction. Secular history gives full details about this conquest. Cyrus eventually took Babylon by turning aside waters of the Euphrates into another channel, so he came in on the riverbed under the two-leaved gates, the gates of the river itself. Cyrus was a legendary figure.
2. VERSE 2
    + God also broke down the gates of Babylon, which had shut Cyrus out and permitted him to go in and capture this strong nation.
3. VERSE 3
    + The rich treasures of Babylon, which the kings of Babylon had taken as spoils of war from all nations, especially from Jerusalem, fell to Cyrus.
4. VERSE 4
    + The question may rightly be asked why God would mark out this lone king and identify him by name. The answer is found here. It was to let His people, Israel, know that He had not forsaken them. They would be able to recognize Cyrus when he appeared in history and they would be assured he was their deliverer. What joyful assurance this must have been to God's people when Cyrus came to the throne. He was and is a character in history. The ruins of his tomb have been found in Iran, which bears this inscription: "I am Cyrus the Great, who gave the Persians an empire and was the King of Asia. Grudge me not, therefore, this monument."

5. VERSE 5

   + This was God's word to Cyrus. Cyrus was a monotheist, as were all the Persians. They did not worship idols, but this does not mean that they knew the true God. Here, God introduces Himself to them as the one God who has no equal, and the One who chose Cyrus.

6. VERSES 6–7

   + Zoroastrianism began and flourished among the Persians. It claimed that Mazda was the god of light. God says He creates light and that Mazda is no god. Darkness was the god of evil. God takes responsibility for darkness even though He does not create evil. The better translation for *"evil"* is "sorrow" or "difficulties," which are the fruits of sin. This is the Old Testament way of saying, *"The wages of sin is death"* (Romans 6:23).

7. VERSE 8

   + God does create all good things and the fruits of good things.

8. VERSES 9–10

   + There may be some who will protest God's taking the future in His hand like this, even choosing and naming a king. These verses are God's answer to that. It reminds us of Romans 9:19–21.

9. VERSE 11

   + God can be proven and tested by prophecy.

10. VERSE 12

    + God claims to be the Creator. Note that He stretched out the heavens and He created all the hosts—bodies of the universe. Don't forget that space is a creation itself.

11. VERSES 13–14

    + The enemies of Israel will finally come to recognize Cyrus as the leader, under the leadership of the Lord God.

12. VERSE 15

    + This is the heart-cry of the prophet in praying that God's ways are unfathomable.

13. VERSE 16

    + Confusion is the end of those who oppose God. The world is moving again toward a tower of Babel.

14. VERSE 17

    + Those who believe God is through with Israel should take a long look at this passage. Israel's salvation is as sure as our salvation; His covenant-keeping is a must.

15. VERSE 18

    + Here we are taken back to the creation and reminded that He did not create the earth and the heavens in vain but that some catastrophe produced this state. (See Genesis 1:2.)

16. VERSE 19

    + Another test of God's dealings is the fact that they are right.

17. VERSES 20–21

    + The whole world is urged to turn to God. God is one God; He is just; He is the Savior.

18. VERSE 22

    + This is the verse that was responsible for the conversion of Charles Spurgeon.

19. VERSE 23

    + Read Philippians 2:10–11.

20. VERSE 24
   + The prophet saw that the righteousness of God alone sufficed for the salvation of man.
21. VERSE 25
   + The Lord alone can justify Israel as He alone can justify us. Notice that *"all the seed of Israel be justified."*

We have now been introduced to Cyrus, who eventually would allow Israel to leave exile in Babylon and return to their Promised Land—the land God had given to them—to rebuild the city walls and temple according to Ezra and Nehemiah. God had a plan and a purpose for the Babylonian captivity, which has yet to come and this is a part of the prophecy that Isaiah predicts. The Lord God keeps talking about idols—false gods—and He emphasizes over and over again that He is the one true God. He intended for Israel to learn a lesson because they were His people, chosen for His purpose. What was His purpose for Israel? What was to come out of the Babylonian captivity?

1. Israel was to witness to the unity of God in the midst of idolatry. (See Isaiah 43:10–12 and all the Scriptures we studied in this lesson).
2. To illustrate to the nations the blessedness of serving the true God. (See 1 Chronicles 17:20–21; Psalm 144:15; Deuteronomy 33:26–29.)
3. To receive, preserve, and transmit the cannon of Scripture. (See Romans 3:1–2; Deuteronomy 4:5–8.)
4. To produce, as to His humanity, the Messiah. (See Isaiah 7:14, 9:6; Matthew 1:1; Romans 1:3; 2 Samuel 7:12–16.)

According to the prophets, Israel, regathered from all nations and restored to her own land, is yet to have her greatest earthly exaltation and glory.

CHAPTER 46

This chapter contains one of the finest satires against idolatry found in the Word of God. Satire uses irony to ridicule the object of its contempt, usually in writing. The chapter opens with the announcement of the defeat of the idols of Babylon. This seems strange since Babylon had not yet come to the front as a world power. Nevertheless, Babylon was a major source of idolatry, and it is fitting that after announcing the defeat of the idols of Babylon, the prophet proceeds to denounce all idolatry, with an injunction to Israel not to forsake their God. With bitter irony and biting ridicule, this chapter portrays the helpless state of the idols to render any real assistance in times of emergency. This sharp distinction between God and idols is emphasized. God had carried and borne Israel through the long, weary centuries of their sinful past. An idol is something you have to bear as a burden and carry if it is to get anywhere.

The real distinction between the true God and idols is simply this: does your God carry you? Or do you carry your god? Is your religion a burden-bearer or is it a burden? This is the basic difference between the true and the false.

1. VERSE 1
   + Bel and Nebo are gods of Babylon. Bel is the shortened form of Baal and is found in the first part of the name Beelzebub. *Beelzebub* means "Satan" or "the devil." *Nebo* means "speaker" or "prophet." I think you can see from these two signs something that we learned in Revelation. Bel is to be personified in the anti-Christ. Nebo, being the speaker and a prophet, is a picture or a type of the false prophet. That is the far-off, distant meaning for us today. Another name for these two is Jupiter for Bel and Mercury for Nebo.

In this modern day, we are not given to idolatry of the same type that Babylon had in its day but Satan is still our enemy and the battles rages on another front. (See Ephesians 6:10–18.) Covetousness is considered idolatry in this day. For instance, read Colossians 3:5 and note especially the last three words: *"which is idolatry."*

2. VERSE 2

    ◆   In times of crisis, the idols could not deliver but were defeated instead.

3. VERSE 3

    ◆   This should constitute a red warning light on the highway Israel was traveling. God had been carrying Israel.

4. VERSE 4

    ◆   Here is a distinction between the true and the false: God had not only been carrying the nation, but He had also carried each individual from the cradle to the grave.

    ◆   The word *"hoar"* means "white" or "white-headed."

    ◆   God carries our sins. *"He hath borne our griefs, and carried our sorrows"* (Isaiah 53:4).

5. VERSE 5

    ◆   The reason that it is so difficult to explain God is because He is infinite while we are finite and live in a finite universe. There is nothing with which to compare God. He cannot be reduced to our terminology without losing all meaning. He cannot be translated into human language. This explains one of the reasons why Christ came in the form of man. Jesus revealed God; Jesus redeemed men.

6. VERSE 6

    ◆   Here begins the satire on idolatry. This is a metallic image that exceeds the wooden image in beauty and value. Here, the wealth of man is expended in making an idol—the best of materials, the genius of mind, the skill of man's hands, and the devotion of his heart. Men worship their own workmanship and, in turn, they actually worship themselves because of what they have done.

7. VERSE 7

    ◆   After such an outlay of money, time, and effort, you would think the idol would reciprocate by doing something for man—at least make his burden lighter. On the contrary, the idol becomes a burden and must be carried as added weight. How utterly ridiculous is idolatry. We might ask ourselves the question: Does our religion carry us or do we carry it? Is it a millstone or a stepping stone?

8. VERSE 8

    ◆   God calls upon men to act as intelligent creatures and not as animals. (See Isaiah 1:18.) If they would only reason away the folly of idolatry, it would deter them from committing an abomination.

9. VERSE 9

    ◆   God suggests that they scan their past history containing the unmistakable leading of the Lord. Is that not enough to stir their hearts?

10. VERSE 10

    ◆   Not only is the past a stimulus to faith but the future is even more so. God has moved into the area where no man or idol dares to go. He moves into the future and records prophecy as if it were history. It always comes to pass in just the way God predicted. This reveals the superiority of God.

11. VERSE 11

    ◆   This is a strange prophecy. He does not predict a glorious future in the immediate days ahead for His people. A ravenous bird is coming up against His people. This has to be Babylon. Jesus predicted that birds would roost in the mustard tree and birds would take the sown seed away. He predicted for our day not worldwide conversion but total apostasy.

12. VERSES 12–13
   + There will be salvation for Israel and God will not delay when that time comes. There is a glorious day beyond the night of weeping, and this is sure because God has spoken it.

CHAPTER 47

This is the fourth occasion in this study in which we have considered the prediction of the doom of Babylon. We saw this in chapters 13, 14, and 21. This is indeed remarkable in view of the fact that Babylon, at this time, was a small and insignificant kingdom. This was almost a century before it would become a world power. It had been in existence since the days of the Tower of Babel and had influenced the world with confusion. There is a spiritual meaning for us that has nothing to do with the Babylon of the past. The Babylon of the past lies under the rubble and ruins of judgment. Its glory is diminished by the accumulated dust of the centuries. However, we can see this Babylonian tendency today in the political realm. The captivity of Judah and the fall of Babylon are clearly set before us here.

There cannot be a shadow of doubt that the ancient, literal Babylon will have a successor in the closing days of this age—not of a material form but of a spiritual and religious character. In Revelation 14:8, we read, *"Babylon is fallen, is fallen."* Then, in Revelation 18:2, we find similar words: *"Babylon the great is fallen… is fallen."* Have we then no interest in Babylon? Surely, we have. The unification of the world politically, welding the present nations of Christendom into oneness, has a corresponding unification of men in the same sphere, religiously, in a universal church, which is clearly foretold in Revelation 17 and 18.

1. VERSE 1
   + *"Come down"* is the command of God to Babylon, similar to how a dog is called to obedience. Babylon is called a *"virgin"* because she had not yet been captured by an army. Before she arrived at the lofty height to which she finally attained, her decline—her fall—is declared in clear terms.

2. VERSE 2
   + This verse describes the indescribable humiliation to which she was to be subjected.

3. VERSE 3
   + Why should God take such awful vengeance upon Babylon? He is not vindictive but He does vindicate His holiness and His righteousness.

4. VERSE 4
   + Israel, in captivity, must look to Jehovah for their deliverance. He has not forsaken them.

5. VERSE 5
   + *"The lady of kingdoms"* is the pet name of Babylon, which speaks of all her comforts, compromise, and confusion. Her fall is inevitable because God has spoken.

6. VERSE 6
   + God delivered His people into the hands of Babylon because they had sinned against Him. He was judging His own people. This is the message of the little prophecy of Habakkuk.

7. VERSE 7
   + God's wrath with His people as mentioned in verse 6 was part of His judgment upon His people, and this fact deceived Babylon. They thought it was by their might and power that they had taken God's people.

8. VERSE 8
   + Babylon was arrogant and careless; not believing that a frightful fall was coming.

9. VERSE 9

   + The suddenness of the fall of Babylon is recorded in Daniel 5. Two things would happen: loss of children and widowhood.

10. VERSE 10

   + Babylon was trusting in her own wickedness, wisdom, and weapons.

11. VERSE 11

   + Again, the swiftness of the destruction of Babylon is forecasted in this verse.

12. VERSE 12

   + God urges Babylon to turn to her witchcraft, which she trusted for a way out. This is a satire which God uses.

13. VERSE 13

   + Confusion characterizes Babylon at this time. The city lives up to its name because Babylon does mean "confusion."

14. VERSE 14

   + Judgment is determined. It will not be deferred.

15. VERSE 15

   + The great economic strength that lay in her commerce could not survive. It dwindled and died.

Now we have discussed the Babylonian captivity and what came out of that captivity. You will find these mentioned in my notes at the end of chapter 45.

When, then, was captivity necessary?

In Jeremiah 25:11–12, we have some indication. This refers us to Leviticus 26:24–43 and 2 Chronicles 36:20–21. The children of Israel had disobeyed God and not observed a Sabbath for a period of 490 years. Therefore, God judged them and made them observe seventy years to make up for the Sabbath years they had missed.

CHAPTER 48

This chapter brings us to the conclusion of the first part of this last major division of Isaiah. The chapter opens with a call to Israel as a whole but before the close of this chapter, there is a distinct difference between the apostate mass of Israel and the remnant of faith, which we notice beginning in verse 12.

1. VERSE 1

   + The whole house of Israel is addressed here—all of those who belonged to the chosen line through Abraham, Isaac, and Jacob. The apostate nation here is given a final injunction to turn back to God. They speak of the God of Israel as if they knew Him. Actually, they had a form of godliness but denied the power thereof.

2. VERSE 2

   + They boast of being citizens of Jerusalem but that is all they are. They are actually strangers to God. God turns from Babylon to those who are called Jews and live that way outwardly. They are of the house of Jacob, even called by that name of honor.

   + Amid those called "Israel," only a few are entitled to that name in its full significance. Paul speaks of this in Romans 9:6: *"For they are not all Israel, which are of Israel."* Paul is not denationalizing any Jew but showing the sovereignty of God in electing Isaac in the place of Ishmael and Jacob in the place of Esau, so the line of promise was not dependent upon accident but upon the sovereignty of God's elective grace. It does not mean that anyone who is by natural birth a Jew is not a Jew. Ishmael could only be Abraham's son, though not in the line of promise. Esau was quite as much the son of Isaac as was Jacob because he couldn't be anything else, but he was not in that line of promise. Thus, all that looks like Israel is not Israel, as far as faith in God is concerned.

3. VERSE 3
   - God had given them ample evidence that He was God by predicting the future, which came to pass as He had said.

4. VERSE 4
   - God knew they were an obstinate people and He piled up evidence to convince them and win their hearts.

5. VERSE 5
   - God told them of the future, lest they give an idol credit for what happened to them.

6. VERSE 6
   - This is the reason God raised up prophets not only to warn but also to speak and predict the future.

7. VERSE 7
   - There was always the danger that these people would smugly say that they already knew these things.

8. VERSE 8
   - They refused to be convinced and turn to God. What a picture of stubbornness. What a picture of the human heart.
   - God will not deal with them according to their sins but He finds the reason within Himself in His mercy and grace.

9. VERSE 10
   - Israel is an elect nation but note the price of election. *"I have chosen thee in the furnace of affliction"* is a statement of historical and doctrinal truth.

10. VERSE 12
    - It would seem here that God is no longer addressing the nation as a whole but confines His word to the remnant labeled *"my called."*

11. VERSE 13
    - He is Creator and Preserver. (See Colossians 1:16–17.)

12. VERSE 14
    - God will deal with Babylon in His own way.

13. VERSES 15–16
    - This is the heart-cry of God in verse 15, and then we see, in verse 16, that here begins the plea of God's messenger, the Lord Jesus Christ.
    - Two of the most famous commentators on the book of Isaiah, C. F. Keil and Franz Delitzsch, said,

    > Since the prophet has not spoken to his own person before, whereas, on the other hand, these words are followed in Isa. 49:1 by an address concerning himself from that servant of Jehovah who announces himself as the restorer of Israel and light of the Gentiles, and who cannot therefore be either Israel as a nation or the author of the prophecies, nothing is more natural than to suppose that the words, "And now hath the Lord," etc., form a prelude to the words of the One unequalled servant of Jehovah concerning Himself which occur in chapter 49. The surprisingly mysterious way in which the words of Jehovah suddenly pass into those of His messenger…can only be explained in this manner.[2]

---

2. C. F. Keil and Franz Delitzsch, *Biblical Commentary on the Old Testament* (Edinburgh: T. and T. Clark, 1866).

+ You will notice that the words, or the voice, is one who is sent from Jehovah. In John 3:34, we find: *"For God giveth not the Spirit by measure."* With the prophets, a partial communication of the mind of God or a fleeting glimpse of His "back side" was all they received, but with Christ, there was no such limit. The Spirit who came with Him, revealed in and by Him, is the very heart of God to man.

14. VERSE 17
   + Note the longing and loving plea of Jehovah to the remnant.

15. VERSE 18
   + Had they obeyed God, they would have experienced both peace and righteousness.

16. VERSE 19
   + God never has been able to bless Israel to the fullest of His promise. That is, likewise, true of the believer. Both Israel and the church have exceedingly precious promises but neither have entered into all the blessings.

17. VERSE 20
   + God urged His people to leave Babylon after the captivity. Only a small remnant returned to build the temple. (See Ezra 2:1, 64; 7:6; and all of Nehemiah.)

18. VERSE 21
   + God takes them back to the deliverance out of Egypt.

19. VERSE 22
   + This is the solemn benediction of this section in which God's servant is set over and against all the idols of the heathen. He alone gives peace.

How Much Do You Remember?

1. In addition to Israel and Jacob, what name does God give to the nation in chapter 44? What meaning does it have?
2. Describe the satires against idolatry found in chapters 44 and 46.
3. Who does Isaiah foretell two hundred years before his existence?
4. Recall the description of the fall of Babylon.

Your Assignment for Next Week:

1. Review your notes from this lesson.
2. Read Isaiah chapters 49, 50, 51, 52, 53.
3. Underline your Bible.

Lesson 16 Notes

_____

_____

_____

_____

_____

_____

_____

Lesson 17
CHAPTERS 49, 50, 51, AND 52

CHAPTER 49

This brings us to the very heart of the book of Isaiah, and to the very heart of the salvation of God. The very "heart of the heart" is found in the fifty-third chapter, with which we are all familiar. Thus far, we have trodden in an outer court. Now we will enter into the holy place, and soon we will be conducted into the Holy of Holies as we arrive at chapter 53.

Israel was the servant of Jehovah but as such, Israel had failed. Now God speaks of another servant of Jehovah, who is the Lord Jesus Christ. This section opens with a discourse of Christ, as truly as the twelve apostles heard such discourses in Galilee. In this chapter, we see Christ moving out to become the Savior of the world. Israel is not forsaken, for her assured restoration to the land is reaffirmed.

In the first part of the chapter, we find Christ speaking in verses 1–6. Then, in verses 7–13, we discover that the Lord God Jehovah is speaking. In verses 14–26, Zion speaks.

1. VERSES 1–3
   - Here, we may boldly say that the speaker is none other than the Lord Jesus Christ, calling on the nations outside of Israel to give ear, for Jehovah had called Him, the virgin's son, and made His name to sound forth even from the first moment of His incarnation. His mouth—that is, His words—have been made so sharp, it is a sword that none, including the Pharisees and Sadducees, the ritualist or the rationalist, could ever stand against. Yet for a time, as an arrow is left in the quiver ready for service, so was He hidden in His lowly home in Nazareth for about thirty years.
   - The term "isles" we have already learned to be the term that is applied to Gentiles.

2. VERSE 4
   - Though He was rejected, and He may look as if He labored in vain, His confidence is in God. Even His death was a victory. The emphasis in this section is on the suffering servant. (See John 1:11.)

3. VERSE 5
   - At His first coming, He did not gather Israel, as they rejected Him. He did something far more wonderful. He wrought salvation for the world. God's purposes were not thwarted by the system of man.

4. VERSE 6
   - God had a far greater purpose in mind than just the regathering of Israel. He was making Christ the light of the world—a light to the Gentiles. (See Acts 13:46–49.)

5. VERSE 7
   - Now we hear Jehovah as He begins to speak. The servant is silent and God addresses Him. He is despised of man from His very soul; He is abhorred, rulers oppress Him; people reject Him. Paul, in 2 Corinthians 6:8, says something similar to what we read here.

6. VERSE 8
   - God heard the prayer of Christ. He whom the nation crucified will be the One kings will bow down to. Every knee must acknowledge His Lordship.

7. VERSE 9
   - The word of reconciliation is now sent to all men.

8. VERSE 10
   + He is speaking here of the physical preservation of the nation.

9. VERSE 11
   + He is here directing our thoughts to the regathering of the nation Israel.

10. VERSE 12
    + Sinim is China, which is eastward. Notice that they will be gathered from all the other directions as well.

11. VERSE 13
    + God's purpose in the earth centers in one nation: Israel. When they are back in the land, both the heavens and the earth can rejoice.

12. VERSE 14
    + Even Israel thinks she is forsaken today.
    + Zion speaks verses 14–21.

13. VERSE 15
    + They had forsaken God.

14. VERSE 16
    + Some people like to have the names of loved ones tattooed on their bodies. God says that He has engraved the name of Israel on the palms of His hands; He cannot forget them.

15. VERSES 17–21
    + God reassures them again that He has neither forgotten nor forsaken them.

16. VERSE 22
    + God assures Israel that the Gentiles will assist Him in the final restoration of the nation to the land. Heretofore, the Gentiles have scattered them. This is rather a remarkable prophecy in this verse.

17. VERSE 23
    + Israel, who is the tail, will someday be the head.

18. VERSES 24–26
    + God will finally redeem Israel. Who is prepared to successfully contradict and refute God's claim?

CHAPTER 50

The person of Christ comes before us more clearly as we come nearer to chapter 53. At first, there was merely a silhouette on every background. Here He is, the suffering servant, subjected to indignities and humiliation. We hear Him speaking in this chapter. This chapter opens with God explaining why He set Israel aside. Isaiah, the prophet, is projected into the future and then looks back to the first coming of Christ. When Christ came, God asked the pressing question found in verse 2, *"When I came, was there no man? when I called, was there none to answer?"* The answer to these two questions is obvious. Only a few shepherds and a delegation of foreigners from the east noticed. The religious rulers were not there; the people were as indifferent and ignorant as the innkeeper at Bethlehem. When Jesus began His ministry, we are told that the common people heard Him gladly. The Pharisees, priests, and scribes became His severest critics. Our Lord's complaint to the nation was, *"Ye will not come to me, that ye might have life"* (John 5:40). John 1:11 says, *"He came unto his own, and his own received him not."*

This chapter is similar to Psalm 2 in structural outline. All three persons of the Godhead speak and the chapter is outlined as follows:

1. First, God the Father states the reason for the rejection of Israel (verses 1–3).

2. Second, God the Son speaks concerning His humiliation (verses 4–9).

3. Third, God the Holy Spirit proclaims that men trust the Son (verses 10–11).

1. VERSE 1

   + Under Mosaic Law, a man could put away his wife on the slightest pretext. (See Deuteronomy 24:1; Hosea 2:2.) A cruel, hardhearted man would take advantage of this to get rid of his wife. Israel is spoken of as the wife of Jehovah. This is the theme of Hosea. God questioned Israel about the grounds by which God set them aside. Certainly God is not cruel or brutal. It was not a whim of God that caused Israel to be set aside but it was because of their sins and iniquity. These are named in the next verse.

2. VERSE 2

   + Here we find the specific sin for which Israel was set aside: the rejection of the Messiah. There was no man to welcome Christ at His birth, nor when He began His ministry. Peter explains this in Acts 2:22–24.

   + Someone may question that the first person of the Godhead is used in this verse. How could it be God the Father speaking? Let the words of our Lord be a sufficient answer: *"He that hath seen me hath seen the Father,"* (John 14:9) and *"I and my Father are one"* (John 10:30).

3. VERSE 3

   + The Lord Jesus Christ controls the universe that He created. The helpless babe on the bosom of Mary could have spoken this universe out of existence.

4. VERSE 4

   + The title by which Christ, the perfect Servant, addresses God is revealing. It is *"Lord God"* (Jehovah Adonai). Christ is speaking here and to Him that word *Adohn* carries with it the idea of the most supreme authority and ownership. It is only used when the utmost reverence is desired to be expressed, and here, the very Lord of glory taking the place of the perfect Servant called Jehovah, "My Lord and My Master," which is the meaning of *Adohn*.

   + Morning by morning from the slumbers of the night, He, Christ, awakes and, as a disciple, a learner, He listens to the living voice of "His Lord and Master." (See John 7:16; 8:28, 38; 12:49–50.)

5. VERSE 5

   + This speaks of His crucifixion. (See Exodus 21:1–6; Psalm 40:6–8; Hebrews 10:5–7.) These passages make it clear that *"opened mine ear"* refers to crucifixion.

6. VERSE 6

   + This was fulfilled when Jesus was arrested. (See Matthew 26:67, 27:26; Mark 14:65.)

7. VERSE 7

   + The confidence of Jesus during the hours of His excruciating suffering was in God. He was doing the Father's will and the Father was well-pleased. Jesus drank the bitter cup pressed to His lips by the Father.

8. VERSE 8

   + This verse refers to the resurrection. (See Romans 4:25.) He is back from the dead, and who can question that He did not make satisfaction for the sins of the world? (See Romans 8:33–34.) Justification is connected with the resurrection of Christ.

9. VERSE 9

   + What will happen to those who come into conflict with Christ? Here, they are like a tattered garment ruined by being moth-eaten, which is a terrible description of slow but certain destruction.

- + This third part of this chapter gives us the consolation that the Holy Spirit gives to the persecuted remnant.

10. VERSES 10–11
   - + The wooing Holy Spirit speaks a soothing, imploring word, urging hearers to trust and rest in God's Servant.
   - + We find a warning word in verse 11. This is in contrast to verse 10. There it is, the wooing word; and here it is, the warning word.
   - + The warning is to those who walk in the light of their own fire, rejecting the One who is the light of the world. This is a word of counsel to those who trust themselves, their ability, and their works for their own salvation.

CHAPTER 51

The impression might be drawn from the last chapter that God has set aside the nation of Israel permanently, but this is a false impression. This chapter precludes any such thought or theory. Just as Israel has a past, rooted in a small beginning, just so today, they are small and set aside but this does not mean that God has forsaken them. Israel is like a train that has been on a sidetrack. God brings the church through on the main line, which is His present purpose in this world. The train on the side is not wrecked and will be brought out at God's appointed time and routed to its eternal destiny.

This chapter is like an alarm clock. Mark the places where the expressions occur like *"Harken unto me,"* *"awake, awake,"* and *"Therefore hear now this."* (See verses 1, 4, 7, 9, 17, 21, and verse 1 of chapter 52). God's timepiece is not a Bulova or Gruen, but Israel. In this chapter, God sounds the alarm to awaken those who are asleep, that they might know that eternal morning is coming soon.

1. VERSE 1
   - + This is a call to every sincere heart in Israel that longs to be righteous and desires to know God. This is not limited to Israel but is a cosmic call to every heart. This is a call to look at the beginning of the nation and the race from which it was taken. All believers know that they have been rescued from the sinking sand and miry clay. They have been lifted from the pit of death and hell.
   - + This verse, and the next few verses, happen to be a wonderful text on which to preach about the freedom to worship and those aspects of life that we find in our own dear country.

2. VERSE 2
   - + This is a call to every pious Israelite to consider his beginning. Abraham and Sarah marked the beginning of the nation. Also, God promised to make them a blessing to the world. The nation Israel failed, but God did not break His promise, as Christ came in fulfillment. (See Genesis 12:1–2; Galatians 3:16; Romans 4:16.)

3. VERSE 3
   - + Zion is Jerusalem, the center of the Land of Promise. The land will be restored as well as the people to the land.

4. VERSE 4
   - + *"My nation"* is Israel. This is a word of glorious anticipation for them.

5. VERSE 5
   - + *"Righteousness"* is Christ. He is made unto us *"righteousness."* The word *"isles"* means *"coast"* and speaks of all the inhabited continents and islands (usually referring to Gentiles). *"Mine arm"* refers to Christ.

6. VERSE 6
   - + This we find described in 2 Peter 3:10.

7. VERSE 7
   - This is a word of encouragement to the faithful remnant in any age.
8. VERSE 8
   - We are on the victory side. Here, the remnant has learned the secret of God's righteousness and grace He has provided for them. They are indeed as sheep in the midst of wolves.
9. VERSES 9–10
   - *"Arm of the LORD"* refers to Christ and the salvation He wrought on the cross. This is clear from chapter 53. *"Rahab"* is Egypt.
10. VERSE 11
    - This is another crystal-clear prophecy that declares the return of the redeemed Israelite back to the land. Nothing in the past can adequately fulfill this prophecy.
11. VERSE 12
    - This is a continuation of the comforts stated first in Isaiah 40. They are the redeemed now, because since chapter 40, the suffering servant has been introduced. As long as man walks this earth uncontrolled in his sinful nature, there is no freedom from fear. Fear is the offspring of forgetting God.
12. VERSE 13
    - Since they had forgotten God, they feared man.
13. VERSES 14–16
    - God delivered Israel from Egypt that He might make them His people. He will perform miracles again that He might say, *"Thou art my people"* (verse 16).
14. VERSE 17
    - This is another sound of alarm. This time, it is to alert them to profit from their present distress. They could make the judgment of God upon them a profitable experience if they learned the lesson of suffering. The nation has suffered more than any other people. History teaches this and it should encourage all of God's people to pray for the peace of Jerusalem.
15. VERSE 18
    - Unfortunately, Israel had not profited from her suffering and was wandering in the dark. There had been no deliverer among her sons.
16. VERSE 19
    - Should not God's people today exercise a sympathy toward Israel? The Christian ought to be the best friend that a Jew has.
17. VERSE 20
    - The nation Israel bears the marks of the rebuke of the Lord.
18. VERSE 21
    - God alerts them to come out of the spiritual stupor in which they exist.
19. VERSE 22
    - God has been pressing the cup of fury to their lips because of the rejection of Christ. The day will come when He will remove the cup.
20. VERSE 23
    - The enemies of Israel will not escape the judgment of God. Every nation that has majored in anti-Semitism has fallen, such as Egypt, Persia, Rome, Spain, Belgium, and Germany. This chapter should alert the believers today that God will yet choose Israel, and that the events in the Near East indicate that we are fast approaching the end time.

CHAPTER 52

This chapter is a vision of Jerusalem during the Kingdom Age. We are standing on the threshold of the kingdom and the King. The alarm clock is still ringing as we enter this chapter. It is the last call and the final invitation is going out. We enter this chapter with great anticipation as we stand on tiptoe on the threshold of the long-awaited event of the future. The long night of weeping has ended. The long-anticipated day has arrived. The gospel of the kingdom has gone out to the world.

This is not another gospel because Paul tells us that there is not another gospel. God has never had but one foundation upon which He saves men and that is the death and resurrection of Jesus Christ. (See 1 Corinthians 15:1–4; Galatians 1:8–9.) The response of men in different ages has varied. Abel brought a little lamb as sacrifice and that lamb pointed to Christ. This message of repentance, the gospel of the kingdom, will go out to the world and multitudes will respond to it. Many expositions place the last three verses of this chapter with Isaiah 53, where they properly belong, but we will follow our accepted chapter divisions and consider the last three verses as an introduction to chapter 53.

1. VERSE 1
   + This is the long-awaited word of Zion and Jerusalem. Her final deliverance has come. The millennial kingdom has arrived. Our Lord said that Jerusalem would be trodden down of the Gentiles till the time of the Gentiles be fulfilled. Those times have ended and Jerusalem is at peace. You can tell from this first verse, and the exposition thereof, that we are talking about the future and about the millennium.

2. VERSE 2
   + The city that for 2,500 years has been captive and trodden down of the Gentiles can now shake off the shackles of slavery.

3. VERSE 3
   + Since God received nothing from those who took His holy city captive, He will give nothing in return.

4. VERSE 4
   + Jacob went down to Egypt by invitation, but his children were made slaves. The Assyrians and others likewise oppressed them.

5. VERSE 5
   + God received no gain from the years of His people's rejection.

6. VERSE 6
   + This verse is a lovely thought. When He was here two thousand years ago, they did not know Christ. They will know Him when He comes again and says, *"Behold, it is I."*

7. VERSE 7
   + Feet are not ordinarily pretty. In fact, they are unsightly. These feet are *"shod with the preparation of the gospel of peace"* (Ephesians 6:15). Preparation means they are ready and willing to preach the gospel under any circumstance. Shod feet move more speedily than bare feet. This is the gospel of the kingdom: *"Thy God reigneth!"* This, as we have indicated, is not another gospel. There is only one gospel—Jesus is the gospel.

8. VERSE 8
   + There will be praise and unity of the faith in that day.

9. VERSE 9

  - Jerusalem is redeemed. The Redeemer has come to Zion. There is joy on the earth. Israel is back in the land. The Lord Jesus Christ is upon the throne of David. The church is the New Jerusalem. The devil is in the bottomless pit. (See Romans 11:1–33; Romans 9:1–12, 25–33.)

10. VERSE 10

  - All this was made possible because God laid bare His mighty arm in redemption at His first coming (see Isaiah 53) and He will redeem and restore Israel at His second coming. All of God's created intelligences will see His salvation.

11. VERSE 11

  - This is a personal cleansing and confession, not the withdrawal from some organization or group of believers or unbelievers.

12. VERSE 12

  - Their return to Israel will not be in panic or fear. God will be their vanguard and their rearguard. He will return them in peace.

13. VERSE 13

  - The next three verses constitute a proper introduction to chapter 53. In this verse, we have the exaltation of Christ. (See Philippians 2:9–11.)

14. VERSE 14

  - This verse sets before us the humiliation of Christ and again we turn to Philippians 2:5–8. After the three hours of darkness upon the cross, the crowd must have been startled when the light broke. He did not look human, just a mass of quivering flesh. It was unspeakable. Little wonder God put a mantle of darkness upon the cross.

15. VERSE 15

  - *"So shall he sprinkle many nations"* could be translated "so will He astonish many nations." This carries out the thought that His death will startle when it is properly understood. The death of Christ should never become commonplace to anyone. His death was different. Let us keep it that way. We have not told it properly unless it startles people.

How Much Do You Remember?

1. Who are the three distinct speakers of chapter 49?
2. What is the structural outline found in chapter 50?
3. Why is chapter 51 likened to an alarm clock?
4. When does the vision of chapter 52 place Jerusalem?

Your Assignment for Next Week:

1. Review your notes from this lesson.
2. Read Isaiah chapters 53, 54, 55, and 56.
3. Underline your Bible.

Lesson 17 Notes

_____

_____

_____

Lesson 18
CHAPTERS 53, 54, 55 AND 56

CHAPTER 53

Here we see the substitutionary death of Christ upon the cross for sinners. Those who are acquainted with God's Word realize that the fifty-third chapter of Isaiah and the twenty-second Psalm give us a more vivid account of the crucifixion of Christ than is found elsewhere in the Bible. This may come as a shock to many who are accustomed to think that the four Gospels alone describe the sad episode of the horrible death of the Son of God. If you carefully examine the gospel account, you will discover that only a few unrelated events connected with the crucifixion are given and that the actual crucifixion is passed over with reverent restraint. The Holy Spirit has drawn a veil of silence over the cross, and none of the lurid details are set forth for the curious mob to gaze and leer upon. It is said of the brutal crowd who murdered Him that they sat down and watched Him. You and I are not permitted to join that crowd. Even they did not see all, for God placed over His Son's agony a cloud of darkness. Some sensational speakers gather to themselves a bit of notoriety by painting, with picturesque speech, the minutest details of what they think took place at the crucifixion of Christ. You and I will probably never know, even in eternity, the extent of His suffering. Very likely, God did not want us to become familiar with that which we need not know. He did not wish us to treat as commonplace that which is sacred. We should remind ourselves constantly of the danger of becoming familiar—too familiar—with holy things.

Isaiah, seven hundred years before Christ was born, allows us to see something of His suffering that we will not find anywhere else. Before going further, we must pause a moment to answer the question that someone, even now, is doubtless asking: "How do you know that Isaiah is referring to the death of Christ? Isaiah was written seven hundred years before Christ was born." That is just the question that the Ethiopian eunuch raised when Philip hitchhiked a ride from him in the desert. The Ethiopian was reading Isaiah 53, we are even told the very verse in the chapter he was reading. (See Acts 8:26–35.) Philip answers the question in this fashion: *"Then Philip opened his mouth, and began at the same scripture, and preached unto him Jesus"* (Acts 8:35). Christ, in John 12:38, quoted from Isaiah 53 and makes application to Himself. Paul, in Romans 5:15–18, quotes from this same chapter in connection with the gospel of Christ. Without attempting to enlarge upon this reference, we affirm that Isaiah 53 refers to Christ, and even more than that, it is a photograph of the cross.

This chapter tells us two things about Christ:

1. The suffering of the Savior (verses 1–9).
2. The satisfaction of the Savior (verses 10–12).

We will not take this chapter verse-by-verse, but render an exposition of the first part, that is, verses 1–9, and then the exposition of the second part, verses 10–12.

You will find that these two sections belong together—suffering and satisfaction. Suffering always precedes satisfaction. There is no short route to satisfaction. Even God did not go that way. He could have avoided the cross and accepted the crown. That was Satan's suggestion. Suffering comes before satisfaction always. Phraseology bears record of that fact: through trial to triumph—sunshine comes after clouds—light follows darkness—and flowers come after the rainclouds. That seems to be God's way of doing things. Since it is His method, then it is the very best method.

1. THE SUFFERING OF THE SAVIOR (verses 1–9).

- This chapter opens with the inquiry: *"Who hath believed our report?"* The prophet seems to be registering a complaint because his message is not believed. This that was revealed to him is not received by men. This is always the sad office of the prophet. His message is rejected until it is too late. God's messengers have not been welcomed with open arms by the world. The prophets have been stoned and the message unheeded.

- There is a peculiar fascination about the fifty-third chapter of Isaiah. There, we see One suffering as no one else suffered. There, we behold One in pain as a woman in travail. We are strangely drawn to Him and His cross. He said, *"And I, if I be lifted up from the earth, will draw all men unto me"* (John 12:32). Suffering has a singular attraction. Pain draws us all together. When we see some poor creature groaning in misery and covered with blood, our hearts instinctively go out in sympathy and somehow we want to help.

- Look with me upon the strange sufferings of the Son of God. Let Him draw our cold hearts into the warmth of His sacrifice and the radiance of His love.

- Isaiah enlarges upon his first question by asking further, *"To whom is the arm of the Lord revealed?"* (verse 1). The term *"arm"* means "power, Christ, strength," symbolic of a tremendous undertaking. When God created the heavens and the earth, it is suggested that it is merely His handiwork.

- Now we have brought before us the person of Christ. We are told something of His origin on the human side in verse 2.

- Christ was a root out of a dry ground. (See Isaiah 11:1, 10; Romans 15:12.) At the time of the birth of Christ, the family of David had been cut off from the kingship. They were no longer princes; they were peasants. The nation Israel was under the iron heel of Rome. The Roman Empire produced no great civilization; they merely were good imitators of great civilizations. There was mediocre achievement and the moral foundation was gone. A strong manhood and a virtuous womanhood were supplanted by the pleasures of sin. The religion of Israel had gone to seed. They merely performed an empty ritual and the heart remained cold and indifferent. Into such a situation Christ came. He came from a noble family that was cut off, from a nation that had become a vassal to Rome, in a day and age that was decadent. The loveliest flower of humanity—Jesus Christ—came from the driest spot and period of the world's history. It was humanly impossible for His day and generation to produce Him, but He came nevertheless, for He came forth from God.

- The prophet focuses our attention immediately upon His suffering and death upon the cross. *"He hath no form nor comeliness; and when we shall see him, there is no beauty that we should desire him"* (verse 2). Some have drawn the inference from this statement that Christ was unattractive and even dare to suggest that He was repulsive in appearance. That cannot be true, for He was the perfect man. The Gospels do not lend any support to such a viewpoint. It was on the cross that this declaration of Him became true in a very real way. His suffering was so intense that He became drawn and His body was out of shape. That cross was not a pretty thing; it was absolutely repulsive to view. Men have fashioned crosses that look attractive, but they do not represent His cross. His cross was not good to look upon; His suffering was unspeakable; His death horrible. He did not even look human after the ordeal of the cross.

- Naturally, we are eager to learn why His death was different and horrible. What is the meaning of the depths of His suffering? Now note very carefully the answer in verses 3 and 4:

  He is despised and rejected of men; a man of sorrows, and acquainted with grief: and we hid as it were our faces from him; he was despised, and we esteemed him not. Surely he hath borne our griefs, and carried our sorrows: yet we did esteem him stricken, smitten of God, and afflicted.

+ The prophet was so afraid that you and I would miss it that he mentioned it three times: "*The LORD hath laid on him the iniquity of us all*" (verse 6); "*Yet it pleased the LORD to bruise him; he hath put him to grief*" (verse 10). We must recognize that it was God who treated the perfect man in such terrible fashion. Therefore, since we do not understand it, we are led to inquire why God should treat Him in this manner. What had He done to merit such treatment? Look for a moment again at that cross. Christ was on the cross six hours, hanging between heaven and earth from nine o'clock in the morning until three o'clock in the afternoon. In the first three hours, man did his worst. He heaped ridicule and insult upon Him, spat upon Him, nailed Him without mercy to the cross, and then sat down to watch Him die. At noon, after He had hung there for three hours in agony, God drew a veil over the sun and darkness covered that scene, shutting out from human eye the transaction between the Father and the Son. For Christ became the sacrifice for the sin of the world. God made His soul an offering for sin and He was treated as sin, for we are told that He was made sin for us who knew no sin. (See Matthew 8:16–17; 2 Corinthians 5:21.)

+ If you want to know if God hates sin, look at the cross. If you want to know if God will punish sin, look at the enduring of the tortures of Christ for its penalty. By what vain conceit can you and I hope to escape if we neglect so great a salvation? That cross became an altar where we behold the Lamb of God, taking away the sin of the world.

+ Now listen again in verses 5 and 6:

  > *But he was wounded for our transgressions, he was bruised for our iniquities: the chastisement of our peace was upon him; and with his stripes we are healed. All we like sheep have gone astray; we have turned every one to his own way; and the LORD hath laid on him the iniquity of us all.*

  He was merely taking your place and mine. He had done nothing amiss. He was holy, harmless, undefiled, and separate from sinners. He was a substitute that the love of God provided for you and me so we might be saved.

+ Surely our hearts go out in sympathy to Him as He expires there upon the tree. Certainly we are not unmoved at such pain and suffering. We would be coldblooded indeed if there were no responsive chord in our own hearts.

+ Some may think that He died a martyr's death. He did not die a martyr's death, for He did not espouse a lost cause! He did not die as martyrs who, in their death, sing praises of joy and confess that Christ was standing by them. He did not die like that, for He was forsaken of God. He said, "*My God, my God, why hast thou forsaken me?*" (Matthew 27:46). His death was different because He died totally, completely alone.

+ As Isaiah saw that and wrote it down, he thought of himself and of us when he said, "*All we like sheep have gone astray*" (verse 6).

2. THE SATISFACTION OF THE SAVIOR (verses 10–12).

+ There is a phrase generally quoted in a wrong sense in connection with verse 3 and verse 10 in which we have the idea that Christ was "a man of sorrows and acquainted with grief," etc. The inference is drawn that Christ was a very unhappy man while here on earth. To fortify this position, a few isolated incidents are quoted in which it says He wept. Let me correct that, if I can. Read on in Isaiah 53 and you will find this: "*Surely He hath borne our griefs, and carried our sorrows*" (verse 4). It was *our* sorrow and grief that He bore. He was supremely happy in His mission here on earth for it is said of Him, "*who for the joy that was set before him endured the cross*" (Hebrews 12:2). Joyfully, He took our place on the cross. He made that cross an altar on which was offered a satisfactory payment for the penalty for your sins and mine. Willingly, He died there, for it is further stated that "*as a sheep before her shearers is dumb, so he openeth not his mouth*" (Isaiah 53:7).

- He not only died for you and for me, He also arose from a grave of victory and ascended back into heaven. At this moment, He is sitting at the right hand of God, and the prophet says, *"He shall see of the travail of his soul, and shall be satisfied"* (verse 11). We have a living, rejoicing Savior, for His suffering led to satisfaction. He took out hell that we might have His heaven. He is happy, for down through the ages and multitudes, millions have come to know Him and found sweet release from guilt, pardon from wrongdoing, and healing from the leprosy of sin. Christ said there is joy in heaven over one sinner that repents (see Luke 15:7) and that number can be multiplied by millions.

3. A SUMMARY OF THE LAST THREE VERSES OF CHAPTER 52 AND ALL OF CHAPTER 53

- Verses 13–15 of chapter 52 are the introduction to chapter 53. This gives us a total of fifteen verses in all, divided into five threes.

- In these five sections of three verses each, we have again a Pentateuch, whose parts have a striking correspondence with the first Pentateuch of the Bible.

- The first three verses (chapter 52:13–15) are the Genesis of the prophecy. In Genesis, we see ruin—sin. This section closes with the prophecy of report going out to those who had never seen or heard of such a marvel—the Gentiles. It has in it all the seed that follows.

- Second, in verses 1–3, we see the Exodus section. Redemption is announced. Salvation is announced and rejected.

- The third section, verses 4–6, brings us to the Levitical section. As that book took us into the sanctuary with the many offerings connected with it, so here we have the one offering that has displaced all these shadows, and by which we have access even unto the holiest. These three verses reveal the secret of those sufferings. Well will it be for us if we listen, not coldly, but with some degree of affection stirred by the revelation. Leviticus then means communion with God or atonement.

- Fourth, we have the section found in verses 7–9 that compares to Numbers, a book of guidance and direction. The pilgrim path of Israel is told with all its desert testings, and their constant failures under those testings. Here, too, we come to just that aspect of the Savior's sufferings as testings from man and His perfect bearing under them because He never failed.

- We now come to the last section (verses 10–12) that compares to the book of Deuteronomy. This describes the faithfulness of God. It is a book of destination. These verses of Isaiah 53 are summing up God's ways with Israel when, with their desert journeys behind them, they are now at the point of their destination.

From first to last, we have kind of a Bible in miniature in this Pentateuch concerning the suffering and satisfaction of our Savior.

CHAPTER 54

Chapter 54 bursts out in exaltation after the prophecies of the sufferings and the sin-bearing and the glory of the servant of Jehovah in chapter 53. Israel is called upon to rejoice with singing and shouting, as her state of barrenness would yield place to fruitfulness. In this chapter, we see the application of Christ's redemption to Israel and the earth. The church is not in view here, as the church is defined as *"a chaste virgin"* (2 Corinthians 11:2) and not a restored wife. People of all dispensations—past, present, and future—are saved by the redemption Christ wrought on the cross. Let the church not rob Israel of the glorious benefits of Christ's redemption portrayed here.

First, we see the regathering and restoration of Israel as the wife of Jehovah in verses 1–10.

Second, we see the rejoicing and righteousness of Israel as the restored wife of Jehovah in verses 11–17.

1. VERSE 1
   - The first word after the crucifixion in Isaiah 53: *"Sing."* It is a call to Israel to sing. In the past, Isaiah has already commented that the travailing of the past only produced vanity and her future is more glorious, as there will be many children.

2. VERSE 2
   - The nation Israel has never occupied the entire land given to them by the Lord. You will read in Joshua 1:4: *"From the wilderness and this Lebanon even unto the great river, the river Euphrates, all the land of the Hittites, and unto the great sea toward the going down of the sun, shall be your coast."* Then, of course, there are other references to the land of Israel. During the millennium, they will occupy the total borders. Also, the city of Jerusalem will push out into the suburban areas, which is already being done.

3. VERSE 3
   - The Gentiles have occupied most of the land of promise. They will have to withdraw to their own borders.
   - The right and left hand stands for both the south and the north, as in Genesis 15:18, Egypt and the Euphrates. Also, for the east and the west, you find that Scripture in Genesis 28:14.
   - There will be much more in their future than what was enjoyed during the reign of Solomon. They are to become the head of the nations.

4. VERSE 4
   - Their past is a cause for shame and deep humiliation but at the same time, it will be all under the blood. This verse is full of the tender lovingkindness of the Lord—His covenant mercies and the glorious future in store for the nation, Israel.

5. VERSE 5
   - God will own them as His redeemed.

6. VERSE 6
   - Israel is today like a wife who has been divorced for adultery, but God will call her back to Himself. Wonderful is the restoring grace of God. He calls Israel back to Himself as a husband receives back his wife he loved in his youth but had cast away because of adultery.

7. VERSE 7
   - The past is forgotten, and although the long centuries slipped by slowly, it will seem to be only a brief moment in comparison to the great blessings for the future. The church has a similar promise, which we find in 2 Corinthians 4:17–18.

8. VERSE 8
   - The wrath of God was small in comparison to His great mercy.

9. VERSE 9
   - God promised Noah never to destroy the earth again with a flood. God has made His promise good and, therefore, He will make His promise good to Israel. The Lord gives a pledge and He never breaks a pledge.

10. VERSE 10
    - This is a glorious promise. Read it again and again until the meaning breaks upon your heart. God's great covenant of peace will never be removed. He conveys that assurance in the illustration when the mountains have departed and the hills have been removed, His kindness will never depart from Israel.

11. VERSE 11
   + Now God begins to comfort Israel that she might rejoice.
12. VERSE 12
   + Compare these descriptions to the New Jerusalem. (See Revelation 21:9–27.) God is a God of beauty. Sin is ugly.
13. VERSE 13
   + This is the day when the knowledge of the Lord will cover the earth. This brings peace.
14. VERSE 14
   + Peace brings righteousness. They belong together. Then comes freedom from fear. (See Psalm 85:10.)
15. VERSE 15
   + No longer will foes attack Israel. They will be far from oppression. Jerusalem will be invincible.
16. VERSE 16
   + God sent the enemies in the past, but He will never permit another to come against them.
17. VERSE 17
   + Even in the past and present, God has been opposed to anti-Semitism. No enemy of God's chosen nation has ever prospered. The witnesses to this truth are many in number. Israel will not be able to claim anything of or by their own merit any more than we can who are justified freely by His grace through the redemption that is in Christ Jesus.

CHAPTER 55

The work of the suffering Servant in chapter 53 makes possible the offer of salvation in this chapter. In chapter 54, the invitation was confined to Israel only. Here, the invitation is extended to the entire world. In chapters 54 and 55, we have the results of the redemption wrought in chapter 53. The gospel went first to Israel and then to the Gentiles. Romans 1:16 says, *"For I am not ashamed of the gospel of Christ: for it is the power of God unto salvation to every one that believeth; to the Jew first, and also to the Greek."*

This verse has yet to find its complete fulfillment in Israel. Today it is worldwide, and the only condition is the thirst of the individual. Although God's salvation is to be proclaimed to every creature, only the thirsty will respond.

This is not a mechanical offer locked up in the airtight compartment of God's election, but it rests upon the free will of each hearer. He is urged; he is commanded to seek the Lord.

1. VERSE 1
   + The first verse of the chapter opens with a sharp form of address: *"Ho!"* It is a heart-cry of God to everyone to pause and to consider His salvation. He wants every weak soul to behold His mighty bared arm in salvation. Though the invitation is ecumenical, it is limited to a certain class and that class happens to be the thirsty ones. Those who have drunk at the waterholes of this world have tasted the flavors of its pleasures and are still thirsty. They are bidden to come to drink of the water of life. For those whose thirst has not been slacked by the man-made cisterns, the invitation is to drink deep and long of the eternal spring.
   + It is a threefold invitation expressed by the thrice repeated *"come."* Three types of drink are offered:
     a. First, *"waters."* This plural form is used, as the water is too wonderful to be expressed in singular form. *"Waters"* also speaks of quantity as well as quality. Water is essential to life and it speaks of the work of the Holy Spirit, as regenerator and life-giver. (See John 3:5.) Water must be received first, as it is life. The invitation of the Lord Jesus Christ was for men to come to Him and drink. The life-giving waters were the Holy Spirit, as He clearly stated.

b. *"Wine"* is the second type of drink offered. This speaks of the drink of the soul, which is joy. Proverbs 31:6 says, *"Give strong drink unto him that is ready to perish, and wine unto those that be of heavy hearts."* Joy always follows the reception of life, never precedes it.

c. *"Milk"* is the third type of drink offered. Milk is essential for growth and development, especially for babies. First Peter 2:2 says, *"As newborn babes, desire the sincere milk of the word, that ye may grow thereby."* The Word of God is the only formula God has for newborn babes.

- These three drinks are listed on God's menu at some exorbitant price, though they are priceless. Money is not the requirement, for they are not for sale at a monetary value. The only requirement is thirst. All are invited to come. Are you thirsty?

2. VERSE 2

- Notice: *"Wherefore do ye spend money for that which is not bread?"* The pleasures of this world are expensive, but they never satisfy. Pleasures of the world are counterfeit; they are like sawdust and can never satisfy the soul. There is a bread that satisfies. John 6:35 says, *"And Jesus said unto them, I am the bread of life: he that cometh to me shall never hunger."*

3. VERSE 3

- *"Incline your ear"* is God's urgent request to pay particular attention to His gracious offer. He is again repeating: *"Come now, and let us reason together"* (Isaiah 1:18). Shut out the luring voices that would distract us.

4. VERSE 4

- Jesus is called *"a witness."* He is yet to become the great Commander.

5. VERSE 5

- The invitation to participate in the sure mercies of David knows no national or racial boundaries, but girdles the globe. (See also Ephesians 2:11–14.)

6. VERSE 6

- The way of God and the way of man are put into contrast and conflict. The objection is often made that this is not a legitimate gospel call for today, as man is not asked to seek God. On the contrary, God is seeking man. This certainly is accurate, but nonetheless, this call is for today as the human aspect is in view here. Human responsibility is not defeated by the sovereign purposes and election of God because His sheep do hear His voice and follow Him.

7. VERSE 7

- Man's way is a wicked way and leads to death. (See Proverbs 14:12; Isaiah 53:6.)

8. VERSE 8

- God's way is different from man's way. The gospel is God's way, and no man could ever have devised it. *"But I certify you, brethren, that the gospel which was preached of me is not after man. For I neither received it of man, neither was I taught it, but by the revelation of Jesus Christ"* (Galatians 1:11–12).

- Proud men would never have chosen this way. Man by wisdom could not have figured it out.

9. VERSE 9

- The gospel could only come by revelation, as man's reason never seems to follow the redemption route.

10. VERSE 10

- In these closing verses, prominence is given to the Word of God. Salvation is a revelation of God. The Word of God is likened to the rain that comes down from heaven. Man does not work his way up to God by some Tower of Babel effort, but he receives God's revelation that comes down from heaven. The rain causes the earth to become fruitful. The seeds germinate and bring forth abundantly.

11. VERSE 11

   - God's Word is rain and seed. It falls upon the dry and desert souls of men. It will germinate in the hearts of many. It will accomplish God's purpose. (See Matthew 13:3–23.) The Word never goes forth without some return.

12. VERSE 12

   - The rain causes the earth to respond with a note of praise to the Creator and Redeemer. *"Because the creature itself also shall be delivered from the bondage of corruption into the glorious liberty of the children of God. For we know that the whole creation groaneth and travaileth in pain together until now"* (Romans 8:21–22).

13. VERSE 13

   - This looks forward to the millennium, when the earth will be redeemed. The curse of sin is expressed by the thorn and the briar. (See Genesis 3:18.)

CHAPTER 56

Here we see the blessing of Israel in the millennium under the new covenant. This chapter, which follows the salvation of God in chapter 53, overtures to Israel in chapter 54, and the world in chapter 55, is not a retreat back to Mount Sinai but rather a victory march through the arch of triumph into the millennium. It is a forward movement that is the logical outworking of what has preceded. It pertains particularly to Israel and radiates out into a widening circle of global benefits. This is all given to us in what we call the New Covenant.

For finding fault with them, he saith, Behold, the days come, saith the Lord, when I will make a new covenant with the house of Israel and with the house of Judah: not according to the covenant that I made with their fathers in the day when I took them by the hand to lead them out of the land of Egypt; because they continued not in my covenant, and I regarded them not, saith the Lord. For this is the covenant that I will make with the house of Israel after those days, saith the Lord; I will put my laws into their mind, and write them in their hearts: and I will be to them a God, and they shall be to me a people. (Hebrews 8:8–10)

In this chapter, our attention is directed from the great events of the future to the more practical aspects of daily life in the kingdom. The emphasis is ethics, not events—practice, not prophecy. All of this should influence our living daily. The study of prophecy is not to entertain the curious or intrigue the intellect, but to encourage holy living.

In the first part of this chapter, verses 1–8, we will see the particulars of the kingdom; in the latter part of the chapter, verses 9–12, we will look at some of the sorry predicaments of Israel during the time of the writing of Isaiah.

1. VERSE 1

   - None of the prophets anticipated a long interval before the establishment of the kingdom. For them, it was an immediate thing. The salvation spoken of here is the national salvation of Israel—a nation born in a day. This is what was in the mind of Paul in Romans 11:26 when he said, *"And so all Israel shall be saved: as it is written, There shall come out of Sion the Deliverer, and shall turn away ungodliness from Jacob."*

2. VERSE 2

   - The Sabbath is to be restored after this day of grace and the church is removed to the place prepared above. This will be during the great tribulation and the millennium. In the meantime, we are not to be judged according to a Sabbath day. The Sabbath was an arrangement between God and Israel. (See Exodus 31:16–17; Ezekiel 20:12.) There was no merit in observing the Sabbath for itself; their lives were to be such that their observance of it meant they kept it.

3. VERSE 3
   - The Gentile in that day is not to feel he is an outsider because of God's particular arrangement with Israel; to the contrary, he is invited to share the blessings.
   - A eunuch could not serve as a priest under the Mosaic economy. A physical handicap will shut no one out in the future.

4. VERSES 4–5
   - The handicapped, the strangers, and all outcasts are invited to accept God's gracious overture of a position that is better than a son or daughter, and a security that is everlasting. This, the law could not afford.

5. VERSE 6
   - The stranger will be given a new heart that he might love the Lord.

6. VERSE 7
   - This is the verse from which the Lord quoted when He cleansed the temple the second time. (See Matthew 21:13.) It was God's original intention that the temple was to be for all people, irrespective of race, tongue, class, or condition. It had long ceased to function as such in the days of Christ. The church today is as far removed from its primary objective as the temple.

7. VERSE 8
   - The kingdom is to be worldwide in its extent and will include members of every family and race in its content. This is the intent.

8. VERSE 9
   - Our vision is shifted from the lofty contemplation of the glorious future kingdom to the sorry condition of the then-existing kingdom of Israel. God was permitting the nations of the world to come in like wild and ferocious beasts and they were to rob the people. Assyria had already broken in and Babylon was soon to follow. Later, others would come to plunder and to destroy Israel.

9. VERSE 10
   - The reason God permitted them to come was because of the weak and inadequate leadership of the people. They were blind as watchmen. They were like dogs that are lazy. They are called dumb dogs. The kings, priests, and false prophets were responsible for the welfare of the nation and its destruction was laid at their door. Do you find anything that sounds familiar here?

10. VERSE 11
    - They were greedy dogs that sought their own personal interest rather than the welfare of the nation. Their covetousness blinded them to the eminent dangers that pressed upon the nation.

11. VERSE 12
    - They drowned their sad plight in drink and faced the future as drunkards and blind optimists.

How Much Do You Remember?

1. What two parts comprise chapter 53?
2. Describe the state of the world when Jesus entered in at His birth (chapter 53).
3. Recall the promise of Isaiah 54:10 and copy it down here:

_____

_____

_____

_____

_____

4. Describe how the offer of salvation changes throughout these chapters.

Your Assignment for Next Week:

1. Review your notes from this lesson.
2. Read Isaiah chapters 57, 58, 59, 60 and 61.
3. Underline your Bible.

Lesson 18 Notes

_____

_____

_____

_____

_____

_____

_____

_____

_____

_____

_____

_____

_____

_____

_____

_____

_____

_____

Lesson 19
CHAPTERS 57, 58, 59, 60, AND 61

CHAPTER 57

This chapter brings us to the final scene before the coming of the King to set up His kingdom. Therefore, we are looking at the days of the great tribulation in this chapter. This chapter brings us to the crossroads where some will die for their faith, and, as John tells us in Revelation, *"These are they which came out of great tribulation, and have washed their robes, and made them white in the blood of the Lamb"* (Revelation 7:14).

1. VERSES 1–2
   - The righteous are removed in verses 1 and 2. This is a picture of 1 Thessalonians 4:13–18 and Revelation 7:14.

2. VERSE 3
   - God addresses the wicked. Even their ancestry is bad. Note the label given to their mothers.

3. VERSE 4
   - They have been the persecutors of the righteous and we find here that God is bringing an indictment against His people called Israel under the most scathing terms.

4. VERSE 5
   - Israel, generally speaking, but not all (because there is still that remnant), are the idolaters who have turned their backs on God and are guilty of gross immorality and murder.

5. VERSE 6
   - They even worship the smooth stones in the brook. They worship everything except the living and true God.

6. VERSE 7
   - Idolatry, associated with the graves on the mountaintops, gives place to scenes of the vilest immorality.

7. VERSE 8
   - Sin is customarily committed in secret, but they have become brazen and they flaunt their sin publicly.

8. VERSE 9
   - This verse has unique interest. Israel, in her lusts, lowered herself to the extent that God says, *"Thou...didst debase thyself even unto hell."* They have sunk so low that they pay homage to Satan's representative, who is "the king"—the anti-Christ.

9. VERSES 10–11
   - The way of wickedness leads to weariness and frustration. There is no hope along the rebellious path they are taking, neither is there remorse on their part. There was no fear of God before their eyes as they continued as liars along their senseless way. God held His peace and did not act. As always, He was patient with them.

10. VERSE 12
    - There is coming a day when the books will be open and their works will be judged. They are cast into the lake of fire.

11. VERSE 13
    - The things they trusted will fail. They will see the utter futility of their way. God is determined that those who trust Him will possess the land. Their rebellion did not frustrate the purpose of God.

12. VERSE 14
    - A way will be made for God's people. The gospel of the cross will no longer be a stumbling block to the Jew.

13. VERSE 15
    - God comforts His own because of who He is—the high and lofty One. He is the God of eternity. How feeble is man with his threescore years and ten. The eternal God promises to take those who do not trust in themselves but trust in Him, and He covers them as a mother hen covers her brood. What a picture of peace and security.

14. VERSE 16
    - He is the eternal God but He will not always be angry with sin, for it is to be removed.

15. VERSE 17
    - God explains why He punishes the wicked. The wicked are covetous and go on in rebellion against God.

16. VERSE 18
    - For those who will forsake the wickedness of their ways, He will heal and save.

17. VERSE 19
    - God alone can speak peace to the heart of the sinner.

18. VERSE 20
    - This is one of the most picturesque descriptions of the wicked in Scripture. Like the troubled and restless sea, the wicked can find no rest or peace in their wicked ways. They continue on like hunted criminals looking for deliverance and safety.

19. VERSE 21
    - This is the second time this statement has been repeated. You will find it also in Isaiah 48:22.

CHAPTER 58

This chapter brings us to the final section of the book of Isaiah. The glory of the Lord had been withheld from Israel. The people were supercilious and cynical about their relationship to God. They were observing forms and dared to question the actions of God toward them. They sat in judgment upon God and His methods. In spite of their outward observance of religion, they were indulging in their own wicked way. This same spirit was manifested after the Babylonian captivity.

What audacity to question God! This is the spirit of the natural man with his outward show of religious form. The heart is far from God and his way is wicked. The veneer of godliness is nauseating to the Lord Jesus Christ.

1. VERSE 1
    - The prophet is commanded by the Lord God to cry aloud a message that is always unpopular. To point out the transgressions and sins of a people who think they are religious is to bring down the bitter displeasure and caustic attitude of the people. Only a brave man will do it.
    - The basic weakness of liberalism is its aim to please the natural man without telling him the real truth about his fatal disease. Here, the Lord God says, *"Shew my people their transgression, and the house of Jacob their sins."*

2. VERSE 2

+ There is an element of biting satire in God's statement. These people were attending the temple worship regularly and going through all the rituals. They were meticulous in following the form of worship. They enjoyed going to church yet their lives were far from being separate and holy.

3. VERSE 3

+ Sarcastically, they ask the reason for fasting and self-infliction if God did not take notice. They evidently had made fasting an important part of their religion. God gave them feast days, but not fast days.

+ They were to afflict their souls in connection with the great Day of Atonement. In times of sin, they were to fast. Fasting was the outward expression of the soul. They had made it a form that ministered to their own ego and pride. Fasting was a private matter between the soul and God, not a public show. Our Lord had much to say about this and specifically about abusing the fast:

> *Moreover when ye fast, be not, as the hypocrites, of a sad countenance: for they disfigure their faces, that they may appear unto men to fast. Verily I say unto you, They have their reward. But thou, when thou fastest, anoint thine head, and wash thy face; that thou appear not unto men to fast, but unto thy Father which is in secret: and thy Father, which seeth in secret, shall reward thee openly.*
>
> (Matthew 6:16–18)

4. VERSE 4

+ God explains why He cannot accept their fasting. They thought it gave them special acceptance with Him.

5. VERSE 5

+ God had not commanded their fasting and their acts of worship were entirely outward.

6. VERSE 6

+ God wanted acts to match their fasts. He wanted to release them from the slavery of empty practices.

7. VERSE 7

+ They were turning their backs on the poor and needy. They even refused to show kindness and love to their fellow Israelite. Their religion was as cold as the north side of a tombstone in January.

8. VERSE 8

+ God could not manifest His blessing and glory to a people who practiced their religion so badly.

9. VERSE 9

+ God wanted to hear their prayers and He wanted to bless. He wanted to open the windows of heaven and pour them out a blessing, but their hearts were not open to receive it.

10. VERSE 10

+ God asked them to practice one specific thing that He might bless and that was to give themselves to the hungry and to satisfy those souls in affliction.

11. VERSE 11

+ God promised to bless them if they would show authenticity in their religion.

12. VERSE 12

+ Their return to God would repair the wreckage of the sins of generations past.

13. VERSE 13

+ God uses another specific with them. He gave the Sabbath day to Israel, as we have indicated before. (See Exodus 31:12–17.) The Sabbath was between God and the children of Israel. Even for them, it was to be more than a form. They made it a day for their own pleasure. It was only a hollow form. They were to enter into that day for rest of body and soul.

14. VERSE 14

+ The horizon here is extended and the future opens before us. They may delay the approaching glory but they cannot destroy God's plan for the coming manifestation of glory.

CHAPTER 59

This chapter continues God's charges against Israel. Their sins have brought about their sad state. Religion had become a cover-up for their sins. God refused to hear their prayers because of their iniquities, not because He was hard of hearing. Their sins are referred to thirty-two times. Many words are used to describe their many sins, for instance: 1. Iniquities, 2. Sins, 3. Defiled with blood, 4. Lies, 5. Perverseness, 6. Vanity, 7. Mischief, 8. Adder's eggs, 9. Spider's web, 10. Viper, 11. Works, 12. Violence, 13. Evil, 14. Wasting, 15. Destruction, 16. Crooked paths, 17. Darkness, 18. Transgressions, 19. Departing, 20. Oppression, 21. Revolt, 22. Conceiving, and 23. Uttering falsehoods. There are twenty-three separate charges against them and nine repeated offenses.

This chapter projects us into the future when the glory of the Redeemer will be revealed. There will be a time of national confession of sin. (See Zechariah 12:11–14.)

1. VERSE 1

+ The reason Israel is not saved is not due to any weakness in the "mighty arm of Jehovah." Neither was it due to a faulty connection with His communication with them.

2. VERSE 2

+ The sins of Israel had separated them from God. Our sin is what separates us from God.

3. VERSES 3–4

+ God lists the specific sins of this ugly brood.

4. VERSE 5

+ A "cockatrice" is a snake. These are serpent's eggs. Sin has a way of multiplying. The spider's web is a flimsy gauze of no value. It is used to snare the food of the spider.

5. VERSE 6

+ Spider's webs are not like the silk of the silkworm. Man's righteousness is not only as dirty rags but it cannot cover the nakedness of man.

6. VERSES 7–8

+ Paul makes this list the universal picture of man. (See Romans 3:15–18.)

7. VERSE 9

+ The change of pronoun here indicates there is another speaker. Instead of "your" and "their," it becomes "we" and "us." They confess now that they are in darkness. Their religious rituals have all been a pretense.

8. VERSES 10–19

+ The charges are specific, and here the confession is specific. Each sin is confessed separately. It is labeled and repudiated. Confession of sins today on the part of Christians should be specific. Usually, they are general in our thoughts and in our prayers. Each sin should be labeled and confessed privately as a sin.

+ Verse 16 is evidently a reference to Christ.

9. VERSES 20–21

- This brings us to the last division of the chapter, and the pronouns change again. The Redeemer will come to Zion. All of God's purposes concerning this earth are moving toward this time. When the Redeemer returns, there will be a great confession of sin.

- God has made a covenant that the Redeemer is coming to Zion. There will never be a time when this promise will be entirely forsaken.

- The Redeemer spoken of here in verses 20–21 is the Lord Jesus Christ. *Redemption* means "to deliver by paying a price." The New Testament records the fulfillment of the Old Testament types and prophecies of redemption through the sacrifice of Christ. The time when the Redeemer will come to Zion is fixed relatively by Romans 11:23–29 as following the completion of the Gentile church—this age.. That is also the order of the great dispensational passage in Acts 15:14–17. In both, the return of the Lord to Zion follows the out-calling of the church.

- The Old Testament redemption can be found mainly in the books of Leviticus, Exodus, and Ruth. Here we find the "kinsman" type of redeemer, which is a beautiful type of Christ.

- The kinsman redemption was of persons of an inheritance. (See Leviticus 25:48; Galatians 4:5.) The redeemer must be a kinsman. (See Leviticus 25:48–49; Ruth 3:12–13; Galatians 4.) The redeemer must be able to redeem. (See Ruth 4:4–6; John 10:11, 18.) Redemption is affected by the kinsman paying the just demand in full. (See Leviticus 25:27; 1 Peter 1:18–19; Galatians 3:13.)

- We find in Romans 11, beginning with verse 23, that Israel is blind in part until the fullness of the Gentiles is manifest. Then all Israel will be saved. How? There will come out of Zion the Redeemer, or the Deliverer, their Kinsman, and He, Christ, will turn away ungodliness from Israel. This is the covenant of God unto them when He will take away their sins.

CHAPTER 60

The theme of this chapter is the Sun of Righteousness rising upon Israel. Israel reflects this glory and light upon the entire earth.

We have come to the full manifestation of the millennial glory. The prophet ascends to new heights of extravagant language. This must not be taken to imply that the meaning of the words is merely symbolic. The literal content of the language is not to be washed out by adopting a low symbolic system of interpretation. Extravagant language is used by the Lord God through the pen of Isaiah because that kind of language alone can describe the exalted state of the millennium.

There is a striking similarity between the description of the earthly Jerusalem and the heavenly Jerusalem. This does not imply that they are one and the same city. The heavenly city comes down from heaven. We would say it becomes a part of the earthly system or we could turn it around and say that the earth becomes a part of the heavenly scheme. Men today are putting satellites into the heavens by shooting rockets upward. God will send a satellite downward from heaven, and its name is New Jerusalem.

1. VERSE 1

- Obviously, the Lord Jesus Christ is the light to which the prophet refers. He is the Light of the World and is called by Malachi the Sun of righteousness: *"But unto you that fear my name shall the Sun of righteousness arise with healing in his wings; and yet shall go forth, and grow up as calves of the stall"* (Malachi 4:2).

- The theme introduced in the previous chapter is continued here. In Isaiah 59:20, He is identified: *"the Redeemer shall come to Zion."*

2. VERSE 2

   + The coming of the light is necessitated by the night of spiritual darkness that has covered the earth. In spite of the preaching of the gospel for two thousand years, there is a wider circle of darkness today than ever before. Light must precede the future blessings. The Sun of Righteousness must rise to bring in the millennial day.

3. VERSE 3

   + The presence of the Redeemer in Zion will bring the Gentiles from afar. Romans 11:15 says, *"For if the casting away of them be the reconciling of the world, what shall the receiving of them be, but life from the dead?"*

4. VERSE 4

   + Rebellious and scattered, they will come to the Land of Promise. The women who are weaker than the men, referred to here as *"daughters,"* will be carried the same way as children are often carried in the east—on the hips of their mothers or older children.

5. VERSE 5

   + The tremendous movements of all peoples toward Jerusalem—by land, sea, and air—will be an occasion of astonishment.

6. VERSE 6

   + Again, wise men, not only from the east, will come with gifts of gold and incense for the Redeemer. Note the omission of myrrh, which spoke of His death at His first coming. This is left out in verse 6.

7. VERSE 7

   + Flocks are brought to Jerusalem for sacrifice. The sacrifices will be reinstituted in the millennial temple. This may be difficult for some to accept but the Old Testament is definite at this point, as you can prove by reading Ezekiel 40–44. Evidently, the sacrifices will point back to the death of Christ, as in the Old Testament they point toward His death.

8. VERSE 8

   + If there is any prophecy in Scripture that suggests the airplane, this is it. Apparently, the direct reference is to the ships upon the sea.

9. VERSE 9

   + Tarshish, as used here, is evidently a reference to all sea-going nations. The ships of the Gentiles will be used to return Israel to the Land of Promise.

10. VERSE 10

    + The nations that once destroyed Israel will not assist in its recovery.

11. VERSE 11

    + The same condition will prevail in the earthly Jerusalem that prevail in the heavenly city.

      And the nations of them which are saved shall walk in the light of it: and the kings of the earth do bring their glory and honour into it. And the gates of it shall not be shut at all by day: for there shall be no night there. And they shall bring the glory and honour of the nations into it.
      (Revelation 21:24–26)

12. VERSE 12

    + *"Every knee should bow...and...every tongue should confess that Jesus Christ is Lord"* (Philippians 2:10–11). In the millennium, men will be forced to bow to Jesus.

13. VERSE 13
    * Trees from all over the world will adorn Jerusalem, which is coming to pass even now.
14. VERSE 14
    * All anti-Semitism will end. Those who once despised Israel will bow down before Israel.
15. VERSE 15
    * Jerusalem will become the center of the earth literally.
16. VERSE 16
    * The riches of Jerusalem, which were taken away by the nations, will be restored with interest.
17. VERSE 17
    * Precious metals will become commonplace again.
    * *"Exactors"* means "tax collectors." Even tax collectors will be righteous in the millennium. Remember, the publicans in Christ's day were tax collectors.
18. VERSE 18
    * Note the radical changes that will take place in the millennium.
19. VERSES 19–20
    * Jesus, the light of the world, will be there. He is likewise the light of the New Jerusalem. Revelation 21:23 says, *"And the city had no need of the sun, neither of the moon, to shine in it: for the glory of God did lighten it, and the Lamb is the light thereof."*
20. VERSE 21
    * Again, this is a clear-cut statement regarding Israel's future. They will be made righteous; they will inherit the land forever.
21. VERSE 22
    * Human strength will be increased without resorting to medication or vitamins. Life will be longer.

CHAPTER 61

Here we find the first and second comings of Christ and particular emphasis on the results of His second coming. This chapter is of peculiar interest in view of the fact that the Lord Jesus opened His public ministry in Nazareth by quoting from it. This chapter continues the full blessings of the millennium with Israel as the center of all earthly benefits. This last section projects us into the total benefits of the thousand-year period.

1. VERSE 1
    * This is the passage that Jesus read in His hometown of Nazareth at the synagogue, which initiated His public ministry:

    > *And he came to Nazareth, where he had been brought up: and, as his custom was, he went into the synagogue on the sabbath day, and stood up for to read. And there was delivered unto him the book of the prophet Esaias [Isaiah]. And when he had opened the book, he found the place where it was written, The Spirit of the Lord is upon me, because he hath anointed me to preach the gospel to the poor; he hath sent me to heal the brokenhearted, to preach deliverance to the captives, and recovering of sight to the blind, to set at liberty them that are bruised, to preach the acceptable year of the Lord. And he closed the book, and he gave it again to the minister, and sat down. And the eyes of all them that were in the synagogue were fastened on him. And he began to say unto them, This day is this scripture fulfilled in your ears.* (Luke 4:16–21)

    * The way Jesus handled the Scriptures is profoundly significant.

2. VERSE 2
   - You will note that Jesus broke off the reading in the middle of this verse with the phrase, *"the acceptable year of the LORD."* He broke off in the middle of the verse, saying that all that went before related to His first coming. He stated definitely that Scripture, up to this point, was fulfilled at His first coming.
   - The following statement, *"and the day of vengeance of our God"* is connected with His second coming. (See Isaiah 34:8.) This method of Christ reveals that the prophets (Isaiah at least) did not distinguish between the first and second comings of Christ. Peter confirms this. (See 1 Peter 1:10–11.)
   - This gives us a system of biblical interpretation. The prophets saw the first and second comings of Christ as two mountain peaks on the horizon. They did not see the wide valley between the two mountain peaks, and it is in this valley that we find the Church Age, the length of which has already extended more than two thousand years.
3. VERSE 3
   - Beyond the *"day of vengeance"* is the peace and prosperity of the millennium. Isaiah is making a play upon words with *"beauty"* and *"ashes"*—it is like saying that he will exchange joy for judgment or a song for a sigh.
4. VERSE 4
   - The land of Israel is yet to receive a face lifting that will restore its beauty.
5. VERSE 5
   - This is a picture of prosperity (Gentiles).
6. VERSE 6
   - It was God's original intention that the entire nation of Israel would be priests. In Exodus 19:6, we read, *"And ye shall be unto me a kingdom of priests, and a holy nation. These are the words which thou shall speak unto the children of Israel."* We too are priests as believers. (See 1 Peter 2:9.)
7. VERSE 7
   - Here we find an expression of fullness of joy.
8. VERSE 8
   - Their lives will adorn their religious ritual.
9. VERSE 9
   - Anti-Semitism will end. Pro-Semitism will begin because they are genuine witnesses for God.
10. VERSE 10
    - The Messiah continues to speak here. He is the Bridegroom. All that are His can join in this song of praise.
11. VERSE 11
    - Not only will there be material benefits and physical improvements, but the true blessings will be spiritual.

How Much Do You Remember?

1. How are the wicked described and what are they likened to in chapter 57?
2. What unpleasant but necessary message must Isaiah deliver in chapter 58?
3. Why was the fasting of the Israelites in chapter 58 unacceptable to God?
4. Recall the passage from chapter 61 that Jesus quoted at the opening of His public ministry in Nazareth.

Your Assignment for Next Week:
1. Review your notes from this lesson.
2. Read Isaiah chapters 62, 63, 64, 65, and 66.
3. Underline your Bible.

Lesson 19 Notes

_____

_____

_____

_____

_____

_____

_____

_____

_____

_____

_____

_____

_____

_____

_____

_____

_____

_____

_____

_____

_____

_____

_____

_____

_____

_____

Lesson 20
CHAPTERS 62, 63, 64, 65, AND 66

CHAPTER 62

In this chapter we find more details concerning the millennial joys of restored Israel. The yearning of the Messiah for Israel to share in the joys yet to come makes this chapter a picture of sheer delight. Blessed are those who hunger and thirst after righteousness—and here we see that thirst and hunger satisfied.

1. VERSE 1
   * This is the longing of the Redeemer for the long-anticipated day. The real Jehovah of hosts will perform this. All of creation and all believers are groaning in their present state as they contemplate the future. Are you weary of the earthly journey and do you desire the fellowship of the Father's house?

2. VERSE 2
   * A new heart, a new situation, and a new righteousness demand a new name. We see this in verse 4.

3. VERSE 3
   * Israel will also have a new position; they will be a crown of glory in the house of the Lord.

4. VERSE 4
   * Israel has been *"Forsaken"*—this is the picture and name of Israel since the crucifixion of Christ.
   * *"Desolate"* is a name as well as a description. In the coming kingdom, they will be called *"Hephzibah,"* which means "delightful." *"Beulah"* is the name given to the land, which means "married."
   * The king is present to protect.

5. VERSE 5
   * He delights over Israel as a bridegroom is delighted over his bride.

6. VERSE 6
   * This longing is contagious. The thirsty soul longs to drink.

7. VERSE 7
   * Only the fulfillment of these long-awaited promises could satisfy the longing soul.

8. VERSE 8
   * The Lord has taken an oath that all will be fulfilled.

9. VERSE 9
   * The kingdom is coming in which all will be fulfilled. Satisfaction will be the trademark when it comes.

10. VERSE 10
    * Such glorious anticipation demands preparation.

11. VERSE 11
    * There are some who declare that the promises to Israel, even if true, should not be a part of the gospel message today. This announcement is pertinent for the present hour, as this verse indicates. The salvation of Israel is part of God's overall plan of salvation. The second coming of Christ means He is returning as He promised. (See John 14:3.).

12. VERSE 12
   + The experience of God's salvation will work a transformation in the nation Israel. The people will be called a holy people and the land will be greatly desired.

CHAPTER 63

The content of the first six verses of this chapter is in contrast to the last section of this chapter. Judgment precedes the kingdom, and this is the divine order. The early church fathers associated these first six verses with the first coming of Christ. They mistook the winepress as the sufferings of Christ on the cross. Such an interpretation is unthinkable, as the blood upon His garments is not His blood but that of others. Also, the "day of vengeance" has been identified already with the second coming of Christ and not His first coming, as the Lord Himself clearly stated back in Isaiah 61:2. (See also Luke 4:18–20.) Most commentators have followed this detour that has eventuated confusion. The Lord Jesus shed His own blood at His first coming, but that is not the picture presented here. He was trodden on at His first coming but here He does the treading.

1. VERSE 1
   + The form here is an antiphony, or a response of two groups to each other.
   + Those who ask the question concerning the one coming from Edom are overwhelmed by His majesty and beauty. There was no majesty and beauty the first time. He comes from Edom in the east and we are told elsewhere that His feet will touch the Mount of Olives on the east. Edom and Bozrah are geographical places and are to be considered as such but this does not exhaust the mind of the spirit. Edom stands for the flesh and the entire Adamic race.
   + The Lord Jesus answers that He is judging in righteousness and that He is always the Savior.

2. VERSE 2
   + The spectators see that there is blood on His beautiful garments just as if He had trodden the winepress.

3. VERSE 3
   + The King picks up the figure of the winepress and states that He has trodden it alone. He is the judge of all the earth.
   + The language here is awe-inspiring and an expression of terror: "trample them in my fury."
   + He went through the winepress for sinners when He was here the first time, and now, those who refuse to accept His salvation must go through the winepress.
   + You will note that it is "their blood" and not His blood; just as grapes burst open, their blood spurts out. This is frightful, but sin is frightful.
   + This links with Revelation 14:15–20, where we have the vintage and the wine of the earth is fully ripe and cast into the great winepress of the wrath of God. It is the eastern figure as they gathered their grapes, threw them into a great winepress, and then, taking off part of their garments, the young men stepped into the winepress with bare feet and trod out the fruit, becoming spattered with the red blood of the grapes.
   + It was always a time of great rejoicing. This was an annual event for the Hebrews. The picture here is God putting into the winepress all the enemies of Israel, all who have sought to destroy His chosen people, and then looking for someone to tread that winepress. There was no one, so He alone tread the winepress.

4. VERSE 4
   + This is His judgment of the earth when He comes and it is defined here as "the day of vengeance."

5. VERSE 5

   + He wrought salvation alone, and judgment is His solo work.

6. VERSE 6

   + This is the end of man's day.

7. VERSE 7

   + The entire content and intent of this chapter changes abruptly at this point. It is like coming out of darkness into sunlight of noonday. It is a transfer from black to white. Our God is *glorious in holiness, fearful in praises, doing wonders* (Exodus 15:11). This is only one aspect of His many attributes. He is good and exhibits lovingkindness. He also is a God of mercy. If these attributes were not in evidence, we would all be consumed.

8. VERSE 8

   + His people here are Israel. It is as if He had high hopes for them but they disappointed Him. Because He was their Savior, they would not lie. Does He not expect us to walk well-pleasing to Him?

9. VERSE 9

   + How tender are these words. He entered into the sufferings of His people.

10. VERSES 10–11

   + This refers directly to Israel but it is a picture of the entire human family. There are some expositors who do not feel that the reference here is to the Holy Spirit, the third person of the Godhead. The Old Testament does not contain such a clear-cut distinction so there is room for argument. I believe, however, the reference here is to the Holy Spirit.

11. VERSES 12–13

   + Again, God looks back in history to their deliverance out of Egypt.

12. VERSE 14

   + Here, He continues that history.

13. VERSE 15

   + The prophet and the people plead with God to look upon their great need and their desire.

14. VERSE 16

   + God was the Father of the nation, Israel, but there is no thought in the Old Testament that He was the Father of the individual Israelite. It was a corporate term and not a personal one in the Old Testament, while it is personal in the New Testament and not corporate. Abraham was the father of the nation and not of each individual Israelite.

15. VERSE 17

   + This is a pleading prayer on the part of Isaiah and the people.

16. VERSE 18

   + The enemies have trodden down God's sanctuary but they, in turn, will be trodden down. In Isaiah's day, this had not yet been fulfilled.

17. VERSE 19

   + They surrender completely to God. This should be the attitude of the Christian today—complete yielding to God the Father through His Son.

CHAPTER 64

This chapter is a prayer of the remnant of God's people continued from the last chapter. This chapter continues the pleading of the hungry hearts for the presence of God in their lives. No child of God today can be immune to such ardent petitions. The Christian can cry, with the same passionate desire, *"Even so, come, Lord Jesus"* (Revelation 22:20).

1. VERSE 1
   * The prophet is a representative of the remnant of Israel in a future day. He is pleading with the heart, welling up with emotion for God to break through the iron curtain of space and come down. He wants, above all else, to have God on the scene.

2. VERSE 2
   * Just as fire makes water boil, so the presence of God would make the nations tremble.

3. VERSE 3
   * The very mountains would melt at His presence. The enemies then would cry for the mountains to hide them.

4. VERSE 4
   * Paul expresses this same thought in 1 Corinthians 2:9: *"But as it is written, Eye hath not seen, nor ear heard, neither have entered into the heart of man, the things which God hath prepared for them that love him."*

5. VERSE 5
   * Here begins the acknowledgment of sins, and at the same time, a confidence in the redemption of the Savior.

6. VERSE 6
   * This verse is familiar because of the extensive use of it in establishing the fact that man has no righteousness. This is not only true of Israel but also of the entire world or "family of mankind."

7. VERSE 7
   * Because of their sins and transgressions, Israel thought God had turned His face from them.

8. VERSE 8
   * This is the recognition of God as Creator, and we have something similar to that expressed in Acts 17:28–29:

     For in him we live, and move, and have our being: as certain also of your own poets have said, For we are also his offspring. Forasmuch then as we are the offspring of God, we ought not to think that the Godhead is like unto gold, or silver, or stone, graven by art and man's device.

9. VERSE 9
   * The prophet pleads for mercy, which God is not reluctant to bestow.

10. VERSE 10
    * This was not true in Isaiah's day but it came to pass shortly afterward in the coming of Babylon against Jerusalem. (See 2 Kings 25:9–10.)

11. VERSE 11
    * The temple was destroyed at the same time Jerusalem was destroyed.

12. VERSE 12
    * The prophet closes with a question. Will God refuse to act? The remainder of the prophecy of Isaiah is God's answer.

13. EXPLORING THE MILLENNIUM
    * There are many thoughts concerning the millennium such as: there will be absolutely no sickness at all during the millennium and death will no longer exist. Let's explore that for just a moment.

In Zechariah 14:18, there is mention of a plague sent by the Lord. Indeed, even in that wonderful millennium age, there will be the possibility of sickness, but only for those who willingly disobey the Word of the Lord.

+ Death will no longer be prevalent but it will be inflicted judicially. Notice carefully in Isaiah 65:18–20 that in the coming day of Jehovah's power, those who enter into the millennial blessing on the earth will, under ordinary circumstances, be granted the gift of long life, such as the patriarchs enjoyed before the flood. In fact, it would seem as though they will live throughout the entire period, unless there is some willful sin that will be dealt with immediately in judgment. Under such circumstances, we read that a sinner dying at the age of one hundred years will be accursed and his death will be as the death of a child.

+ This shows us that the Kingdom Age will not be like the eternal state known as the kingdom of God, in which sin can never again lift up its head and death will be absolutely unknown. It will still be possible for man to sin against divine light, even though there be no adversary to tempt him, but such behavior will not be tolerated when righteousness reigns. Therefore, there will be no immediate judicial dealings.

+ It will be a period of a thousand years without war. (See Micah 4:3; Isaiah 2:4.)

+ Poverty will be abolished, as we will see in Isaiah 65:21–23.

+ Changed conditions of the lower creation will come about, as is seen in Isaiah 65:25 and Isaiah 11:6–9.

+ So, regardless of what we have thought in times past about the millennium, it will be a time of righteousness and a time when Satan is bound, but there is still the old Adamic nature to deal with. It will exist, and when it does show its ugly head, the Lord will deal with it immediately. Otherwise, those who serve and delight in being with the Lord will live throughout that period.

CHAPTER 65

In the last chapter, we saw the fervent prayer of the prophet and the people pleading with the King to break through all barriers and come back to the earth. This chapter and the following and final chapter will contain His answer. God charges them with their sins and unfaithfulness. Nevertheless, He has preserved a remnant through which He will fulfill all His promises and prophecies. Again, He gives a vision of the kingdom and a prospectus of the eternal position of Israel in the *"new heavens and a new earth"* (verse 17).

1. VERSE 1
   + These are the Gentiles to whom the gospel has now come. Paul says that Isaiah was bold, indeed, as a loyal Israelite to make such a prediction. *"But Esaias [Isaiah] is very bold, and saith, I was found of them that sought me not; I was made manifest unto them that asked not after me"* (Romans 10:20).

2. VERSE 2
   + This is the Jew to whom God first gave the gospel. Paul continues to quote from Isaiah in Romans 10:21: *"But to Israel he saith, All day long have I stretched forth my hands unto a disobedient and gainsaying people."*

3. VERSE 3
   + This is the reason that the blessings were withheld from Israel.

4. VERSES 4–5
   + This is a partial list of the reasons for Israel's rejection.

5. VERSES 6–7
   + Israel walked in pride as they practiced the externalities of a God-given religion. Their hearts were far from God. They practiced iniquity as easily as they practiced the rituals of religion.

6. VERSE 8

    *   In spite of their sins, God would not totally exterminate them.

7. VERSE 9

    *   A seed out of Jacob could refer to Christ but more particularly, it refers to the remnant out of Israel here in this verse.

8. VERSE 10

    *   For the sake of the remnant, God will make good His promises.

9. VERSES 11–12

    *   For the remainder of the nation that went headlong without heeding the Word of God, there remains nothing but punishment.

10. VERSE 13

    *   The remnant will survive. God cannot exterminate Himself in sin.

11. VERSE 14

    *   There is a distinction between the nation and the remnant, and here, the remnant is called *"my servants"* and the nation Israel is referred to as *"ye shall cry."*

12. VERSES 15–16

    *   The remnant will survive. The nation at large will perish. All sinners who refuse God's grace will be punished irrespective of nation, race, or condition.

13. VERSE 17

    *   Here we have the creation of the new heavens and the new earth. They seem to precede, chronologically, the setting up of the kingdom here. It is equally as clear in Revelation 21:1 that the new heavens and the new earth follow the millennium. Radical transformation will take place on the earth during the kingdom that is tantamount to a new earth. Such radical changes will take place on the earth with the rapture of the church. I have taken the position that the new heavens and the new earth come into existence after the millennium. I believe this verse refers to just that. God says here is Isaiah: *"For, behold, I will create new heavens and a new earth."* What happens during the millennium is merely a shadow of what is to come.

14. VERSE 18

    *   Here, Isaiah definitely returns to millennial blessings and Jerusalem will be a rejoicing people and a people full of joy.

15. VERSE 19

    *   This is quite a change for Jerusalem. There will be no more weeping and only joy will be in the people.

16. VERSE 20

    *   Longevity of life that predated the patriarchs will be one of the features of the kingdom. Notice: *"for the child shall die an hundred years old."*

17. VERSE 21

    *   Prosperity is another feature of the kingdom.

18. VERSE 22

    *   Permanence and stability will likewise mark the millennium.

19. VERSE 23

    *   No fruitless effort or frustration will exist. All efforts will be blessed.

20. VERSE 24
   * Prayer in that day will receive a new potency and speed in receiving an answer.
21. VERSE 25
   * The sharp fang and bloody claw will no longer rule animal life. The law of the jungle will be changed to conform to the rule of the King. There will be nothing to hurt, harm, or make afraid in the whole world. This is the long-awaited kingdom of Christ.

CHAPTER 66

This brings us to the last chapter of Isaiah. One final flash of the prophecy passes before our eyes. There is likewise the flash from judgment fires that are still burning. These but warn us that the kingdom has not yet come, and before that day, *"the slain of the Lord shall be many"* (verse 16). Isaiah does not conclude like a fairy tale in which everyone lives happily ever after. There is no sweetness here. There is the rugged reality of judgment upon sin that must inevitably precede the establishment of the kingdom. The kingdom is coming, for this is the persistent purpose of God, and none can deter Him. All of God's children can *"rejoice…with Jerusalem"* (verse 10).

1. VERSE 1
   * The kingdom is one thousand years but it is also eternal. The eternal character of the kingdom is before us in this final scene. There will be a millennial temple but will it be necessary for eternity? Surely, the church of the Lord Jesus in the New Jerusalem will have no temple because we read:

     To him that overcometh will I grant to sit with me in my throne, even as I also overcame, and am set down with my Father in his throne. He that hath an ear, let him hear what the Spirit saith unto the churches.   (Revelation 3:21–22)

   * It has never been the conception of God's people that He could dwell in a temple: *"But will God indeed dwell on the earth? behold, the heaven and heaven of heavens cannot contain thee; how much less this house that I have builded"* (1 Kings 8:27).
2. VERSE 2
   * God has created this vast universe and He is above and beyond it. Nevertheless, He will dwell with the humble and contrite heart that knows it is poor. What deference!
3. VERSE 3
   * The sacrificial system will be dispensed with after the millennium. To offer an ox without spiritual comprehension was the same as murder. Everything in eternity must point to Christ or that which was once commanded becomes sin.
4. VERSE 4
   * For those who refused to answer the call of God, there will be delusion and fear.
5. VERSE 5
   * God will make the distinction between the true and the false. The Pharisee who was meticulous in his religious practice will be cast out. The publican who stood afar off and repented will be received.
6. VERSE 6
   * God will finally deal with the enemies of Israel. (See Revelation 16:17.)
7. VERSE 7
   * Before the great tribulation, Christ was born of this nation called Israel.
8. VERSE 8
   * They will be born a nation in a day, in the time of the great tribulation.

9. VERSE 9
   * God will see that all of this is accomplished. The 144,000 who are sealed at the beginning of the great tribulation survive intact throughout the entire period of suffering.

10. VERSES 10–11
   * Every Christian who has prayed for the peace of Jerusalem will rejoice when the kingdom is ushered in with Jerusalem as the center. Remember, we are in the millennium in this chapter.

11. VERSE 12
   * Now peace will come to this city, whose name means "peace." The Gentiles will no longer tear down Jerusalem but will come to walk in the light of the city.

12. VERSE 13
   * How tender is God toward His people, Jerusalem.

13. VERSE 14
   * Joy awaits those who enter into God's feelings for this city.

14. VERSE 15
   * Nevertheless, the Lord is coming in judgment upon His enemies.

15. VERSE 16
   * The fires of judgment cannot be quenched until they have burned out entirely.

16. VERSE 17
   * God will judge the wicked.

17. VERSE 18
   * All nations must appear before Him:

     When the Son of man shall come in his glory, and all the holy angels with him, then shall he sit upon the throne of his glory: and before him shall be gathered all nations: and he shall separate them one from another, as a shepherd divideth his sheep from the goats. (Matthew 25:31–32)

18. VERSE 19
   * Many Gentiles will be saved in the kingdom.

19. VERSE 20
   * The nations will worship in Jerusalem. Zechariah makes this very definite. Just as the Queen of Sheba came in Solomon's day, thus will the kings of the earth come to Jerusalem.

20. VERSE 21
   * Again, the prophet states that Israel will be a nation of priests.

21. VERSE 22
   * God's purposes and promises for Israel are as eternal as the new heavens and the new earth.

22. VERSE 23
   * The redeemed of all ages will worship God throughout eternity. That is the engaging business of eternity.

23. VERSE 24
   * Hell is eternal. The book of Isaiah closes with a warning to the human race. *"He that hath an ear, let him hear"* (Revelation 2:11, see also 2:17; 3:6, 13).

Now that we have studied this great book, I pray that it will be a blessing to all who read the notes and all who open the Word of God and study it along with the notes. Now, may the Lord Jesus give you encouragement and wisdom to teach these lessons to others as well.

Blessing, and honour, and glory, and power, be unto him that sitteth upon the throne, and unto the Lamb for ever and ever.

(Revelation 5:13)

How Much Do You Remember?

1. Describe the transformation that will occur in the nation of Israel after the experience of God's salvation (chapter 62).
2. Recall the imagery and symbolism of the winepress from chapter 63 in terms of Jesus's first and second comings.
3. Compare and contrast the millennium and the eternal kingdom with information from the notes on chapter 64.
4. What known features mark the kingdom? The millennium? (Chapter 65)
5. Summarize the final chapter of Isaiah. What will the judgment look like?

Lesson 20 Notes

_____

_____

_____

_____

_____

_____

_____

_____

_____

_____

_____

_____

_____

_____

_____

_____

_____

_____

_____

_____

_____

_____

_____

ABOUT THE AUTHOR

Dr. Alan B. Stringfellow (1922–1993), a Bible teacher and minister of the gospel for more than four decades, specialized in Christian education. Long concerned with the struggle most people have in understanding the Bible, he set out to write a study course that would bring believers more knowledge and a greater appreciation of God's Word. He wrote *Through the Bible in One Year, Great Truths of the Bible, Great Characters in the Bible,* and *Insights on the Book of Revelation* for laymen, to be taught by laymen. Dr. Stringfellow trained at Southwestern Baptist Theological Seminary in Fort Worth, Texas, after which he served at Travis Avenue Baptist Church in Fort Worth; First Baptist Church of West Palm Beach, Florida; First Baptist Church of Fresno, California; and First Baptist Church of Van Nuys, California.